Ajax Programming for the Absolute Beginner

Jerry Lee Ford, Jr.

Course Technology PTR
A part of Cengage Learning

COURSE TECHNOLOGY
CENGAGE Learning™

Australia, Brazil, Japan, Korea, Mexico, Singapore, Spain, United Kingdom, United States

COURSE TECHNOLOGY
CENGAGE Learning™

Ajax Programming for the Absolute Beginner: Jerry Lee Ford, Jr.

Publisher and General Manager, Course Technology PTR: Stacy L. Hiquet

Associate Director of Marketing: Sarah Panella

Manager of Editorial Services: Heather Talbot

Marketing Manager: Mark Hughes

Acquisitions Editor: Mitzi Koontz

Project Editor: Jenny Davidson

Technical Reviewer: Keith Davenport

PTR Editorial Services Coordinator: Jen Blaney

Interior Layout Tech: Value-Chain

Cover Designer: Mike Tanamachi

Indexer: Katherine Stimson

Proofreader: Sara Gullion

For product information and technology assistance, contact us at
Cengage Learning Customer & Sales Support, 1-800-354-9706

For permission to use material from this text or product, submit all requests online at **cengage.com/permissions** Further permissions questions can be emailed to **permissionrequest@cengage.com**

All trademarks are the property of their respective owners.

Library of Congress Control Number: 2008928834

ISBN-13: 978-1-59863-564-5
ISBN-10: 1-59863-564-6

Course Technology
25 Thomson Place
Boston, MA 02210
USA

Cengage Learning is a leading provider of customized learning solutions with office locations around the globe, including Singapore, the United Kingdom, Australia, Mexico, Brazil, and Japan. Locate your local office at: **international.cengage.com/region**

Cengage Learning products are represented in Canada by Nelson Education, Ltd.

For your lifelong learning solutions, visit **courseptr.com**

Visit our corporate website at **cengage.com**

Printed in Canada
1 2 3 4 5 6 7 11 10 09

To my mother and father for always being there, and to my wonderful children, Alexander, William, and Molly, and my beautiful wife, Mary.

ACKNOWLEDGMENTS

There are several individuals to whom I owe many thanks for their help and assistance in the development of this book. I'll start by thanking Mitzi Koontz, who served as the book's acquisitions editor. Special thanks also go out to Jenny Davidson for serving as the book's project editor. I also want to thank Keith Davenport for all the valuable input and advice. In addition, I would like to thank everyone else at Course Technology PTR for all their hard work.

About the Author

Jerry Lee Ford, Jr. is an author, educator, and an IT professional with over 18 years of experience in information technology, including roles as an automation analyst, technical manager, technical support analyst, automation engineer, and security analyst. He is the author of 28 books and co-author of two additional books. His published works include *AppleScript Studio Programming for the Absolute Beginner, Microsoft Windows PowerShell Programming for the Absolute Beginner, Microsoft Visual Basic 2005 Express Edition Programming for the Absolute Beginner, Microsoft VBScript Professional Projects, Microsoft Windows Shell Scripting and WSH Administrator's Guide, Microsoft Windows Shell Script Programming for the Absolute Beginner, Learn JavaScript in a Weekend, Second Edition*, and *Microsoft Windows XP Professional Administrator's Guide.* Jerry has a master's degree in business administration from Virginia Commonwealth University in Richmond, Virginia, and he has over five years of experience as an adjunct instructor teaching networking courses in information technology.

TABLE OF CONTENTS

Chapter 4   UNDERSTANDING THE DOCUMENT OBJECT MODEL...... 91

Part III   BUILDING AJAX APPLICATIONS....................................... 111

Chapter 5   AJAX BASICS... 113

Chapter 8 **WORKING WITH CASCADING STYLE SHEETS.............. 195**

Chapter 9 **WORKING WITH AJAX AND PHP............................ 223**

INTRODUCTION

Welcome to *Ajax Programming for the Absolute Beginner!* Ajax (Asynchronous JavaScript and XML) is a collection of web development technologies that can be used to create web applications that provide levels of responsiveness previously unheard of. As a result, when combined with high-speed internet connections, you can use Ajax to develop web applications that behave and respond like desktop applications.

In recent years, web developers have begun to make major investments in Ajax, using it to create a whole new generation of web applications. For example, Google has used Ajax in the creation of all its latest applications, including Google Suggest, Google Maps, and Gmail. Amazon.com has used Ajax in the development of its A9.com search engine as well as to enhance and improve its main website. Websites like Ask.com and Snap.com have used Ajax to make major improvements to their search engines. Other companies have used Ajax to help develop entire office suites of free online applications. For example, ThinkFree Online (www.thinkfree.com) can create text documents, spreadsheets, and presentations all of which are 100 percent compatible with Microsoft Office. Google's Google Docs Online office suite (docs.google.com) is another example of online applications developed using Ajax.

When it comes to web development, Ajax is truly the "next big thing." Ajax is becoming an essential ingredient in the makeup of modern web applications. Ajax is being used in the development of all kinds of exciting new applications and rightly so, given its ability to support the creation of web applications with desktop-like performance.

Using Ajax programming techniques you can transform the way your web applications look and feel, providing your visitors with a significantly enriched experience. By learning how to create Ajax applications, you will develop a highly marketable set of skills that are currently in high demand. To help you accomplish this goal, this book uses a hands-on instructional approach, emphasizing learning by doing, which is accomplished through the development of a series of computer games.

So, whether you are a student who has just signed up for an introductory web development class that uses Ajax, a hobbyist who wants to have some fun, or a web developer interested in expanding your skill set, this book will help you get off to a good start. By the time you are done, you will be ready to begin taking your web applications to the next level.

WHY AJAX?

Ajax changes the way in which web applications are designed, replacing requests for new web pages and screen refreshes with small data queries to web servers. By requesting less data, the web servers are able to respond quicker. Ajax data requests are made asynchronously, meaning that users no longer have to sit and wait for the web server to fulfill a request. Instead, the user can continue to work with the web application while Ajax collects and processes the web server's data in the background, and when it is time to do so, Ajax can use the data to dynamically update the web page without forcing a page reload. The end result is a streamlined, faster, and more desktop-like experience.

Because it relies on commonly available technologies like JavaScript and XML, Ajax is readily available and supported by all major computer operating systems and web browsers. You do not have to download and install any special software to work with Ajax, and the people who visit your website do not have to install anything to view and interact with your Ajax applications.

WHO SHOULD READ THIS BOOK?

Ajax Programming for the Absolute Beginner is designed to teach first-time programmers, computer enthusiasts, and web developers interested in adding Ajax to their bag of tricks. An understanding of HTML is required for you to complete this book. While previous programming experience is certainly helpful, as is a basic understanding of JavaScript, the DOM, CSS, the `XMLHttpRequest` object, and XML, you do not need to be an expert with any of these technologies. You will learn all that you need to know about each of these technologies as you make your way through this book.

In addition to teaching you everything you need to know to get up and running quickly, this book will make your learning experience as enjoyable as possible. This will be accomplished using a games-based instructional approach in which you will learn Ajax programming through the creation of web-based computer games. If this approach to learning sounds interesting and fun to you, then keep reading. It won't be long before you are creating all kinds of fun and exciting web applications.

WHAT YOU NEED TO BEGIN

Ajax is not something that you can buy in a box or download from the internet. It is a collection of related technologies that are readily available to everyone. Because it is based on technologies like JavaScript, XML, and the DOM, it is readily available. You do, however, need a few tools and resources to get started. Ajax uses JavaScript as its programming language. In order to develop JavaScript code, you need a text or code editor. If you already have a code editor that you are using to develop your HTML pages, odds are it will support JavaScript as well. Otherwise, you can use any plain text editor, such as Windows Notepad, when developing Ajax applications.

In addition to an editor, you will need access to one or more web browsers like Internet Explorer, Safari, Firefox, or Opera to test your web applications. Because Ajax applications are designed to work with web servers, you also need access to a web server and the ability to develop programs that run on the server. For most people this means signing up with one of the many available web service providers.

Most Ajax applications involve the development of some server-side programs. In this book, server-side applications (programs that run on web servers) are developed using PHP. Although the use of PHP will be minimal, to follow along with and test the execution of all of the examples in this book, you will want to make sure that your service provider supports the execution of PHP.

Working with Different Web Browsers

Ajax uses JavaScript as its programming language. As such, Ajax is susceptible to all of the same problems that JavaScript programmers face. One of these compatibility issues involves the browser. Due to internal design differences, different web browsers work differently with JavaScript and therefore with Ajax. To properly test your Ajax applications, you should use all major web browsers, including those listed below, to make sure that they behave as you expect them to.

- Internet Explorer
- Apple's Safari
- Mozilla Firefox
- Opera

Most of the figures and examples that you will see in this book are demonstrated using Internet Explorer 7. Except where noted, all of the examples that are presented in this book should work exactly the same on all of the major web browsers.

What You Need to Know

In order to take advantage of this book, you need to be familiar with the basics of HTML development and, of course, you need a website that you can work with and are interested in making more responsive and dynamic. Beyond that, this book will provide everything else you need to know. This includes an overview of how to program using JavaScript and the Document Object Model. This book also provides a basic review of XML and CSS.

Ajax applications have a server-side component needed to make them work. There are many different server-side programming languages from which to choose, including Ruby on Rails, PHP, Java Servlets, and ASP. Of these, PHP is arguably the most popular and easiest to work with and is the server-side programming language that this book uses. You will not have to become a PHP guru in order to make your way through this book. However, a basic understanding of PHP will be helpful. To make sure you have a basic understanding of PHP programming, this book provides a quick server-side PHP programming primer.

 Most web hosts support PHP. In fact, it is most likely provided as a free service as part of your web hosting agreement. To make sure it's available, visit your provider's website.

How This Book Is Organized

Although this book has been designed to be read sequentially from cover to cover, it covers a wide variety of topics and you may want to pick and choose which ones you review based on your background and previous experience. *Ajax Programming for the Absolute Beginner* is organized into five parts. Part I of this book consists of a single chapter that provides an overview of Ajax and its capabilities. You will also see numerous real-world examples of Ajax in action to help better demonstrate its capabilities.

Part II consists of three chapters that offer an overview of JavaScript and the browser's Document Object Model (DOM). JavaScript serves as Ajax's programming language and a good understanding of its syntax and usage is critical to your success as an Ajax developer. You will learn how to create JavaScripts that store data and apply conditional and looping logic. You will learn how to organize your program code into functions. You will also learn how to work with browser and JavaScript objects and respond to events like mouse clicks and keyboard input. The last chapter in this part provides an overview of the Document Object Model and demonstrates how to use it to access and modify different parts of web pages.

Part III consists of two chapters that are designed to provide the information you need to begin developing Ajax applications. This includes learning how to communicate with and retrieve information from web services and to update web pages without requiring any page refreshes. You will then learn how to use Ajax to perform an assortment of different tasks.

Part IV consists of four chapters, each of which addresses a unique topic that is important to rounding out your Ajax skills. The first chapter demonstrates the benefits of using XML in place of plain text when retrieving data from web servers. The second chapter explains how to use cascading style sheets or CSS to control the presentation and formatting of information displayed on your web pages. The third chapter demonstrates how to work with PHP to develop server-side program code that supports your Ajax applications. The last chapter rounds things out by addressing a number of important design issues that you need to take into consideration as you develop your Ajax applications.

Part V consists of two appendices. The first appendix provides an overview of all the game projects presented throughout this book and explains how to download the book's source code from its companion website. The second appendix provides a list of online resources you can visit to continue your Ajax education and further your programming knowledge.

The basic outline of the book is as follows.

- **Chapter 1, "An Ajax Overview."** This chapter provides a broad overview of Ajax and the technologies that comprise this exciting web development tool. This includes a review of Ajax's major features and capabilities and its strengths and weaknesses. You will also see examples of websites currently using Ajax to improve their applications and provide visitors with a better, faster experience.

- **Chapter 2, "An Introduction to JavaScript."** Ajax uses JavaScript as its programming language. A solid understanding of JavaScript is therefore key to your success as an Ajax developer. This chapter provides a little background information on how JavaScript came to be and how it is used in Ajax applications. You will then begin learning the basics of JavaScript programming. You will learn how to add JavaScript to your HTML pages and the rules you need to follow to comply with JavaScript syntax requirements. You will also learn how to store data and to apply both conditional and looping logic.

- **Chapter 3, "A Deeper Dive into JavaScript."** This chapter rounds out your JavaScript education, teaching you how to respond to events and manage forms. You will learn how to create functions and to control the execution of those functions, using them to interact with web servers and retrieve the data needed by your Ajax applications. You will also learn how to store and process collections of related data using arrays.

- **Chapter 4, "Understanding the Document Object Model."** All modern web browsers define the content displayed within web pages in a hierarchical fashion using the DOM. Using the DOM, Ajax programmers are able to dynamically insert and display information retrieved from web servers, without requiring time-consuming and resource-wasting page refreshes. This chapter defines and explains the DOM and demonstrates how to use it within your Ajax applications.

- **Chapter 5, "Ajax Basics."** This chapter ties together all of the information already discussed in this book and explains how to use it in the formulation of different types of Ajax applications. You will learn how to work with the XMLHttpRequest object to retrieve text from web servers. You will also create your first Ajax game.

- **Chapter 6, "Digging Deeper into Ajax."** This chapter delves deeper into Ajax, introducing you to XML and the retrieval of JavaScript from the web server. You will learn how to create an Ajax application that uses Google Live search to retrieve data and will be introduced to different Ajax frameworks, which you can use to simplify and reduce the amount of time and effort required to build Ajax applications.

- **Chapter 7, "Working with XML."** Rather than relying on plain text, this chapter teaches you how to use XML to transport complex collections of data. You learn how to define XML elements and to extract XML data using properties. You also learn how to process XML data. In addition, you will also learn about JavaScript Object Notation or JSON, which provides an alternative to XML as a means of transporting complex collections of data.

- **Chapter 8, "Working with Cascading Style Sheets."** A big part of Ajax web development involves the dynamic display of data in your web pages. This is accomplished by displaying data returned in response to background requests made to web servers. This chapter explains how cascading style sheets or CSS control and manage the display and appearance of server data. You will learn how to make elements visible and invisible and to control their location, color, font, and border.

- **Chapter 9, "Working with Ajax and PHP."** Rather than displaying entirely new web pages in response to every request made to web servers, Ajax allows you to retrieve only the data you need from the web server and to use that data to update the display of a web page without having to reload everything. Because of this change in design, new programs have to be developed on web servers that are designed to work with this new programming model. This chapter demonstrates how to use PHP as the web server's development language.

- **Chapter 10, "Important Ajax Design Issues."** As is the case with all new technologies, Ajax has a number of technical hurdles to overcome. This chapter provides a review of these problems and discusses the ways that Ajax developers are working to overcome them.

- **Appendix A, "What's on the Companion Website?"** This appendix reviews the Ajax projects presented in this book and made available for download on this book's companion website (www.courseptr.com/downloads).

- **Appendix B, "What Next?"** This appendix provides additional guidance and advice on how to continue your Ajax education. You will find information regarding additional reading resources as well as a listing of websites and blogs where you can read what other people are saying about Ajax.

CONVENTIONS USED IN THIS BOOK

To help make this book as easy as possible to read and understand, a number of conventions have been applied to help highlight critical information and to emphasize specific points. These conventions are as follows.

- *Italics.* Whenever I introduce an important programming term for the first time, I will highlight the work using italics to give it additional emphasis and to let you know this is a term that you will want to make sure you understand and remember.

These are tips on how to do things differently and point out different techniques that you can do to become a better programmer.

From time to time, I will point out areas where you are likely to run into problems and then provide you with advice on how to deal with these situations or, better yet, prevent them from happening in the first place.

Tricks are programming shortcuts that will help to make you a better and more efficient programmer.

CHALLENGES

At the end of each chapter, you will find instructions that guide you through the development of a new computer game. Immediately following each game project, you will find a series of suggestions or challenges that you should be able to apply to improve the game and further the development of your programming skills.

Part

I

Introducing Ajax

AN AJAX OVERVIEW

Ajax represents a powerful new way of developing web applications. It does away with the traditional model of breaking down web applications into multiple pages that must constantly be loaded and reloaded. Instead, Ajax supports the development of applications that seamlessly update page content, pulling data from the web server behind the scenes, without requiring any page reloads. The end result is a faster, more desktop-like end-user experience. This chapter provides an overview of Ajax and the different technologies that it uses to provide web developers with the tools needed to create a new generation of powerful, fast, and responsive applications. This chapter will also provide an overview of a number of different Ajax applications, offering examples of the kinds of things that Ajax is capable of performing.

Specifically, you will learn:

- About Ajax and the different technologies that it comprises
- How traditional web applications differ from Ajax applications
- How to create your first Ajax application
- About different examples of Ajax as used in various web applications

PROJECT PREVIEW: THE JOKE OF THE DAY APPLICATION

In this chapter and in each of the chapters that follow, you will learn how to create an Ajax game application. Learning application development by creating computer games is not only instructional but helps make learning fun. This chapter's game project is the Joke of the Day application. It begins by displaying a web page showing the opening punch line of a joke, as demonstrated in Figure 1.1.

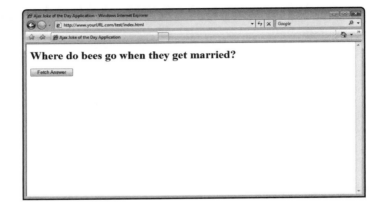

FIGURE 1.1

The Joke of the Day application demonstrates basic Ajax execution through the telling of a funny joke.

As you can see, the application's opening page consists of an HTML header and a button that when pressed uses Ajax to send a request to the web server. In response, a text file stored on the web server is returned to the browser, where its contents are then displayed in the browser, immediately under the application's button control, as demonstrated in Figure 1.2.

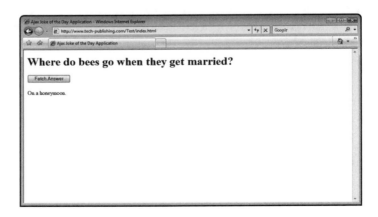

FIGURE 1.2

The joke's punch line is provided by the web server and dynamically displayed in the browser window, no screen refresh required.

INTRODUCING AJAX

Ajax, also known as Asynchronous JavaScript and XML, is a term used to refer to a collection of related web technologies. These technologies offer web developers the ability to create web applications that are able to dynamically interact with users and to work behind the scenes with web servers to retrieve application data. The data can then be displayed in the browser without requiring any page refreshes. The end result is the development of web applications that look and feel like desktop applications.

By 2005, many websites, most notably Google, were hard at work developing a whole new generation of applications (Google Maps, Google Suggest, etc.). Then on February 18, 2005 Jesse James Garrett wrote an article titled "Ajax: A New Approach to Web Applications," coining the term Ajax for the very first time. From here, things really took off.

Ajax applications are faster and more responsive than traditional web-based applications. Improved performance is attained by modifying web applications so that they exchange smaller amounts of data with web servers. As a result, web servers no longer have to generate and return entire web pages in response to every user request or interaction with the application. Since only small amounts of data are exchanged in place of web pages, web page refreshes can be eliminated.

 As this book will demonstrate, Ajax provides access to an enormously powerful set of development capabilities. However, just because you can use Ajax to perform all kinds of tasks does not mean that you should use it. Like all good things, Ajax is often best used in moderation. For example, if you need for the user to fill out and submit a form, you can do so without using Ajax. However, if you need to dynamically update a web page, then Ajax is the way to go.

With Ajax, data exchanged between web browsers and web servers is passed asynchronously behind the scenes. This means that Ajax applications can submit requests to the web server without having to pause application execution and can process the requested data whenever it is returned. Instead of submitting data to the web server using a form, Ajax applications submit requests using a special browser object known as the XMLHttpRequest object. This object is the key component of Ajax that enables asynchronous communication.

 Prior to Ajax, web developers had access to a collection of client-side web development technologies collectively referred to as DHTML. Using DHTML, web developers are able to dynamically update web pages using data collected from the user when interacting with the application.

DHTML is a collection of technologies, including HTML, CSS, JavaScript, and the DOM that when used together provide web page developers the ability to create dynamic web page effects like animation, graphical rollovers, and dynamic menus. It is strictly used to develop client-side automation and effects. Ajax embraces all of the same technologies as DHTML and adds the XMLHttpRequest object and XML into the mix.

Ajax Technologies

Ajax is a collection of technologies all of which have been around for a number of years. Each of these technologies was developed for various reasons that had nothing to do with Ajax. However, because of their complementary nature, web developers have discovered that when used together, these technologies provide a robust and powerful environment for creating and running web applications. The individual technologies that make up Ajax include:

- **JavaScript.** The programming language used to develop Ajax applications, tying together the interaction of all of the other Ajax technologies.
- **XML.** Provides a means of exchanging structured data between the web server and client.
- **The** XMLHttpRequest **object.** Provides the ability to asynchronously exchange data between web browsers and a web server.
- **HTML and CSS.** Provides the ability to mark up and style the display of web page text.
- **The Document Object Model or DOM.** Provides the ability to dynamically interact with and alter the web page layout and content.

Traditional Web Development Versus Ajax Development

Until the last couple years, web applications have lagged well behind desktop applications in regard to their look and feel, made all the worse by performance problems brought on by slow internet connections. However, with the advent of Ajax, all this is beginning to change. Using Ajax, web developers can now create robust web-based applications capable of rivaling their desktop counterparts. When combined with today's high-speed internet access and powerful web servers, Ajax applications are capable of offering a level of performance that makes web-based applications a viable option for today's computer users.

Thanks to Ajax, web applications no longer have that web feel. For example, rather than forcing customers to move from one screen to another when making purchases, Ajax applications can seamlessly allow customers to select merchandise, add it to a shopping cart, and then complete the purchase all from the same web page, without once ever forcing a screen refresh or requiring the customer to advance through a series of screens.

Traditional web applications are made up of any number of loosely integrated web pages, which are then displayed in a predefined order through links embedded within HTML pages.

As such, in order to work with traditional web applications, the user must move from web page to web page interacting with a different portion of the application in a step-by-step process. Each time the customer clicks on a link to the next inventory page, a brief wait ensues while the customer waits for that page to be loaded.

Using this traditional approach, HTTP requests are submitted to the web server in response to user actions. Upon receiving the request, the web server satisfies the request by returning a new web page, which the web browser then displays. This interaction is depicted in Figure 1.3.

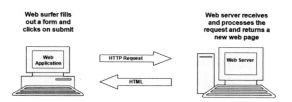

Web surfer fills out a form and clicks on submit

HTTP Request

HTML

Web server receives and processes the request and returns a new web page

FIGURE 1.3

The traditional design of most web applications involves a lot of page refreshes and waiting.

When processing the incoming request, the web server may perform any number of actions, including retrieving data from files, databases, or applications that run on the server. Once it has collected the data needed to satisfy the request, the web server may need to further process this data before generating the HTML page into which it will be embedded.

 The data retrieved from the web server can be a plain text file stored on the web server or it may be data retrieved from a server-side database or generated after some processing has occurred on the web server. A number of different server-side programming languages are available. These languages include PHP, ASP, Ruby on Rails, and Java Servlets.

Consider a typical online merchant example. The merchant's web application might require customers to review dozens of different pages in order to locate and select different items for purchase. Once the user has finished shopping and has selected all of the items she wants to purchase, a summary page is generally displayed requesting the customer to confirm the contents of her cart. From here, the application must then load a page that contains a form into which credit card information must be entered. Once submitted to the application's web server for processing, the user must wait for a purchase confirmation page to be returned. After clicking on a button to provide confirmation and complete the transaction, the customer must wait for the web server again to complete the purchase, after which a final page, serving as a receipt, is displayed. At every step within the application, the customer must wait as the web server processes the user's input and downloads new web pages for display. Using

Ajax, you can change this application model so that only the absolute minimum amount of data needed to be exchanged is passed between the web browser and the server. This speeds things up a lot.

By passing data in place of web pages, and allowing data to be displayed within an existing web page, web application developers are able to give their applications a desktop-like feel. This replaces the loosely integrated web pages with a tightly integrated presentation. Ajax applications also help to better balance the use of resources. This is accomplished by adding an additional layer, referred to as the Ajax engine, into the mix as depicted in Figure 1.4.

FIGURE 1.4

Ajax applications are much more responsive and result in a better end user experience.

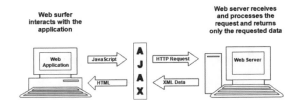

Once the initial web interface page is loaded, communication between the web browser and web server can be performed by passing data in place of entire web pages. Because small amounts of data can now be passed asynchronously, network payload is decreased and things speed up. Asynchronous processing is accomplished through the execution of JavaScript function calls. Asynchronous processing also significantly cuts down on wait time by eliminating the need for page refreshes. In fact, while waiting for new data to be returned from the web server, the user is free to use other parts of the applications. Small amounts of data sent back by the web server may be sent as plain text. On the other hand, larger and more complicated collections of text are usually sent using XML.

 In addition to plain text and XML, Ajax applications also support the exchange of data using *JavaScript Object Notation* or *JSON*. This book will show you how to work with both plain text and XML. Although its usage is not demonstrated, more information on JSON is provided in Chapter 7, "Working with XML."

Asynchronous processing also reduces the web server's workload, allowing more work to be done on the client computer when necessary. As the workload on the web server is reduced, the web server is able to respond more quickly and to handle an increased number of connections from other customers.

EXAMPLES OF REAL WORLD AJAX APPLICATIONS AND WEBSITES

Enough with all this talk about Ajax and what it is capable of doing. Let's spend a few minutes looking at some examples of Ajax in action. Specifically, let's look at a number of well known and not so well known websites and look at examples of how they have used Ajax to enhance their web applications. By the time you have completed this whirlwind tour, you should have a pretty good idea of the many different kinds of tasks that you can use Ajax to tackle.

Search Engine Makeovers

One of the earliest adapters of Ajax was large search engines, which realized that Ajax could be used to greatly improve a search engine's ability to provide users with a better experience. Using Ajax, search engine developers were able to go beyond just displaying a list of URLs and website descriptions and discovered that they could provide web surfers with all kinds of additional information, quickly retrieved behind the scenes based on visitor behavior.

A9.com

Amazon.com was one of the earliest websites to take advantage of Ajax. It used Ajax to help build its A9.com search engine (www.a9.com), as shown in Figure 1.5, which web surfers can use to search both the internet and amazon.com's online catalog.

FIGURE 1.5

The A9.com website allows you to search either the internet or amazon.com.

When used to perform a search, the results returned by A9.com look very much like those of any other search engine. Using Ajax, the developers of this search engine added a Site Info feature that displays additional information about a website when the user moves the mouse pointer over the link, as demonstrated in Figure 1.6. Everything works quite seamlessly, without any screen refreshes. Web surfers with high-speed internet access experience almost no wait time at all.

FIGURE 1.6

The information displayed for each website includes additional links, each of which is clickable.

Ask.com
The developers of the Ask.com website's search engine (www.ask.com) have used Ajax to enhance their search engine, allowing web surfers to preview websites as demonstrated in Figure 1.7 and to use this information when deciding whether to click on the site's URL.

Only URL links that are preceded by graphical binoculars can be previewed. To preview the site, simply move the mouse pointer over the binoculars. The preview picture that is displayed is not collected in real time and therefore it may be a little out of date.

Suggest Styled Applications
Another really neat use of Ajax is in the use of suggestion-based search engines, which retrieve data from the web server based on user keystrokes. There are many variations of this type of Ajax application.

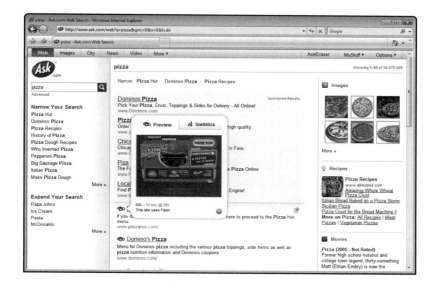

FIGURE 1.7

In addition to previewing a picture of the website, Ask.com also provides statistical information about the site.

Google Suggest

Google was one of the first web companies to heavily invest in Ajax. It used Ajax in the development of a whole new generation of online applications including Google Gmail, Google Maps, and Google Suggest (http://www.google.com/webhp?complete=1&hl=en), which is pictured in Figure 1.8.

FIGURE 1.8

Google Suggest monitors user keystrokes and displays lists of related topics from which to choose.

To use Google Suggest, all you have to do is begin typing. As you type, the application passes your keystrokes behind the scenes to one of Google's servers and retrieves a list of topics that match what you have typed so far. As you continue to type, Goggle Suggest continues to update the list of topics that is displayed. You can either enter your own unique search term or select one of the entries that is displayed to initiate an internet search.

Amazon Zuggest

An interesting variation of Suggest is Amazon Zuggest (http://www.francisshanahan.com/zuggest.aspx), as demonstrated in Figure 1.9. This application monitors user keystrokes, retrieving and displaying items from amazon.com's catalog that match up against whatever you enter. The more you type, the better the application is able to hone in on what you are looking for.

FIGURE 1.9

Amazon Zuggest is an application that searches amazon.com and displays items that match up against keyboard input.

Online Ajax Dictionaries

Another great use of suggestion-based searching is in the development of dictionary and thesaurus type applications. One such application is ObjectGraph (http://www.objectgraph.com/dictionary/), as demonstrated in Figure 1.10.

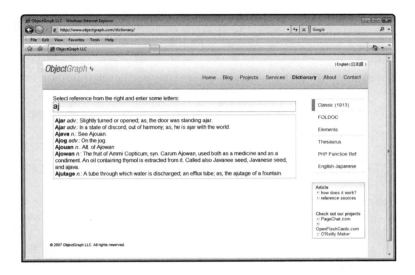

FIGURE 1.10

ObjectGraph
retrieves
dictionary words
on the fly as you
type.

Google Maps

One of Google's best known and most popular applications is Google Maps (maps.google.com). As shown in Figure 1.11, Google maps provide a global view of the Earth, allowing visitors to view detailed pictures of any individual spot on the globe. Using Ajax, Google maps allows you to click on and drag the map to reveal different locations. Based on user input, new map images are returned from the server and displayed in the map portions of the applications, with near instantaneous results and no page refreshes.

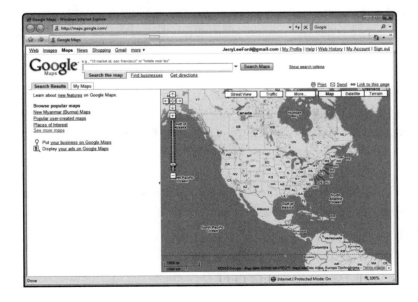

FIGURE 1.11

Google Maps can
be used to zoom in
on and display
detailed images of
maps for any part
of the world.

Netflix

Another website that has made notable use of Ajax is Netflix (www.netflix.com). Netflix is an online DVD rental service with over 6 million subscribers. Customers can search for and order movies, which are then either downloaded to the customer's computer or mailed to their residence. As Figure 1.12 demonstrates, the Netflix website uses Ajax to display additional information about movies in a popup when the customers move the mouse pointer over its title.

FIGURE 1.12

Netflix lets customers retrieve and view additional information for any movie in the company's inventory.

Virtual Desktop Applications

Among the newest generation of applications now available on the internet are applications that let you run a virtualized computer operating system within your web browser. One example of such an application is ajaxWindows (www.ajaxwindows.com), as shown in Figure 1.13.

Figure 1.14 shows an example of ajaxWindows in action. As you can see, its overall appearance resembles that of a Windows operating system. Included as part of the operating systems are a number of common desktop applications, including a word processor called ajaxWrite and a paint program named ajaxSketch.

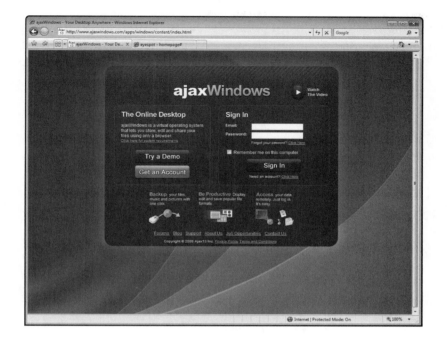

FIGURE 1.13

The ajaxWindows
online desktop
application lets
you remotely run a
virtual operating
system in your
web browser.

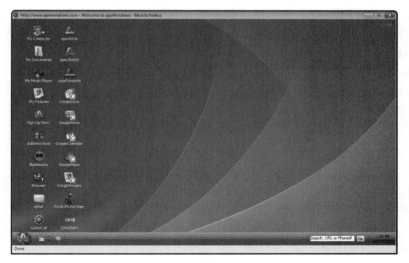

FIGURE 1.14

ajaxWindows
provides access to
a virtualized
Window's-like
desktop.

ajaxWrite and ajaxSketch are just two of a number of applications supplied as part of ajaxWindows. In addition to accessing these applications through the ajaxWindows application, you can also access and run them directly within your browser. For example, by visiting http://us.ajax13.com/en/ajaxwrite/ you can launch ajaxWrite. As demonstrated in Figure 1.15, ajaxWrite very much resembles Microsoft Word. It can be used to create, edit, write, and print text documents. It can even save documents in Microsoft Word format, which can be stored online or saved directly to your computer's hard drive.

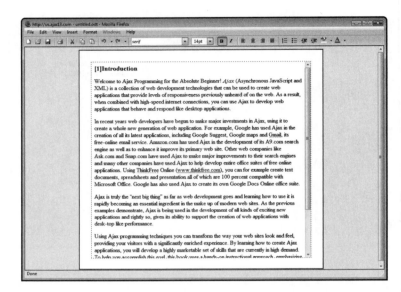

Photo Management Using Flickr

Another prominent web application built in part using Ajax is Flickr (www.flickr.com). Flickr is an online photo management tool that is capable of rivaling most desktop photo management programs. As demonstrated in Figure 1.16, Flickr lets you upload and manage all your personal photos.

Flickr provides users with access to an application called Organizr. Using this application, Flickr users can organize and manage their uploaded photos. Organizr allows users to drag and drop photos and to create and modify photo descriptions and groupings. Organizr looks and feels like a desktop-based photo management program.

Ajax Instant Message Applications

Another category or application that Ajax is commonly used to develop is instant messaging. One such instant message application is ajax im (www.ajaxim.net). As shown in Figure 1.17, ajax im (asynchronous JavaScript and xml instant messenger) is a browser-based IM client that allows users to send and receive text messages to one another without ever refreshing the browser window.

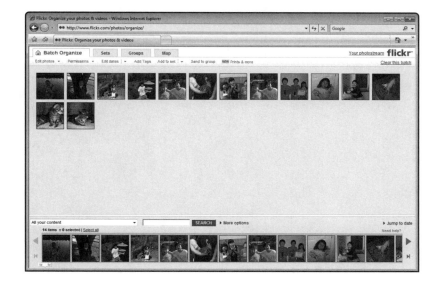

FIGURE 1.16

Flickr allows you to upload, edit, organize, and share your personal photos and videos.

FIGURE 1.17

Ajax im is a browser-based instant message client.

Online Calendars

Another interesting category of applications that Ajax has been used to create is online calendar and time management applications. One such application is calendar hub (www.calendarhub.com), as shown in Figure 1.18. CalendarHub lets you view calendar data using a day, week, month, and list views. You can post as many calendar entries and to-dos as you want. You can even share your calendar with others and receive notifications via email.

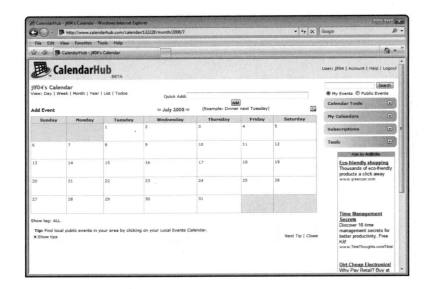

FIGURE 1.18

CalendarHub is a free online calendar application that supports individual and group calendar use.

Using Ajax, CalendarHub supports a drag and drop interface that allows you to move calendar entries around and add new entries to the calendar without any page refreshes.

BACK TO THE JOKE OF THE DAY APPLICATION

It is now time to turn your attention to the development of this chapter's Ajax project, the Joke of the Day application. This application, when loaded into the web browser, will present the user with a web page that displays the opening line for a joke. Underneath the joke is a button that, when pressed, instructs the application to retrieve the joke's punch line using Ajax, which is stored in a plain text file on the application's web server.

Since this book has yet to introduce you to the intricacies of Ajax development, such as JavaScript or how to work with the XMLHttpRequest object, don't worry if you do not fully grasp what each individual code statement in the application is doing. As long as you can understand the HTML portions of the examples, you should be in good shape. For now, try to keep your focus on the overall process of converting a traditional web application into an Ajax application. Everything will become clear as you make your way through this book, and by the time you are done, simple applications like the Joke of the Day application will seem quite elementary to you.

Designing the Application

To help keep things simple, the development of this application will be performed in five steps, as outlined here:

1. Create a new HTML page.
2. Create the application's text file.
3. Test the HTML version of the application.
4. Enhance the application using Ajax.
5. Execute your new Ajax application.

The first three steps will demonstrate how to create and execute the application using HTML by following the traditional web development approach, and the last two steps will show you how to modify the application using Ajax. Although this initial application is relatively simple, it will walk you through the basic development steps required to update any typical web page using Ajax. As long as you follow along carefully with the instructions provided in each step, you'll have your own copy of this application up and running in no time.

 In order to follow along with this example you need access to a web server where you can upload your web pages. If you do not have a website, now would be a good time to sign up with a web host and get started. To find a web host, visit www.google.com and perform a search on "web host." You will find plenty of web host providers ready and willing to help you get started. If you already have access to a website to which you can upload your web pages, I suggest that you begin by creating a subfolder in your web directory and that you do all of your Ajax work in it as you work your way through this book. This way, you won't mess up anything on your website while learning and experimenting with Ajax.

Step 1: Writing the Application's HTML

The first step in creating the Joke of the Day application is to create an HTML version of the application. To do so, open your preferred code or text editor—Microsoft Notepad or any text editor that can save plain text files will do—and create and save a new file named index.html. Once this has been completed, you need to add the application's HTML statements, which are shown next, to the file.

```
<HTML>
  <HEAD>
    <TITLE>HTML Joke of the Day</TITLE>
  </HEAD>
  <BODY>
    <H1>Where do bees go when they get married?</H1>
    <A href="joke.txt">Fetch Answer</A>
  </BODY>
</HTML>
```

As you can see, this version of the Joke of the Day application is a typical HTML page, consisting of head and body tags. The head section includes a title tag that displays the name of the application and the body section contains a level 1 heading that displays the application's joke, followed by a link to another file named joke.txt where the joke's punch line is stored. The joke.txt file is a plain text file made up of a single line of text. When clicked, the link opens and then displays the contents of the file in the web browser.

 If you want, you could modify this example to open another HTML page that displays the punch line instead of a text file.

Step 2: Creating the Application's Text File

Now that you have the index.html page created, it is time to create the joke.txt file. Do so by opening your preferred text file editor and typing the sentence shown in Figure 1.19 into it.

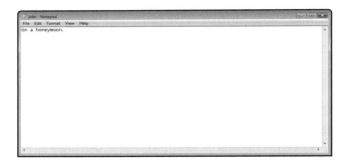

You can use any plain text editor to create the application's text file.

As you can see, this file consists of a handful of words, saved as a plain text file. Once you have keyed in the file's text, save the file in the same place that you saved the index.html file.

Step 3: Uploading and Testing the HTML Version of the Application

Once you have created both the index.html and joke.txt files, you need to upload them to your web server for testing. You may be able to perform this step using FTP or using a web-based administrative interface provided by your web host provider. Consult with your web host to see which of these options are available to you.

Once you have uploaded these two files to your web server, you should be ready to test this temporary HTML version of the Joke of the Day application. To do so, open your web browser and type the URL for the index.html web page. The URL that you use will vary based on the name of your website's URL and the location on that web server where you uploaded the application's files. For example, the following URL would be used to load the application into your web browser if your website's URL was www.tech-publishing.com and you elected to create a subfolder named "test" into which you placed the application's files.

```
http://www.tech-publishing.com/test/index.html
```

TRICK Actually, since all you are working with at this point is HTML, you can test your application directly from your desktop without first uploading its HTML files to your web server. To do this, all you have to do is start up your web browser and instead of loading index.html by specifying its URL, you click on the File menu and select the Open command and then specify the name and location of the HTML file. To work, a copy of the joke.txt file must reside in the same folder as the index.html file.

Once loaded into your web browser, you should see the web page shown in Figure 1.20 appear, displaying the application's joke and a link labeled Fetch Answer.

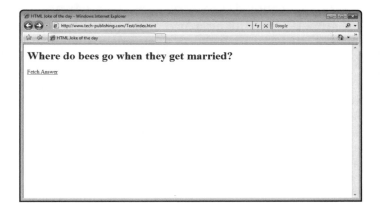

FIGURE 1.20

The HTML version of the Joke of the Day application relies on a link to the text file containing the joke's punch line.

To view the joke's punch line, click on the link. Within a few moments, the browser window will blink and the contents of the joke.txt will load, as shown in Figure 1.21. As you can see, this is a pretty standard HTML application. It involves loading an initial web page, after which additional data is presented by loading new web pages into the browser window while the user waits for the browser's window to reload.

HINT Since this application was small and does not make use of large amounts of graphics or sounds, everything happens pretty quickly, so you may not notice a significant delay. However, if the web page was loaded down, the delay would have been more obvious.

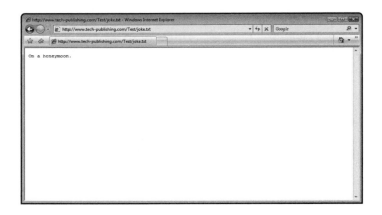

FIGURE 1.21

To open and display the contents of the text file, the browser must load it, replacing the currently open HTML page.

Step 4: Turning the HTML Application into an Ajax Application

Now that you have the HTML version of the Joke of the Day application up and running, you are ready to convert it to an Ajax application. Do so by opening the index.html application in your preferred code or text editor and modifying it as shown here:

 Beginning new Ajax applications by first developing them as HTML applications is a very popular approach to Ajax development. Applying Ajax to an existing HTML page is often easier than trying to develop a new Ajax application from scratch. In addition, since Ajax does have a number of limitations that have yet to be completely overcome, as discussed in Chapter 10, "Important Ajax Design Issues," having an HTML and an Ajax version of your application provides the ability to service web surfers whose computers can and cannot support Ajax applications. You will learn more about dealing with this type of situation in Chapter 3, "A Deeper Dive into JavaScript."

```
<HTML>

  <HEAD>

    <TITLE>Ajax Joke of the Day Application</TITLE>

    <SCRIPT language = "javascript" type = "text/javascript">

      var Request = false;

      if (window.XMLHttpRequest) {
        Request = new XMLHttpRequest();
```

```
      } else if (window.ActiveXObject) {
        Request = new ActiveXObject("Microsoft.XMLHTTP");
      }

      function retrieveJoke(url, elementID) {

        if(Request) {
          var RequestObj = document.getElementById(elementID);
          Request.open("GET", url);
          Request.onreadystatechange = function()
          {
            if (Request.readyState == 4 && Request.status == 200) {
                RequestObj.innerHTML = Request.responseText;
            }
          }
          Request.send(null);
        }
      }

  </SCRIPT>

</HEAD>

<BODY>

  <H1>Where do bees go when they get married?</H1>

  <FORM>
    <INPUT type = "button" value = "Fetch Answer"
      onclick = "retrieveJoke('joke.txt', 'DivTarget')">
  </FORM>

  <DIV id="DivTarget"> </DIV>

</BODY>

</HTML>
```

As you can see, the Ajax version of the Joke of the Day application involves the addition of a considerable number of new statements. Since this book has yet to review the intricacies of creating Ajax applications, this chapter won't go into great detail about what each and every one of the new statements in index.html does. Instead, let's keep things at a reasonably high level. Figure 1.22 breaks down the new code statements that you have added to the Ajax version of the application.

```
<html>

  <head>

    <title>Ajax Joke of the Day Application</title>

    <script language = "javascript" type = "text/javascript">

      var Request = false;                                        } Variable

      if (window.XMLHttpRequest) {
        Request = new XMLHttpRequest();                             XMLHttpRequest
      } else if (window.ActiveXObject) {                            Object
        Request = new ActiveXObject("Microsoft.XMLHTTP");
      }

      function retrieveJoke(url, elementID) {

        if(Request) {

          var RequestObj = document.getElementById(elementID);

          Request.open("GET", url);

          Request.onreadystatechange = function()
          {
            if (Request.readyState == 4 && Request.status == 200) {   Function
              RequestObj.innerHTML = Request.responseText;
            }
          }

          Request.send(null);

        }
      }

    </script>

  </head>

  <body>

    <H1>Where do bees go when they get married?</H1>

    <form>                                                          Event Driven
      <input type = "button" value = "Fetch Answer"                 Function call
        onclick = "retrieveJoke('joke.txt', 'DivTarget')">
    </form>

    <div id="DivTarget"> </div>                                     Placeholder
                                                                    for Text
  </body>

</html>
```

JavaScript (brace spanning the script section)

Form (brace for the form section)

Div Tags (brace for the div section)

FIGURE 1.22

The HTML page has been turned into an Ajax application through the addition of a number of new code components.

As Figure 1.22 shows, most of the new statements that have been added to index.html make up a JavaScript, which begins and ends with <script> and </script> tags. Within the script, variables are used to store data, an XMLHttpRequest object is set up to enable communication with the application's web server, and a function is used to set up a connection to the web server and retrieve a text string containing the joke's punch line.

The rest of the statements added to index.html are used to create a form made up of a button that, when clicked, triggers an event that results in the execution of a function named retrieveJoke(). There is also a pair of Div tags in the body section that provide the application with a placeholder where the joke's punch line will be displayed.

Hopefully, you already know how to work with forms and Div tags. Just in case, this book will briefly touch on them as well as introduce you to programming with JavaScript and the XMLHttpRequest object in Chapters 3 and 4.

Step 5: Executing Your New Ajax Application

Once you have created the Ajax version of the Joke of the Day application, you will need to upload it to your website before you can test its execution. Once you have done this, open your web browser and enter the URL for the index.html web page. For example, the following URL would be used to load your Ajax application if your website's URL was www.yourURL.com and you elected to create a subfolder named "test" into which you placed the application's files.

```
http://www.yourURL.com/test/index.html
```

Once loaded, your copy of the Joke of the Day application should operate exactly as was demonstrated at the beginning of this chapter, instantly displaying the joke's punch line when the Fetch Answer button is pressed, without any page refresh.

The Final Result

All right, at this point your new Ajax version of the Joke of the Day application should be ready for testing. To test the application, you had to upload the modified version of the HTML page to your web server and then load it using your web browser. Once loaded, you were able to view the application's new interface and click on its button control in order to retrieve and load the punch line for the application's joke. Assuming that you followed along carefully when creating this new application and that you did not run into any problems uploading it to your web server, everything should work as described.

In the event that you run into any errors, make sure you have entered the correct URL for the application into your browser. If your URL is okay, go back and double-check the statements that make up the Ajax version of the application and look for any mistakes that you may have made when keying it in.

You will find a copy of this application's source code files on the book's companion website, located at http://www.courseptr.com/downloads.

SUMMARY

This chapter provided an introduction to Ajax. You learned how to use the different technologies that Ajax harnesses in order to build fast and responsive desktop-like applications. You learned how Ajax applications differ from traditional HTML applications and reviewed a number of different websites where Ajax has been used, examining how Ajax was used to enhance and improve the application. You also learned how to create your first Ajax application, which you created by modifying an existing HTML application to communicate with and retrieve a text file from a remote web server.

Before you move on to Chapter 2, "An Introduction to JavaScript," consider setting aside a little extra time to improve the Joke of the Day application by addressing the following challenges.

CHALLENGES

1. The joke told by the Joke of the Day application is somewhat bland. Why not spice it up a bit by replacing it with a joke that reflects your own sense of humor?

2. Consider creating a copy of the Joke of the Day application, perhaps making a Joke of the Week application, and set it up to tell a different joke.

Part

II

Learning JavaScript and the DOM

AN INTRODUCTION TO JAVASCRIPT

J avaScript is the programming language that binds together HTML with all of the other technologies that make up Ajax applications. As such, a good understanding of how to program with JavaScript is essential to Ajax developers. The focus of this chapter and the next chapter is to help you build a good JavaScript foundation, providing you with an understanding of basic JavaScript programming concepts needed to support the development of Ajax applications.

Specifically, you will learn:

- About JavaScript's origins and browser compatibility
- How to create and embed JavaScript in web pages
- How to formulate JavaScript statements and comply with JavaScript syntax
- How to collect, store, and modify data using variables
- How to apply conditional and iterative programming logic

PROJECT PREVIEW: THE NUMBER GUESSING GAME

Since the objective of this chapter is to teach you the fundamentals of JavaScript programming, this chapter will end by showing you how to create a JavaScript game called the Number Guessing game. As demonstrated in Figure 2.1, this game begins by displaying a popup dialog window that challenges the player to try to guess a number from 1 to 10.

FIGURE 2.1

To submit a guess, the player must type in a number and click on the OK button.

Once a guess has been submitted, the popup dialog window disappears and the player's guess is analyzed to determine whether it is correct, too low, or too high. If the player's guess was incorrect, a dialog similar to the one shown in Figure 2.2 is displayed, giving the player a hint to help guide her next guess.

FIGURE 2.2

The player's guess was too low.

The player may make as many guesses as required to guess the game's secret number. Figure 2.3 shows the message that is displayed once the player finally guesses the secret number.

FIGURE 2.3

The player has won the game.

As shown in Figure 2.4, at the end of each game the player is prompted to play another round. If the player types the letter y and clicks on the OK button, a new secret number is generated and everything starts over again. Otherwise, game play ends.

FIGURE 2.4

The player is prompted to play another round.

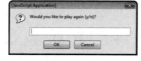

Once the player has decided to stop playing the game, the popup dialog window shown in Figure 2.5 is displayed, thanking the player for playing the game.

FIGURE 2.5

The game thanks
the player for
taking the time to
play the game.

JAVASCRIPT—AJAX'S PROGRAMMING LANGUAGE

JavaScript is a computer programming language designed to execute within web browsers. JavaScript is used in the development of small programs referred to as scripts, which are embedded inside HTML pages. When executed, these scripts provide the ability to add interactive content to any web page. JavaScript is an interpreted programming language, which means that scripts written in JavaScript are not converted into an executable form until the HTML page that contains them is processed. As such, JavaScript is a little slower than compiled programming languages, which are converted or compiled into executable code at the end of the development process, allowing for faster execution.

JavaScript is an object-based programming language. It sees everything within HTML files and the browser as *objects*. To Javascript, the browser is an object; browser windows are objects as are form text fields and buttons. Resources like image files are also viewed as just another type of object. Every object has *properties*, which describe some feature or aspect of the object. For example, a button can display text, which can be specified using its text property. Graphic images also have properties. Using these properties you can, for example, specify the size of graphics displayed in web pages.

In addition to properties, objects also have *methods*, which are collections of script statements that when called upon to execute, enable the objects with which they are associated to perform certain predefined actions. For example, you can add custom methods to your JavaScripts that when called upon to execute, will perform actions like opening and closing browser windows. Using object properties and methods, the JavaScripts that make up your Ajax applications can dynamically alter the content and presentation of web pages.

One important feature of JavaScript that is essential to Ajax programming is the ability to execute program code based on the occurrence of different events. An *event* is an action that is initiated whenever the user interacts with your web application. As covered in Chapter 3, events occur when web pages are opened and closed. Events also occur whenever the user clicks on the text fields, buttons, or other objects displayed on web pages.

A Little JavaScript Background Information

JavaScript was developed in 1995 by Netscape Communication Corporation in order to provide web page developers with greater control over the presentation of their web pages.

JavaScript's original name was LiveScript. Later, when Java arrived on the scene and began to receive massive amounts of attention, Netscape decided to rename it to JavaScript. Beyond the similarity of their names, Java and JavaScript have little in common.

Using JavaScript, web page developers were able to incorporate programming logic into the client-side portion of their applications and web pages. JavaScript provides web page developers with the ability to integrate graphics effects like rollover images and text in their web pages. Using JavaScript in conjunction with the DOM (covered in Chapter 4, "Understanding the Document Object Model"), web developers were able to exercise precise control over the content of both web pages and the browser that loaded and displayed them.

Realizing the popularity of Netscape's JavaScript programming language, Microsoft decided to develop its own version of the programming language which it named Jscript. Unfortunately, Microsoft Jscript was not 100-percent compatible with JavaScript, which led to much confusion and helped to begin the web browser wars. To try to make things better, Netscape began working with the European Computer Manufacturing Association or ECMA to standardize JavaScript, which it did in the form of ECMAScript.

In recent years, many of the differences between JavaScript and Jscript have disappeared as web browser developers moved towards embracing the ECMAScript version of JavaScript. However, small differences still exist today in the manner in which different web browsers support JavaScript. Where relevant, this book will point out these differences and explain how to overcome them as you develop your Ajax applications.

Browser Compatibility Issues

One major area of concern for Ajax developers is browser compatibility. Unfortunately, even though Netscape and Microsoft's browser war has been over for many years, there are still many differences in the ways that modern web browsers support JavaScript. Things are made even more complicated by the fact that there are so many different web browsers in use. Examples of popular web browsers include:

- Internet Explorer (www.microsoft.com/Windows/Downloads/IE)
- Firefox (www.mozilla.com/en-US/firefox/)
- Safari (www.apple.com/safari/)
- Konqueror (www.konqueror.org)
- Flock (www.flock.com)
- Opera (www.opera.com)

Because of compatibility differences between different browsers, web pages sometimes look and behave differently depending on which browser has been used to load and execute them.

A big part of Ajax development is developing an understanding of existing compatibility issues and dealing with them.

> Because differences in JavaScript support exist between the main web browsers, you will want to test your Ajax applications using more than one browser. At a minimum, you will want to test your Ajax applications using Internet Explorer, Firefox, and Safari.

One very important difference between web browsers is the manner in which they support the creation of the XMLHttpRequest object. This object provides Ajax applications the ability to asynchronously request and process data retrieved from web servers. You will learn all about this object and how to create and work with it in Chapter 3, "A Deeper Dive into JavaScript."

> Unfortunately there are also differences in JavaScript support for different versions of the same browser. To combat this, you may want to test your Ajax applications using previous versions of the major web browsers.

WORKING WITH JAVASCRIPT

JavaScripts are embedded inside the head or body sections of an HTML page. JavaScripts are inserted into HTML pages using <SCRIPT> and </SCRIPT> tags. Figure 2.6 outlines the syntax that must be followed when using these tags.

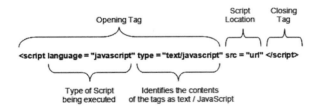

FIGURE 2.6

The syntax required to add a JavaScript to an HTML file in your Ajax applications.

As you can see, the syntax outlined in Figure 2.6 includes a number of arguments, all of which are located in the opening <SCRIPT> tag. The language attribute is used to specify JavaScript as the scripting language in use. The type attribute is always text/javascript and the scr attribute is used to specify an optional external file where the JavaScript can be stored.

> The language attribute represents an old way of specifying script type. The HTML 4.0 specification states that the type attribute is the proper way to specify script type. You can use both attributes if you want. This will help ensure that older browsers will be able to run your JavaScripts.

Creating a Simple JavaScript

Now that you have seen the syntax required to work with the `<SCRIPT>` and `</SCRIPT>` tags, let's look at an example of how to use them to add a simple JavaScript to an HTML page. To begin, create and save the HTML page shown here, assigning it a name of `hello.html`.

```
<HTML>
  <HEAD>
    <TITLE>My first JavaScript</TITLE>
  </HEAD>
  <BODY>
  </BODY>
</HTML>
```

As you can see, this is a pretty ordinary HTML page. Now add the following JavaScript statements to its head section.

```
<SCRIPT language = "javascript" type = "text/javascript">
  document.write("Hello World!");
</SCRIPT>
```

When you are done, the HTML page should look like the example shown here:

```
<HTML>
  <HEAD>
    <TITLE>My first JavaScript</TITLE>
    <SCRIPT language = "javascript" type = "text/javascript">
      document.write("Hello World!");
    </SCRIPT>
  </HEAD>
  <BODY>
  </BODY>
</HTML>
```

You should recognize the first and last JavaScript statements as being the script's opening and closing tags. The second statement instructs the browser to write a text string of `"Hello World!"` on to the current document (web page).

Executing Your JavaScript

To run your new JavaScript, open the web page in which it resides using your web browser. Since this example consists of only HTML and JavaScript and there is no interaction with any web server, you do not even have to upload it to your web browser. Double-click on it and it will automatically be loaded into your default browser. Alternatively, you can open and execute it by starting your web browser and then executing the Open command located on the File menu. For example, the following procedure outlines the steps involved in loading the HTML page using Internet Explorer.

1. Start Internet Explorer.
2. Click on File and then click on Open. The Open dialog window is displayed.
3. Type the location of your HTML page and click on OK or click on the Browse button to locate your HTML file and then click on OK. Internet Explorer will open your HTML page and automatically run its embedded JavaScript, as demonstrated in Figure 2.7.

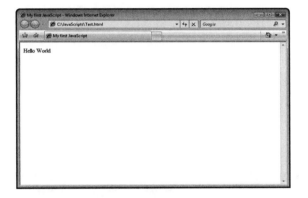

FIGURE 2.7

Using Internet Explorer to execute an HTML page with an embedded JavaScript.

If the words `Hello World` do not appear then you have most likely made a typo, which you should be able to locate and fix by re-checking the HTML file.

FOUR WAYS OF WORKING WITH JAVASCRIPT

In addition to embedding JavaScripts in either the head or the body section of HTML pages, you can also store your JavaScripts in external files. You can also integrate JavaScript statements directly into an HTML tag. All four of these options are examined in the sections that follow.

Embedding JavaScripts in the HEAD Section

By convention, most Ajax developers place their application's JavaScripts in the head section of their HTML pages. JavaScripts embedded in the head section can be set up to automatically or conditionally execute when HTML pages load. Most Ajax developers place all JavaScript functions and most variable declarations in the head section in order to ensure they are defined and available before the rest of the HTML page loads, but do not automatically execute them when the HTML page loads.

A *variable* is a pointer to a location in computer memory where data is stored. A *function* is a named collection of JavaScript statements that can be called on to perform a task.

The following HTML page includes a JavaScript embedded in the head section. The JavaScript automatically executes when the HTML page loads.

```
<HTML>
  <HEAD>
    <TITLE>Demo: Automatic JavaScript execution</TITLE>
    <SCRIPT language = "javascript" type = "text/javascript">
      window.alert("Boo!");
    </SCRIPT>
  </HEAD>
  <BODY>
  </BODY>
<HTML>
```

Take note of the use of the window object's alert method (window.alert) in the preceding example. This method lets you display a text message with an OK button in a popup dialog window and is great for displaying individual messages that do not require user interaction. The following statements outline the syntax required to work with the alert method.

```
window.alert("message");
```

You will learn more about how to work with objects and their methods in Chapter 3.

When loaded, this HTML page displays a text message in a popup dialog, as demonstrated in Figure 2.8.

FIGURE 2.8

An example of a JavaScript that is automatically executed when its HTML page loads.

As this example demonstrated, any time you embed a JavaScript inside an HTML page's head section, it will automatically execute when the page loads. However, if you organize your JavaScript using functions, those functions only execute when called upon to run. For example, the following HTML page contains an embedded JavaScript made up of a function named `ScareUser()` that does not execute when the HTML page is initially loaded.

```
<HTML>
  <HEAD>
    <TITLE>Demo: Organizing Javascript into functions</TITLE>
    <SCRIPT language = "javascript" type = "text/javascript">
      function ScareUser() {
        window.alert("Boo!");
      }
    </SCRIPT>
  </HEAD>
  <BODY>
  </BODY>
</HTML>
```

Because the JavaScript statements are now stored inside a function, they do not execute unless called upon to run from elsewhere in the HTML page. You will learn all about functions and how to use them in Chapter 3.

Embedding JavaScripts in the BODY Section

JavaScripts can also be placed in the body section of HTML pages. Scripts embedded in the body section are automatically executed when the page loads. The following example demonstrates how to embed a JavaScript in an HTML page's body section.

```
<BODY>
  <SCRIPT language = "javascript" type = "text/javascript">
    document.write("Boo!");
  </SCRIPT>
</BODY>
```

If your Ajax applications require it, you can embed multiple JavaScripts in the same HTML page, as demonstrated here:

```
<BODY>
  <SCRIPT language = "javascript" type = "text/javascript">
    document.write("Boo!");
```

```
</SCRIPT>
<BR>
<SCRIPT language = "javascript" type = "text/javascript">
  document.write("Did I scare you?");
</SCRIPT>
</BODY>
```

Placing JavaScripts in External Files

Large Ajax applications often consist of complex HTML pages and a lot of JavaScript. When programmers embed a lot of JavaScript inside complex HTML files, the resulting code can become hard to understand and manage. One common way Ajax developers deal with this problem is to store the JavaScript and HTML code in separate files.

 TRICK If you store your Ajax application's JavaScripts in external script files, you can better handle cross-browser issues by creating different JavaScripts for different browsers and then calling upon the appropriate external file based on which browser is being used.

To store a JavaScript in an external file, save it in a plain text file with a .js file extension. Once you have done this, you can refer to it using the scr attribute, as demonstrated here:

```
<SCRIPT src="Test.js" language="javascript" type="text/javascript">
</SCRIPT>
```

The external JavaScript file can contain one or more JavaScripts. One thing that it cannot contain is HTML. Otherwise, an error will occur. The JavaScripts that you store in external files can be of any length.

There are a number of reasons that Ajax developers like to store JavaScripts in external files. Moving JavaScript statements out of HTML pages makes the pages smaller and easier to manage. External JavaScript files can be referenced and used by more than one Ajax application. Should you need to later modify an external JavaScript, you can do so without having to modify every HTML page that references it, which would be the case if you hard coded the JavaScript in every page that referenced it.

Embedding JavaScripts in HTML Tags

In addition to placing your JavaScripts in an HTML page's head or body section or in an external file, you can also embed individual JavaScript statements within HTML tags, as demonstrated here:

```
<BODY onLoad = document.write("Boo!")> <BODY>
```

Here, the JavaScript statement `onLoad=document.write("Boo!")` has been embedded within a `<BODY>` tag. This statement instructs the browser to display the specified text when the browser loads the HTML page.

Embedding individual JavaScript statements in HTML tags gives you an easy way to execute individual JavaScript statements. However, as covered in Chapter 3, to initiate the execution of JavaScripts placed in the head or body section or scripts stored externally, you need to call on JavaScript functions. Learning how to set this up is a key step in becoming an effective Ajax developer.

Understanding JavaScript Statement Syntax

JavaScript is a case-sensitive programming language. This differs from HTML, which allows you to use different capitalization when formulating HTML tags. You must use correct spelling and capitalization when formulating JavaScript statements. For example, JavaScript requires that when you refer to the `document` object and its methods and properties, you use all lowercase spelling. If you do not an error will occur.

Except for its strict application of case-sensitivity, JavaScript is a very flexible programming language that does not impose many rules regarding the formulation of scripts. Statements generally begin and end on the same line. However, you can begin on one line and continue a statement onto the next line if you need to. You can even put multiple statements on the same line by separating them with semicolons (;). Javascript uses semicolons to identify the end of statements. However, you are not required to add them. Still, it is considered to be a good programming practice to end all JavaScript statements with semicolons.

 TRICK   JavaScript also allows you to make liberal use of white space. Any number of blank lines can be inserted between script statements in order to make them more readable.

Dealing with Browsers That Do Not Support JavaScript

One of the challenges that Ajax developers face is that many people surfing the web are using web browsers that either do not support JavaScript or that have been configured to disable JavaScript support. One way of addressing this issue is to use HTML comment tags to hide JavaScript statements from browsers that cannot understand them. HTML comments are embedded within `<!--` and `-->` characters. Browsers will ignore any text placed inside these characters.

All browsers know not to display the <SCRIPT> tags, whether they support JavaScript or not. However, browsers that do not support JavaScript do not know what to do with the statements located inside the <SCRIPT> tag and will display the script statements as part of the HTML page. To prevent this from happening, all you have to do is enclose the JavaScript statements located in the <SCRIPT> and </SCRIPT> tags within HTML comments, as demonstrated here:

```
<HTML>
  <HEAD>
    <TITLE>Demo: Hiding JavaScript from non-supporting browsers</TITLE>
  </HEAD>
  <BODY>
    <SCRIPT language = "javascript" type = "text/javascript">
    <!-- Start hiding JavaScript statements
      document.write("Boo!");
    // End hiding JavaScript statements -->
    </SCRIPT>
  </BODY>
</HTML>
```

When coded this way, browsers that do not support JavaScript will ignore the JavaScript statements as comments.

Documenting Your Scripts Using Comments

In order to make your JavaScripts easier to understand and maintain, it is recommended that you get into the habit of embedding comment statements that document what is going on into your Ajax applications. Comments have no effect on the performance of JavaScripts. JavaScript supports two types of comments. For starters, you can add a comment line at any location within a script by typing // followed by the text of your comment, as demonstrated here:

```
//The following statement displays a scary message
document.write("Boo!");
```

You can also append a comment to the end of any statement, as demonstrated here:

```
document.write("Boo!");  //This statement displays a scary message
```

JavaScript also allows you to create multi-line comments by placing text inside opening /* and closing */ characters, as demonstrated here:

```
/* The following statement displays a short but very scary message directly
on the browser window */
document.write("Boo!");
```

WORKING WITH DIFFERENT TYPES OF VALUES

Ajax applications store and manipulate data as they execute. JavaScript makes an implicit determination about every type of data that it works with. This value assignment has a direct effect on how JavaScript handles the data. Table 2.1 lists the different types of values that JavaScript supports.

TABLE 2.1	JAVASCRIPT SUPPORTED VALUES
Value	**Description**
Boolean	A value indicating a condition of either true or false
Null	An empty value
Numbers	A numeric value
Strings	A string of text enclosed in matching quotation marks

You can store and manipulate data in your JavaScripts using variables. A *variable* to a location in memory where an individual piece of data is stored.

Creating Javascript Variables

Before you can use a variable in a Javascript, you must declare or define it. Variable declaration can be done either explicitly or implicitly. To explicitly declare a variable, you can use the var keyword, as demonstrated here:

```
var playerName = "Wing Commander";
```

Here, a variable named playerName has been defined and assigned a value of Wing Commander. To implicitly declare a variable, reference it for the first time, as demonstrated here:

```
playerName = "Wing Commander";
```

Explicit variable declaration is a good programming practice. It helps make your scripts easier to read and understand.

Assigning Variable Names

JavaScript is very flexible in its support of variable names. There are, however, a few rules that you must follow, as outlined here:

- Variable names can only consist of uppercase and lowercase letters, the underscore character, and the numbers 0 through 9.
- Variable names cannot begin with a number.
- Variable names cannot contain spaces.
- Reserved words cannot be used as variable names.

Remember that variables are case-sensitive. If you declare a variable with the name `playerCount`, you must refer to it using the exact same case throughout your JavaScript. Another important point to consider when assigning variable names is that good variable names are descriptive of their contents or purpose. For example, `PlayerName` is much more descriptive than `pn`.

Understanding Variable Scope

The term *scope* refers to the location within JavaScripts where a variable exists and can be accessed. JavaScript supports two types of variable scopes, global and local. Variables with a global scope can be accessed by any JavaScript embedded within an HTML page. Local variables are variables created within functions. Local variables can only be accessed by statements located within the functions where they are defined.

 An understanding of scope is often difficult for new programmers to understand. Do not worry if the idea of scope seems a little vague at this point. The concept will become clearer as you gain further programming experience.

Working with Global Variables

A *global variable* is a variable that can be referenced and modified by any script statement located in the web page. Global variable can be defined in a couple of ways, including:

- An initial reference to a new variable from inside a function without using the `var` keyword.
- Defining a variable outside of a function (with or without the `var` keyword).

Working with Local Variables

Local variables are explicitly declared inside functions using the `var` keyword. A *function* is a named collection of code statements that can be called on for execution from different locations within a script or HTML page. As an example of how to create a local variable, take a look at the following statements.

```
function DisplayGreeting() {
  var greetingText = "Hello World!";
  document.write(greetingText);
}
```

Here, a function named `DisplayGreeting()` has been created that when called upon to execute will declare a local variable named `greetingText`, assign a text string to it, and then display the text string in the browser window. The value assigned to `greetingText` is inaccessible outside of the function.

Doing a Little Math

When working with numeric data, JavaScript lets you perform arithmetic calculations using the operators listed in Table 2.2. Using these operators, you can develop statements that perform virtually any type of calculation and then assign the result to a variable.

TABLE 2.2   JAVASCRIPT MATHEMATICAL OPERATORS

Operator	Description	Example
+	Adds two values together	`playerScore = 5 + 10`
-	Subtracts one value from another	`playerScore = 10 - 5`
*	Multiplies two values together	`playerScore = 5 * 10`
/	Divides one value by another	`playerScore = 10 / 5`
-x	Reverses a variable's sign	`count = -count`
x++	Post-increment (returns x, then increments x by one)	`x = y++`
++x	Pre-increment (increments x by one, then returns x)	`x = ++y`
x--	Post-decrement (returns x, then decrements x by one)	`x = y--`
--x	Pre-decrement (decrements x by one, then returns x)	`x = --y`

Use of the first four operators listed in Table 2.2 should be self explanatory. However, the remaining operators require additional explanation. The x++ and ++x operators provide the ability to increment a value of x by 1. The difference in the way these two operators work is when the update occurs. Suppose for example that you had two variables, `playerScore` and `noOfHits`. If `noOfHits` was set equal to 100 and the following statement was then executed, the value assigned to `noOfHits` would be incremented by 1 and a value of 101 would then be assigned to `playerScore`.

```
playerScore = ++noOfHits;
```

Using the x++ operator, as shown here, results in a different result.

```
playerScore = noOfHits++;
```

What happens here is that the value of noOfHits (e.g., 100) is first assigned to playerScore and only once this has occurred is the value of noOfHits incremented to 101. The --x and x-- operators work identically to the ++x and x++ operators except that they decrement a variable's value by 1.

Assigning and Modifying Variable Values

As you have already seen, to assign an initial value to a variable, you need to use the = operator. Likewise, to modify a variable's assigned value all you have to do is assign it a new value using use the = operator, as demonstrated here:

```
playerScore = 0;
.
.
.
playerScore = 100;
```

In addition to the = operator, JavaScript lets you modify variable values using any of the operators listed in Table 2.3.

TABLE 2.3	JAVASCRIPT ASSIGNMENT OPERATORS	
Operator	**Description**	**Examples**
=	Sets a variable value equal to some value	x = y + 1
+=	Shorthand for x = x + y	x += y
-=	Shorthand for x = x - y	x -= y
*=	Shorthand for x = x * y	x *= y
/=	Shorthand for x = x / y	x /= y
%=	Shorthand for x = x % y	x %= y

To better understand how to work with the operators shown in Table 2.3, take a look at the following example.

```
<HTML>
  <HEAD>
    <TITLE>Demo: Using JavaScript operators</TITLE>
  </HEAD>
  <BODY>
    <SCRIPT language = "javascript" type = "text/javascript">
    <!-- Start hiding JavaScript statements
      var x = 3;
      var y = 10;
      var z = 0;
      z = x + y;
      document.write("x + y = " + z);
      z += 2
      document.write("<BR>x += y = " + z);
      z -= 5
      document.write("<BR>x -= y = " + z);
      z *= 3
      document.write("<BR>x *= y = " + z);
      z /= 2
      document.write("<BR>x /= y = " + z);
      z %= 4
      document.write("<BR>x %= y = " + z);
    // End hiding JavaScript statements -->
    </SCRIPT>
  </BODY>
</HTML>
```

 Take note of the use of the `<BR>` **tag located inside the** `document.write()` **statement. This tag provides a means of controlling line breaks with JavaScripts. Also take note of the use of the + operator, which when used with strings instead of numeric data, lets you join two strings together to form a new string.**

As you can see, three variables named x, y, and z have been defined and assigned initial starting values. Next, six pairs of statements are used that demonstrate the use of a particular operator. For example, the first pair of statements adds x and y and assigns the result to z. The resulting value is then written to the browser window. Figure 2.9 shows the output that is produced when this script is executed.

FIGURE 2.9

A simple example
of how to work
with JavaScript
operators.

Comparing Different Values

One very common task in most Ajax applications is the comparison of values. Depending on the result of that analysis, the application will alter its execution. For example, an application might take one action if a value was greater than 100 and a different action if the value was less than 100. As shown in Table 2.4, JavaScript supports a number of different comparison operators.

TABLE 2.4	JAVASCRIPT COMPARISON OPERATORS	
Operator	**Description**	**Example**
==	Equal to	x == y
!==	Not equal to	x !== y
>	Greater than	x > y
>=	Greater than or equal to	x >= y
<	Less than	x < y
<=	Less than or equal to	x <= y

Note that when checking to see if two values are equal, JavaScript requires that you use the == comparison operator and not the = assignment operator. For example, the following statements check to see if the values assigned to two variables are equal.

```
if (x == y) {
document.write("Bingo!");
}
```

By modifying this example, as shown below, you can easily adjust it to formulate a test that checks to see if the value of x is greater than or equal to y.

```
if (x >= y) {
document.write("Bingo!");
}
```

APPLYING CONDITIONAL LOGIC

Conditional programming logic enables you to alter the logical execution flow of your Ajax applications based on the result of comparison operations. Specifically, conditional logic allows you to execute one set of statements when the tested condition proves `true` and a separate set of statements when the tested condition evaluates as `false`.

Introducing the if Statement

Using the `if` statement you can check whether a logical condition is `true` or `false` and conditionally execute one or more statements. In its simplest form, the syntax of the `if` statement is outlined here:

```
if (condition)
   statement
```

Here, *condition* is an expression, enclosed within parentheses that evaluates as being either `true` or `false`. The easiest way to learn how to use the `if` statement is to observe it in action, so take a look at the following example.

```
<HTML>
  <HEAD>
    <TITLE>Demo: Working with the if statement</TITLE>
  </HEAD>
  <BODY>
    <SCRIPT language = "javascript" type = "text/javascript">
    <!-- Start hiding JavaScript statements
      var playerScore = 99;
      if (playerScore < 100) document.write("You lose, try again.");
    // End hiding JavaScript statements -->
    </SCRIPT>
  </BODY>
</HTML>
```

Here, the value assigned to a variable named playerScore is checked to see if it is less than 100, and if it is, the string "You lose, try again." is displayed. However, if the value assigned to playerScore is not less than 100, the string is not displayed.

Multi-line if Statements

Using the { and } characters, you can use the if statement to create a code block made up of any number of statements, all of which are executed in the event the tested conditional proves true. To see how this works, take a look at the following example.

```
<HTML>
  <HEAD>
    <TITLE>Demo: Working with the if statement</TITLE>
  </HEAD>
  <BODY>
    <SCRIPT language = "javascript" type = "text/javascript">
    <!-- Start hiding JavaScript statements
      var playerScore = 101;
      if (playerScore > 100) {
        document.write("You win!");
        window.alert("Winner!");
      }
    // End hiding JavaScript statements -->
    </SCRIPT>
  </BODY>
</HTML>
```

Here, two statements are executed if the value of playerScore is greater than 100.

Providing for Alternative Conditions

Using an optional else keyword, you can modify an if statement code block to execute an alternative set of statements in the event the tested condition evaluates as false. An example demonstrating how this works is provided here:

```
<HTML>
  <HEAD>
    <TITLE>Demo: Working with the if statement</TITLE>
  </HEAD>
  <BODY>
    <SCRIPT language = "javascript" type = "text/javascript">
```

```
<!-- Start hiding JavaScript statements
  var playerScore = 99;
  if (playerScore <= 100) {
    document.write("You lose, try again.");
  }
  else {
    document.write("You win!");
  }
// End hiding JavaScript statements -->
</SCRIPT>
  </BODY>
</HTML>
```

Here, the text string "You lose, try again." is displayed if playerScore is less than or equal to 100, and a string of "You win!" is displayed if playerScore is not less than or equal to 100. Note that the statements associated with the else keyword are embedded inside the opening { and closing } characters.

Nesting if Statements

One powerful way of using the if statement is to embed or nest it within another if statement code block in order to set up more complex and sophisticated conditional logic. The following statements provide an example of how you might use nested if statements.

```
<HTML>
  <HEAD>
    <TITLE>Demo: Working with the if statement</TITLE>
  </HEAD>
  <BODY>
    <SCRIPT language = "javascript" type = "text/javascript">
    <!-- Start hiding JavaScript statements
      var gameOver = false;
      var playerScore = 199;
      if (gameOver == true) {
       if (playerScore <= 100) {
         document.write("You lose, try again.");
        }
        else {
         document.write("You win!");
        }
```

```
      }
      else {
        document.write("It is not over yet. Try again.");
      }
    // End hiding JavaScript statements -->
    </SCRIPT>
  </BODY>
</HTML>
```

Here, the value of gameOver is checked to see if it is equal to true. If it is, the embedded if statement code block executes, evaluating the value of playerScore, executing either of two statements depending on whether playerScore is less than or equal to 100.

Working with the switch Statement

JavaScript also supports the execution of conditional logic using the switch statement. This statement evaluates a series of conditional tests or cases, executing code statements belonging to the first case statement that evaluates as true. The syntax of the switch statement is outlined here:

```
switch (expression) {
  case label:
    statements;
  break;
  .
  .
  .
  case label:
    statements;
  break;
  default:
    statements;
}
```

Here, the value of the expression is compared against the value of each case. The statements belonging to the first case statements whose value equals that of the expression is executed. If no case statements prove true, the statements belonging to the default statement are executed. Note that the default statement is optional and if omitted, no action occurs in the event that none of the case statements evaluate as true.

Note that the break statement located at the end of each case is optional. When present, the break statement tells the script to exit the switch statement when a match is found. If you were to remove the optional break statements, the script would execute the statements belonging to any case statement whose value matched the value of the expression.

To get a better feel for how to work with the switch statement, take a look at the following example,

```
<HTML>
  <HEAD>
    <TITLE>Demo: Working with the switch statement</TITLE>
  </HEAD>
  <BODY>
    <SCRIPT language = "javascript" type = "text/javascript">
    <!-- Start hiding JavaScript statements
      var fruit = window.prompt("Pick a fruit: apple, orange or pear?");
      switch (fruit) {
        case "apple":
          document.write("The apples are nice and red this year.");
          break;
        case "orange":
          document.write("The oranges were hand picked this morning.");
          break;
        case "pear":
          document.write("Pears are on sale for half off today.");
          break;
        default:
          document.write("Sorry, this fruit is not in stock.");
      }
    // End hiding JavaScript statements -->
    </SCRIPT>
  </BODY>
</HTML>
```

Here, the user is prompted to type in the name of a fruit. The user's input is then analyzed using a switch code block and 1 of 4 messages is written to the browser window, depending on the user's input. Figures 2.10 and 2.11 demonstrate the execution of this example using the Firefox browser.

TRICK

Take note of the variable declaration statement in the previous example. It uses the `window` object's `prompt` method to display a message in a popup dialog window that prompts the user to enter a response and click on the dialog's OK button. The following statements outline the statement's syntax.

```
window.prompt("message" [, "default"]);
```

Here, *message* is a text string displayed in the dialog window and *default* is an optional parameter that when specified, displays default text in the popup dialog's entry field.

You should use the `window` object's `prompt` method when you want to collect a quick piece of data from the user. It will save you the trouble of having to define an HTML form in which to collect the data. You will learn more about how to work with objects and their methods in Chapter 3.

FIGURE 2.10

Prompting the user for input using a popup dialog window.

FIGURE 2.11

Using the `switch` statements to analyze and process user input.

Working Efficiently with Loops

Loops are collections of statements that are repeatedly executed. Loops provide you with the ability to process large amounts of data or to repeatedly execute a repetitive task using just a few lines of code. This greatly simplifies script development and maintenance.

Working with the for Statement

Using the for statement you can set up a loop that executes until a tested condition becomes false. This loop uses a variable to manage loop execution. The for loop is made up of three parts: a starting expression, a tested condition, and an increment statement. The syntax of this statement is outlined here:

```
for (expression; condition; increment) {
  statements;
}
```

All the statements embedded within the loop's starting and ending brackets are executed every time the loop iterates (repeats). To better understand how to work with the for statement, consider the following example. Here a loop has been set up to iterate 10 times. At the beginning of the loop's first iteration, the value of i is set to 1. The loop repeats 10 times, terminating when the value of i reaches 11.

```
<HTML>
  <HEAD>
    <TITLE>Demo: Working with the for loop</TITLE>
  </HEAD>
  <BODY>
    <SCRIPT language = "javascript" type = "text/javascript">
    <!-- Start hiding JavaScript statements
      document.write("Watch me count to 10: <BR>");
      for (i=1; i<11; i++) {
        document.write(i,"<BR>");
      }
    // End hiding JavaScript statements -->
    </SCRIPT>
  </BODY>
</HTML>
```

Figure 2.12 shows the output that is displayed when this example executes.

Working with the while Statement

Using the while statement, you can set up a loop that executes as long as a tested condition remains true. The syntax for this statement is outlined here:

```
while (condition) {
  statements;
}
```

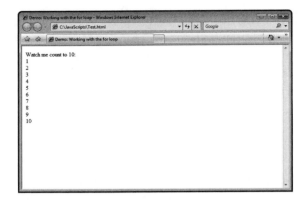

FIGURE 2.12

Setting up a for
loop to count
from 1 to 10.

As an example of how to work with the `while` statement, take a look at the following HTML
page.

```
<HTML>
  <HEAD>
    <TITLE>Demo: Using a while loop to count down to launch</TITLE>
  </HEAD>
  <BODY>
    <SCRIPT language = "javascript" type = "text/javascript">
    <!-- Start hiding JavaScript statements
      var countdown = 10;
      document.write("<B>Prepare to launch.</B><BR><BR>");
      while (countdown > 0) {
        document.write(countdown, "<BR>");
        countdown--;
      }
      document.write("<BR><B>Blastoff!</B>");
    // End hiding JavaScript statements -->
    </SCRIPT>
  </BODY>
</HTML>
```

Here, a loop has been set up that runs as long as the value of a variable named `countdown`
is greater than 0. Each time the loop iterates, the value of `countdown` is decremented by 1.
Figure 2.13 shows the output that is displayed when this example is executed.

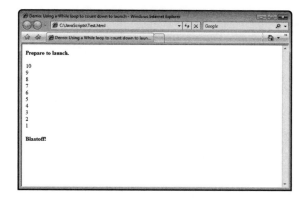

Working with the do...while Statement

A third type of loop supported by JavaScript is created by the `do...while` statement, which executes a loop until a tested condition becomes `false`. The syntax of this statement is outlined here:

```
do {
  statements;
} while (condition)
```

Although similar to the `while` loop, the `do...while` loop distinguishes itself in that it always executes at least once because the tested condition is not checked until the end of the loop's first execution. The following example demonstrates how to work with the do...while loop.

```
<HTML>
  <HEAD>
    <TITLE>Demo: Using a do...while loop to count down to launch</TITLE>
  </HEAD>
  <BODY>
    <SCRIPT language = "javascript" type = "text/javascript">
    <!-- Start hiding JavaScript statements
      var countdown = 10;
      document.write("<B>Prepare to launch.</B><BR><BR>");
      do {
        countdown--;
        document.write(countdown, "<BR>");
      } while (countdown > 0)
      document.write("<BR><B>Blastoff!</B>");
    // End hiding JavaScript statements -->
```

```
    </SCRIPT>
  </BODY>
</HTML>
```

The results that are generated are exactly the same as those that were generated using the while loop example.

Altering Loop Execution

By default, loops execute from beginning to end, over and over again. However, there will be times in which you will want to halt loop execution or skip individual loop iterations. This can be accomplished using the break and continue statements. The following example demonstrates how to use the break statement. Here, the break statement is used to stop a loop when the value assigned to a variable named countdown is set to 5.

```
<HTML>
  <HEAD>
    <TITLE>Demo: An example of how to use the break statement</TITLE>
  </HEAD>
  <BODY>
    <SCRIPT language = "javascript" type = "text/javascript">
    <!-- Start hiding JavaScript statements
      var countdown = 10;
      document.write("<B>Prepare to launch.</B><BR><BR>");
      while (countdown > 0) {
        document.write("countdown = ", countdown , "<BR>");
        if (countdown == 5 ) {
          document.write("<BR><B>Countdown aborted!</B>");
          break;
        }
        countdown--;
      }
    // End hiding JavaScript statements -->
    </SCRIPT>
  </BODY>
</HTML>
```

Figure 2.14 shows the output that is displayed when this example executes.

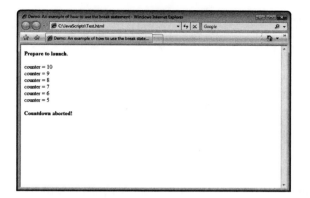

FIGURE 2.14

Using the break keyword to prematurely terminate a loop's execution.

Skipping Loop Iterations

Unlike the break statement, which halts loop execution, the continue statement only terminates the current iteration of the loop, allowing the loop to continue its execution. For example, the following HTML page contains a JavaScript that has been set up to execute 10 times. When the loop begins its execution, the value assigned to i is 10. Each time the loop iterates the value assigned to i is automatically decremented by 1. As soon as i is set to 0, the loop stops executing.

```
<HTML>
  <HEAD>
    <TITLE>Demo: An example of how to use the continue statement</TITLE>
  </HEAD>
  <BODY>
    <SCRIPT language = "javascript" type = "text/javascript">
    <!-- Start hiding JavaScript statements
      document.write("<B>Prepare to launch.</B><BR><BR>");
      for(i=10; i>0; i--) {
        switch (i) {
          case 10:
            continue;
          case 8:
            continue;
          case 6:
            continue;
          case 4:
            continue;
          case 2:
```

```
        continue;
      }
    document.write(i, "<BR>");
    }
    document.write("<BR><B>Blastoff!</B>");
  // End hiding JavaScript statements -->
  </SCRIPT>
  </BODY>
</HTML>
```

Within the loop, a `switch` statement code block has been set up that looks for the values 10, 8, 6, 4, and 2, executing a `continue` statement whenever the value assigned to i is set to one of these values. As a result, only the numbers 9, 7, 5, 3, and 1 are displayed. Figure 2.15 shows the output that is generated when this example runs.

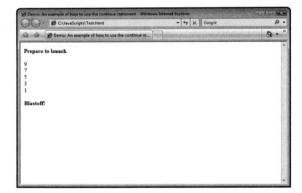

FIGURE 2.15

Using the break keyword to prematurely terminate a loop's execution.

BACK TO THE NUMBER GUESSING GAME

Okay, it is now time to turn your attention back to the development of this chapter's application project, the Number Guessing game. This game, when loaded into a web browser, will challenge the player to guess a number from 1 to 10 in as few guesses as possible. Development of this game will help to reinforce the topics covered in this chapter and prepare you for the development of Ajax applications.

Designing the Application

As with all of the game projects that are presented in this book, you will complete the development of this application by following a specific series of steps, as outlined here:

1. Create a new HTML page.
2. Start the development of the application's JavaScript.
3. Develop the rest of the application's programming logic.
4. Execute your new application.

Step 1: Writing the Application's HTML

The first step in creating the Number Guessing game is to create a new HTML page, which you can do using your preferred code or text editor. Add the following statements to your new HTML file and then save it with a name of `NumberGuess.html`.

```
<HTML>

  <HEAD>
    <TITLE>The number guessing game</TITLE>
  </HEAD>

  <BODY>

  </BODY>

</HTML>
```

As you can see, there is nothing fancy with the application's HTML code. It consists of the standard head and body tags. The head section includes a title tag, displaying a text string identifying the game. The body section is currently empty.

Step 2: Beginning the Application's Script

The execution of the Number Guessing game is controlled by a JavaScript embedded inside the body section of the HTML page. Begin the development of this script by adding the statements shown below to the body section of the HTML file.

```
<SCRIPT language = "javascript" type = "text/javascript">
<!-- Start hiding JavaScript statements

  //Define script variables
  var randomNo = 0;
  var gameOver = false;
  var keepPlaying = false;
  var guess = "";
```

```
var msg = "I am thinking of a number from 1 - 10. Try to guess it:"
var reply = "";

// End hiding JavaScript statements -->
</SCRIPT>
```

As you can see, these statements define a JavaScript containing six variable declarations. randomNo will be used to store the game's randomly generated number. gameOver and keepPlaying are used to manage loops that control the game's execution. guess and reply will be used to store player input, and msg is used to store a text string that is displayed in one of the game's popup dialog windows.

Step 3: Adding the Application's Controlling Logic

The rest of the JavaScript used in the Number Guessing game is shown next and should be added to the script file, immediately after the six variable declaration statements and before the closing </SCRIPT> tag.

```
//This loop allows the player to play as many games as desired
while (gameOver == false) {

  randomNo = 1 + Math.random() * 9; //Generate a random number
                                    //from 1 - 10
  randomNo = Math.round(randomNo);  //Turn the number into an integer

  keepPlaying = false;  //Set value to indicate that the current
                        //round of play should continue

  //Loop until the player guesses the secret number
  while (keepPlaying == false) {

    //Prompt the player to guess the secret number
    guess = window.prompt(msg + randomNo);

    //Analyze the player's guess
    if (guess == randomNo) {    //See if the player guessed the number

      window.alert("Correct! You guessed the number.");
      reply = window.prompt("Would you like to play again? (y/n)");
```

```
    if (reply == "y") {  //See if the player wants to play again
      keepPlaying = true;
      gameOver = false;
    } else {              //Let the current round of play continue
      keepPlaying = true;
      gameOver = true;
    }
  } else {
    if (guess > randomNo) { //See if the player's guess is too high
      window.alert("Incorrect. Your guess was too high.");
    } else {                //See if the player's guess is too low
      window.alert("Incorrect. Your guess was too low.");
    }
  }
}


}


window.alert("Game over. Thanks for playing.");  //Thank the player
```

As you can see, the execution of these statements is controlled by a `while` loop, which has been set up to repeatedly execute as long as the value assigned to a variable named `gameOver` is set to `false`. Next, a random number from 1 to 10 is generated using the `Math` object's `random()` method. Since the `random()` method returns a value between 0 and 1, the value that is returned is multiplied by 9 and then incremented by one in order to generate a number in the range of 1 to 10.

 The `Math` object's `random()` method is used to retrieve a random number between 0 and 1. This method's syntax is shown here:

```
Math.random()
```

You can store the randomly generated number returned by the `random()` method in a variable for later processing.

At this point the value assigned to `randomNo` is a decimal number between 1 and 10. However, the game is designed to work with integer values so the value of `randomNo` is rounded to the nearest whole number using the `Math` object's `round()` method. Next, the value of `keepPlaying` is set to `false`, preparing for the execution of another `while` loop, which is responsible for collecting and processing player guesses.

The Math object's round() method is used to round a decimal number to the nearest integer value. This method's syntax is shown here:

```
Math.round(x)
```

Here, *x* represents a decimal number to be rounded. Note that if the value that is passed to the round() method is .5 or greater, the number that the function returns is the next highest integer value. Otherwise, the value of the next lowest integer is returned.

Within the inner loop, the player is prompted to enter a guess using the window object's prompt() method. The player's input is then stored in a variable named guess. Next, an if statement code block is set up to analyze the player's input. If the player's guess is incorrect, a message is displayed letting the player know if the guess was too low or too high. If the player's guess is correct, a message is displayed congratulating the player using the window object's alert() method. If this is the case, the window object's prompt() method is then used to display a popup dialog window that prompted the player to play again. If the player responds by entering a y, then the values of keepPlaying and gameOver are modified. Setting keepPlaying to true causes the inner loop to terminate its execution and setting gameOver to false ensures that the outer loop keeps executing. If the player elected not to play, then both keepPlaying and gameOver are set equal to true, terminating both the inner and outer loop, thereby ending the game. The last statement in the script is executed at the end of the game, displaying a text message that thanks the player for playing the game.

Step 4: Testing Your New Application

All right, assuming that you have followed along carefully with the instructions that have been provided, your copy of the Number Guessing game should be ready for execution. Simply upload it to your website and then use your web browser to load it. If you run into any problems, double-check your typing and look for typos or missing statements.

You will find a copy of this application's source code files on the book's companion website, located at http://www.courseptr.com/downloads.

SUMMARY

This chapter provided an overview of JavaScript, giving you an understanding of basic JavaScript programming concepts required to support the development of Ajax applications. You learned about JavaScript's origins and issues surrounding browser compatibility. You also learned how to create and embed JavaScripts in your web pages in order to make them more interactive. This chapter explained how to formulate JavaScript statements and to comply with JavaScript syntax and showed you how to collect, store, and modify data using variables and to work with conditional and iterative programming logic.

Before moving on to Chapter 3, consider setting aside a little extra time to make improvements to the Number Guessing game by addressing the following challenges.

CHALLENGES

1. As currently written, the Number Guessing game challenges the player to guess a number from 1 to 10. Consider making the game more challenging by increasing the range supported by the game to 1 to 100 or 1 to 1000.

2. Rather than just telling the player when guesses are too high or too low, consider modifying the game to provide additional feedback when the player's guess gets close to the secret number.

A DEEPER DIVE INTO JAVASCRIPT

This chapter rounds out the book's review of JavaScript programming. You will learn how to create and execute functions. The use of functions is a fundamental feature utilized in most Ajax applications. You will also learn how to manage collections of data using arrays. This chapter will also review the usage of the `<DIV>` `</DIV>` and `<SPAN>` `</SPAN>` tags, whose use is essential to the development of Ajax applications that dynamically update text displayed on web pages. This chapter will also explain how to work with different browser events and how to develop applications that can react to events when they occur, enabling you to create all sorts of interactive applications.

Specifically, you will learn how to:

- Organize JavaScript statements into functions and to set up these functions to process and return data
- Dynamically modify the display of text within your applications
- Use arrays in order to more efficiently store and process large amounts of data
- Trigger function execution using browser events

PROJECT PREVIEW: THE ROCK, PAPER, SCISSORS GAME

This chapter's game project is the Rock, Paper, Scissors game. This application pits the player against the computer. As demonstrated in Figure 3.1, this game is played by clicking on one of the three button controls.

FIGURE 3.1

To play the Rock, Paper, Scissors game, click on one of the three application buttons.

As soon as one of the buttons is clicked, the game generates a random move on behalf of the computer and then analyzes the result to determine whether the player won, lost, or tied. The winner of the game is determined using the following set of rules:

- Rock crushes scissors
- Paper covers rock
- Scissors cut paper
- Matching moves result in a tie

Figure 3.2 shows an example of a typical round of play. Here, the player submitted a move of Rock and a move of Paper was generated on behalf of the computer.

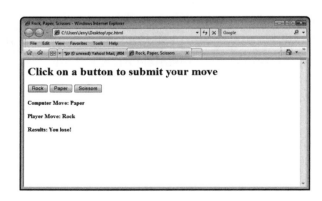

FIGURE 3.2

The application generates a move on behalf of the computer.

Although the application does not interact with a web server behind the scenes and is not technically an Ajax application, this application ties together many of the JavaScript programming concepts that are covered in this and the previous chapter. This application also gives you the opportunity to work on an application that dynamically updates its own content, which is an essential feature of Ajax applications.

IMPROVING JAVASCRIPT ORGANIZATION WITH FUNCTIONS

To be able to create Ajax applications that interactively communicate with web servers, you need a means of submitting requests and processing the data that is sent back. This is accomplished through the use of functions. A *function* is a collection of program statements called upon to perform a specific task. Ajax programmers store JavaScript functions in the head section of HTML pages or in external files referenced within the head section. This ensures that they are loaded and available as soon as the web pages that contain them are loaded. This makes functions easier to locate and maintain.

Avoid placing your functions in the body section of your HTML pages. If your JavaScripts attempt to execute a function buried at the bottom of the body section of your HTML page before that function has been loaded, an error will occur. Instead, place all your functions in the head section of your HTML pages and you will not only avoid errors but will make your JavaScript more manageable.

Ajax developers use functions to control the execution of statements designed to manage communication with web servers and to control the application of dynamic updates to web pages.

Organizing Code Statements into Functions

Functions must be defined before they can be executed. The syntax required to define a function is outlined here:

```
function FunctionName(p1, p2,....pn) {
  statements;
return
}
```

FunctionName represents the name assigned to the function. The function name is always followed by a pair of parentheses, which are used to define one or more (optional) command-separated arguments that the function is designed to process. The parentheses are required, even if the function does not define any arguments. Functions can contain any number of statements that are placed within the function's opening and closing curly braces. Functions can also contain an optional `return` statement. When present, the `return` statement allows the function to return data back to the statement that called it.

The following example shows a function named ValidateAge, which accepts a single argument—the user's age. The function uses this argument to determine whether the user is old enough to use the application that contains the functions. If the user is less than 18 years old, a message is displayed advising the user not to use the application. The return statement has been added to explicitly return control of the script back to the calling statement. However, since the function is not designed to return any data, the return statement could have been omitted without affecting the execution of the function.

```
function ValidateAge(age) {
  if (age < 18) {
    window.alert("Please leave. You are too young to play.");
  }
  return
}
```

Defining a function within a JavaScript does not cause that function to execute. The function must be called on to execute. If your Ajax applications contain functions that are never called upon to run, then the code statements inside those functions will never execute. Once written, you can call upon a function to execute as many times as necessary during application execution. Functions can be used to reduce the size of applications by eliminating the need to duplicate a particular section of programming logic.

Controlling Function Execution

There are two ways of calling on JavaScript functions to execute. The first is simply to type in its name, as demonstrated here:

```
ShowInstructions();
```

Here, a function name ShowInstructions() has been called upon to execute. Note that the opening and closing parentheses are required, even when the function call does not involve the passage of any arguments for processing. When called this way, the specified function executes, and when done, processing flow is returned and then the next statement in the script (immediately following the function call) is executed.

Functions that have been set up to process arguments can be passed data as part of the function call, as demonstrated here:

```
TerminateGame(100);
```

Here, a function named TerminateGame() is called and passed a value of 100. You can pass as many arguments to a function as it has been set up to handle, provided you separate each argument using commas, as demonstrated here:

```
TotalPlayerScores(100, 125, 333);
```

You must make sure functions are capable of handling all of the arguments passed to them or an error will occur.

The second way of calling on a function is to use the function as part of an expression. When used this way, a function can return a value to a calling statement (provided the function was set up to do so). For example, the following statement executes a function named `DeterminePlayerAge()` and then stores the result that this function returns in a variable named `playerAge`.

```
playerAge = DeterminePlayerAge();
```

To better understand how to call on functions, let's look at a couple of quick examples. In the following example, a function named `ValidateAge()` has been added to the head section of the HTML page. It is executed by a `ValidateAge(userAge);` statement located in the body section. The function call includes the passing of a single argument called `userAge`. When called, the function maps the `userAge` variable to its `age` argument. The function then displays either of two messages based on the value of the argument.

```
<HTML>
  <HEAD>
    <TITLE>Demo: Executing statements stored in a function</TITLE>
    <SCRIPT language = "javascript" type = "text/javascript">
    <!-- Start hiding JavaScript statements
      function ValidateAge(age) {
        if (age >= 18) {
          window.alert("Welcome! Let's play.");
        } else {
          window.alert("Please leave. You are too young to play.");
        }
      }
    // End hiding JavaScript statements -->
    </SCRIPT>
  </HEAD>
<BODY>
  <SCRIPT language = "javascript" type = "text/javascript">
  <!-- Start hiding JavaScript statements
    var userAge;
    userAge = window.prompt("Enter your age:","");
    ValidateAge(userAge);
  // End hiding JavaScript statements -->
```

```
    </SCRIPT>
  </BODY>
</HTML>
```

Figures 3.3 and 3.4 show an example.

FIGURE 3.3

Collecting user input using a popup dialog window.

FIGURE 3.4

Using a function to analyze player input.

This last example demonstrates how to call on and process the value returned by a function.

```
<HTML>
  <HEAD>
    <TITLE>Demo: Using functions to enhance script organization</TITLE>
    <SCRIPT language = "javaScript" type = "text/javascript">
    <!-- Start hiding JavaScript statements
      var age;
      function GetUserAge() {
        var userAge;
        userAge = window.prompt("Enter your age: ","");
        return userAge;
      }
    // End hiding JavaScript statements -->
    </SCRIPT>
  </HEAD>
  <BODY>
    <SCRIPT language = "javaScript" type = "text/javascript">
    <!-- Start hiding JavaScript statements
      age = GetUserAge();
      if (age >= 18) {
        window.alert("Welcome! Let's play.");
      } else {
```

```
        window.alert("Please leave. You are too young to play.");
      }
    // End hiding JavaScript statements -->
    </SCRIPT>
  </BODY>
</HTML>
```

Here, a function named GetUserAge() has been defined. When called for execution, the function prompts the user to enter her age and assigns the input to a variable named userAge, which is then passed back to the calling statement using a return statement. The function is called by a statement located in the body section, which takes the value returned by the function and assigns it to a variable named age.

DEVELOPING APPLICATIONS THAT RESPOND TO EVENTS

Most of the JavaScripts that have been presented so far have executed in a top-down fashion, with the browser executing each JavaScript starting with its first statements and continuing on to the last statement. The only exception to this has been examples that placed code statements in functions located in the head section of the HTML page, which were called by functions located in the body section of the HTML page.

Developing Event-Driven Scripts

An *event* is something that occurs within the browser. Events occur when the user uses the mouse to click on something. Events also occur when the mouse moves, keys on the keyboard are pressed, and windows are opened and closed or resized. Browsers automatically recognize events and react to them. For example, if the user clicks on a link embedded within a web page, the onClick event occurs. The browser's default response in this example is to load the web page or resource specified by the link.

By creating functions and associating them with specific events using event handlers, you can develop Ajax applications that react to user actions, retrieving and then displaying data as needed from web servers. An *event handler* is a mechanism that detects the occurrence of an event and reacts to it. Upon detecting the occurrence of a specified event, an event handler can either execute a JavaScript statement or a JavaScript function. You might set up an event handler that calls upon a function that displays a confirmation dialog box requiring users to confirm their age before allowing the application to proceed.

Events are associated with individual objects. If an event is triggered for an object, the object's event handler, if defined, executes. Event handlers are easy to set up. All you have to do is insert HTML tags that define objects. The following example demonstrates how to define an event handler that automatically executes when the web page loads.

```
<BODY onLoad = "window.alert('Boo!')">
```

As you can see, the event handler used in this example executes when the load event occurs. When this happens, an alert dialog is displayed. You can execute any JavaScript statement as an event handler. However, the real power of event handlers occurs when you set them up to execute functions.

Working with Different JavaScript Events

As shown in Table 3.1, JavaScript is capable of reacting to all kinds of events, such as when a page loads, unloads, changes size, or when the user interacts with a page using the keyboard or mouse.

TABLE 3.1   JAVASCRIPT EVENTS AND EVENT HANDLERS

Event	Handler	This event occurs when:
abort	onabort	An action is aborted
blur	onblur	An item loses focus
change	onchange	When data associated with a control is changed
click	onclick	When an element is clicked
dblclick	ondblclick	When an element is double-clicked
dragdrop	ondragdrop	An element is dragged and dropped
error	onerror	A JavaScript error occurs
focus	onfocus	An element receives focus
keydown	onkeydown	A keyboard key is pressed down
keypress	onkeypress	A keyboard key is pressed down and released
keyup	onkeyup	A keyboard key is released
load	onload	A web page is loaded
mousedown	onmousedown	One of the mouse buttons is pressed
mousemove	onmousemove	The mouse is moved
mouseout	onmouseout	The mouse is moved off of an element
mouseover	onmouseover	The mouse is moved over an element
mouseup	onmouseup	The mouse's button is released
reset	onreset	A form's Reset button is clicked
resize	onresize	An element is resized
submit	onsubmit	A form's Submit button is clicked
unload	onunload	The browser unloads a web page

As you can see in Table 3.1, each event that JavaScript recognizes has an accompanying event handler. Using these event handlers, you can set up the automatic execution of functions defined within web pages. You will see examples of how to work with a number of these events and event handlers in the sections that follow.

Reacting to Window Events

One important category of events that is important to many types of Ajax applications are events that are triggered in response to changes that affect the browser window. These types of events include the `load`, `unload`, and `resize` events. As shown in Table 3.1, each of these events has a corresponding event handler. To create Ajax applications that can react to these events, embed the appropriate event handlers into the HTML page's `<BODY>` tag. The following example demonstrates how to work with all three of these events.

```
<HTML>
  <HEAD>
    <TITLE>Demo: Working with window and frame events</TITLE>
  </HEAD>
  <BODY onLoad = "window.alert('Page loaded!')"
    onResize = "window.alert('Ouch, that hurts!')"
    onUnload = "window.alert('Goodbye cruel world...')"
  </BODY>
</HTML>
```

Figures 3.5 through 3.7 show the output that it generates when the application is executed.

FIGURE 3.5

The onLoad event handler executes when the web page initially loads.

FIGURE 3.6

The onResize event handler executes whenever the user tries to change the size of the web page.

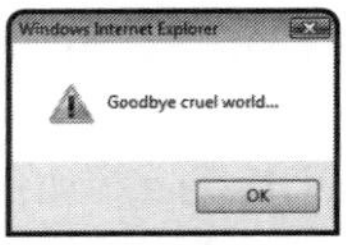

FIGURE 3.7

The onUnload event handler executes when the user closes the web browser or loads a new web page.

Processing Mouse Events

Another group of events used in Ajax applications are triggered when the user works with the mouse when interacting with the applications. These types of events include the onMouseOver and onMouseOut events. The use of these two events is demonstrated in the following example.

```
<HTML>
  <HEAD>
    <TITLE>Demo: Working with mouse event handlers</TITLE>
    <SCRIPT language = "javascript" type = "text/javascript">
    <!-- Start hiding JavaScript statements
      function DisplayMessage(msgInput) {
        document.getElementById('Msg').innerHTML = msgInput;
      }
    // End hiding JavaScript statements -->
    </SCRIPT>
  </HEAD>
  <BODY>
    <A HREF="http://www.courseptr.com"
      onMouseOver = 'DisplayMessage("May the force be with you!")';
      onMouseOut = 'DisplayMessage("Beware the dark side.")';>
      Go to www.starwars.com</A>
    <P><B><DIV id="Msg"> </DIV></B></P>
  </BODY>
</HTML>
```

Here a link has been defined that displays a label of Go to www.starwars.com. Next, the onMouseOver and onMouseOut event handlers are used to call on a function named DisplayMessage() and pass it a text string. When called, the function retrieves an object reference to the web page's <DIV> </DIV> tags using the getElementByID() method and then uses the object's innerHTML property to display the text string passed to it inside the <DIV> </DIV> tags.

Figure 3.8 shows how the application looks when the example is first loaded.

When called as a result of the execution of the MouseOver event (e.g., when the user moves the mouse over the link), the message May the force be with you! is displayed, as shown in Figure 3.9.

When the MouseOut event is used to call on the DisplayMessage() function, the message Beware the dark side. is displayed, as shown in Figure 3.10.

Note that in the previous example, the onMouseOver and onMouseOut event handlers have been used to set up an automated effect referred to as a rollover.

Processing Forms

Forms are used in many Ajax applications as a means of collecting information that is then sent to the web server for processing. Forms are created by defining individual form elements like buttons and text fields using the <FORM> </FORM> tags. When used in conjunction with

JavaScript, forms can be processed and validated. To connect a form control to a JavaScript function, use the control's `onclick` attribute to trigger the execution of functions, as demonstrated here:

```
<HTML>
  <HEAD>
    <TITLE>Demo: Working with mouse event handlers</TITLE>
    <SCRIPT LANGUAGE = "JavaScript" TYPE = "Text/JavaScript">
      function SayName() {
        document.getElementById('trgtDiv').innerHTML = "Hello " +
          document.getElementById('nameField').value;
      }
    </SCRIPT>
  </HEAD>
  <BODY>
    <FORM>
      Enter your name: <INPUT type = "text" id="nameField"> <BR>
      Click here to process: <INPUT type = "button" value = "OK"
        onclick = "SayName()">
    </FORM>
    <DIV id = "trgtDiv"> </DIV>
  </BODY>
</HTML>
```

Here a form made up of a text field and a button element has been set up to prompt the user to type in his name and click on the button. When clicked, the `onClicked` event hander assigned to the button control executes a function named `SayName()`. When executed, the function displays a text string, just below the button control, that welcomes the user. This text string is made up of the word `Hello` concatenated to a text string retrieved from the form's text field element. Figure 3.11 shows an example of this application in action.

DIV AND SPAN TAGS

Ajax applications are all about the dynamic updating of web page contents without requiring web pages to be refreshed. One very popular and functional way of achieving this goal is through the use of the <DIV> </DIV> and <SPAN> </SPAN> tags. These two sets of tags allow you to apply changes to any text enclosed within them. Although commonly used to apply style attributes, such as color, font, and various other presentation attributes, these tags can also be used in your Ajax applications to facilitate dynamic text replacement.

Working with the <DIV> </DIV> Tags

The <DIV> </DIV> tags are used to create logical divisions within web pages, acting much like the <P> </P> tags in this regard, except that the <DIV> </DIV> tags allow you to divide pages up into larger divisions. <DIV> </DIV> tags are block-level elements. Using these tags, you can apply different `style` attributes to an entire section of a web page as demonstrated here:

```
<DIV style = "Color : Green">
  <H1> Once upon a time...</H1>
</DIV>
```

Here, any text placed within the two tags is displayed in green. In addition to applying different styles to web pages, you can use the <DIV> </DIV> tags to refresh the displays of text. In order to use these tags in this manner, you must first assign a name, using the `id` attribute to the sections of your web pages outlined with <DIV> </DIV> tags.

```
<DIV name = "OpeningLine" style = "Color : Green">
  <H1> Once upon a time...</H1>
</DIV>
```

Here, a name of `OpeningLine` has been added to the opening <DIV> tags, allowing this division of the web page to be programmatically referenced and updated as necessary.

Working with the <SPAN> </SPAN> Tags

The <SPAN> </SPAN> tags are similar to the <DIV> </DIV> tags, except that instead of dividing pages up into larger sections, the <SPAN> </SPAN> tags allow you to apply style changes and test replacements inline. This means that any text enclosed within these tags is affected by whatever changes you specify while any outlying text remains unaffected.

```
<SPAN style = "Color : Red">Once upon a time...</SPAN>
```

Like the <DIV> </DIV> tags, you can assign a name to any pair of <SPAN> </SPAN> tags, allowing you to later reference and update their content, as demonstrated here:

```
<SPAN name = "" style = "Color : Red">Once upon a time...</SPAN>
```

Programmatically Replacing Text without Screen Refresh

To better understand how to dynamically replace text within your web pages, let's take a look at an example that uses the <DIV> </DIV> tags to surgically update text. Let's begin by creating a new HTML page made up of the following statements.

```
<HTML>
  <HEAD>
    <TITLE>Demo: Dynamically displaying text</TITLE>
    <SCRIPT language = "javascript" type = "text/javascript">
    <!-- Start hiding JavaScript statements
      function GreetPlayer() {
        document.write("Well, hello there.");
      }
    // End hiding JavaScript statements -->
    </SCRIPT>
  </HEAD>
  <BODY onload = "GreetPlayer()">
    <H1>Knock Knock!</H1>
  </BODY>
</HTML>
```

Once created, load this example into your browser. When you do, you may be surprised at the results that are displayed. Instead of displaying a level 1 heading of Knock Knock! followed by a text string of "Well, hello there.", only the text string written by the JavaScript is displayed. The reason for this is that when the JavaScript's GreetPlayer() function is executed, its document.write statement automatically clears out any text displayed on the web page before writing its own text string, as demonstrated in Figure 3.12.

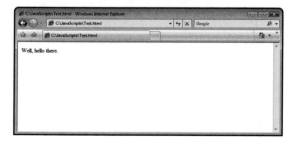

Ajax application developers overcome this type of problem using the <DIV> </DIV> and <SPAN> </SPAN> tags, as demonstrated next. Here, the previous example has been updated. Instead of attempting to use the document.write() method to update the display of text on the web page, the GreetPlayer() function has been updated to post its text string inside the page's <DIV> </DIV> tags.

```
<HTML>
  <HEAD>
    <TITLE>Demo: Dynamically displaying text</TITLE>
    <SCRIPT language = "javascript" type = "text/javascript">
    <!-- Start hiding JavaScript statements
      function GreetPlayer() {
        document.getElementById('GreetingMsg').innerHTML = "Well, hello there."
      }
    // End hiding JavaScript statements -->
    </SCRIPT>
  </HEAD>
  <BODY onload = "GreetPlayer()">
    <H1>Knock Knock!</H1>
    <DIV id="GreetingMsg"> </DIV>

  </BODY>
</HTML>
```

To fully understand what is happening here, you need to know more about the methods and properties used in the GreetPlayer() function. For starters, the document object's getElementByID() method is used to retrieve an object reference, to the object created by the <DIV> </DIV> tags. This is accomplished by passing the name of GreetingMsg() to the method as an argument. Next, the resulting object reference's innerHTML property is used to write a new text string to the web page, replacing the empty text string currently displayed by the <DIV> </DIV> tags. The end result of all this is that instead of clearing the web page and then writing out text, this modified HTML page simply replaces the text string specified inside the <DIV> </DIV> tags. No muss, no fuss, and no page refresh required! Figure 3.13 shows how the result of this example differs from the previous version of the HTML page.

TRAP Like all things, overuse of the <DIV> </DIV> and <SPAN> </SPAN> tags can create problems in the event that any text that is updated using them is not obvious. It is essential that any changes that are made are easily noticeable. At the same time, it is equally important that you do not overuse these tags, a condition sometimes referred to as *divitis*, creating too much confusion and making web pages difficult for users to keep up with.

MANAGING COLLECTIONS OF DATA

Depending on what your Ajax applications are designed to do, there may be times when working with data a piece at a time is no longer practical, which would be the case in an application designed to process a list of data keyed in by the user or retrieved from a web server. In these types of situations, you can use arrays to store and help manage application data.

An *array* is an indexed list of values. Arrays can be used to store any type of value supported by JavaScript. As demonstrated next, arrays must be declared prior to using them.

```
weapons = new Array(5);
weapons[0] = "Ray Gun";
weapons[1] = "Pulsar Cannon";
weapons[2] = "Phaser Pistol";
weapons[3] = "Photon Torpedo";
weapons[4] = "Cyber Tank";
```

In the first statement, an array named weapons has been declared using the new keyword. This array is capable of storing 5 values. The last five statements assign values to the array. The array's index begins at 0 and goes to 4.

TRICK As a shortcut for creating small arrays, you can also create what is known as a *dense array*. A dense array is an array that is populated during declaration. The following example demonstrates how to set up a dense array named supplies. This array is made up of six items.

```
supplies = new Array("pen", "paper", "ink", "pencil", "tape",
"staples");
```

Note that when created this way, an array is made up of a comma-separated list of items enclosed inside parentheses, preceded by the name of the array. This array is functionally equivalent to the following array.

```
supplies = new Array(6);
supplies[0] = "pen";
supplies[1] = "paper";
supplies[2] = "ink";
supplies[3] = "pencil";
supplies[4] = "tape";
supplies[5] = "staples";
```

Accessing Individual Array Elements

Accessing values stored in an array is easy. All you have to do is specify the name of the array followed by the index position of the value (embedded inside a pair of square brackets). To see how this works, take a look at the following example.

```
<HTML>
  <HEAD>
  <TITLE>Demo: Working with an array</TITLE>
  </HEAD>
  <BODY>
    <SCRIPT language = "javascript" type= "text/javascript">
    <!-- Start hiding JavaScript statements
      weapons = new Array(5);
      weapons[0] = "Ray Gun";
      weapons[1] = "Pulsar Cannon";
      weapons[2] = "Phaser Pistol";
      weapons[3] = "Photon Torpedo";
      weapons[4] = "Cyber Tank";
      document.write("The 3rd item in the weapons array is " + weapons[2]);
    // End hiding JavaScript statements -->
    </SCRIPT>
  </BODY>
</HTML>
```

JavaScript arrays are zero based. Therefore, the third item stored in the array is located at index position 2 (e.g., weapons[2]). Figure 3.15 shows the output produced when this example executes.

FIGURE 3.15

Processing array items by referencing their index position.

Using Loops to Process Arrays

Processing the contents of arrays an element at a time can become tedious, especially if those arrays contain dozens, hundreds, or thousands of items. Instead, it is usually much easier and more efficient to process array contents using a for loop, as demonstrated in the following example:

```
<HTML>
  <HEAD>
  <TITLE>Demo: Processing array contents using a loop</TITLE>
  </HEAD>
  <BODY>
    <SCRIPT language = "javascript" type = "text/javascript">
    <!-- Start hiding JavaScript statements
      var lengthOfArray;
      weapons = new Array(5);
      weapons[0] = "Ray Gun";
      weapons[1] = "Pulsar Cannon";
      weapons[2] = "Phaser Pistol";
      weapons[3] = "Photon Torpedo";
      weapons[4] = "Cyber Tank";
      lengthOfArray = weapons.length;
      document.write("<B>Weapons Inventory</B><BR>");
      for (var i = 0; i < lengthOfArray; i++) {
        document.write(weapons[i], "<BR>");
      }
```

```
      // End hiding JavaScript statements -->
    </SCRIPT>
  </BODY>
</HTML>
```

Here, an array named weapons has been set up and populated with 5 items. A loop is then used to process the contents of the array, beginning at weapons[0], incrementing by 1 each time the loop iterates, and ending when the last item is processed. Note the use of the array object's length property, which has been used to retrieve a numeric value representing the length of the weapons array, assigning that value to a variable named lengthOfArray. Figure 3.16 demonstrates the output that is displayed when this example is executed.

FIGURE 3.16

Using a loop to process the contents of arrays.

Sorting the Contents of Arrays

Like all objects, arrays have properties and methods. One particularly useful method is the sort() method, which can be used to sort the items stored in an array. The following example demonstrates how to use this method to produce a sorted list of array contents.

```
<HEAD>
  <TITLE>Demo: An example of how to sort the contents of an Array</TITLE>
</HEAD>
  <BODY>
    <SCRIPT language = "javascript" type = "text/javascript">
    <!-- Start hiding JavaScript statements
      supplies = new Array("pen", "paper", "ink", "pencil", "tape");
      document.write(supplies.sort());
    // End hiding JavaScript statements -->
    </SCRIPT>
  </BODY>
</HTML>
```

As you can see, this example creates and populates a dense array named `supplies`. The array's `sort()` method is then used to sort the contents of the array, which are displayed in the browser window. Note that the entire contents of the array were processed without using a loop. When this example is run, a list of array items, separated by commas, is displayed on a single line.

BACK TO THE ROCK, PAPER, SCISSORS APPLICATION

Okay, now it is time to turn your attention back to the development of this chapter's game project, the Rock, Paper, Scissors game. This game will make use of the `<SPAN> </SPAN>` tags to dynamically update the display of text on web pages, which is an essential feature of most Ajax applications. When loaded into the web browser, this application will challenge the player to compete against the computer in a game of Rock, Paper, Scissors.

Designing the Application

Like the other application projects that you have already worked on in this book, the Rock, Paper, Scissors game will be created in a series of five steps, as outlined here:

1. Create a new HTML page.
2. Add a form to collect user data.
3. Format and display text output.
4. Develop the game's controlling logic.
5. Execute your new Ajax application.

The first several steps are devoted to developing the HTML portion of the application, and the remaining steps focus on developing the application's controlling logic using JavaScript and then executing it.

Step 1: Writing the Application's HTML

The first step in the development of the Rock, Paper, Scissors game is to create the application's HTML page. Begin by opening your preferred text or code editor and then create and save a new file named `rpc.html`. Once you have completed this task, add the following HTML statements to the file:

```
<HTML>
  <HEAD>
    <TITLE>Rock, Paper, Scissors</TITLE>
  </HEAD>
  <BODY>
  </BODY>
</HTML>
```

As you can see, there is nothing exceptional about the Rock, Paper, Scissors game's HTML page. It is made up of the typical head and body tags. The head section includes a title tag that displays the application's name.

Step 2: Creating a Form

Now it is time to display a form that will display three button controls labeled Rock, Paper, and Scissors. The player will click on these buttons when playing the game in order to submit moves. To add the form to the HTML page, along with a descriptive heading, add the following statements to the body section of the HTML page.

```
<H1>Click on a button to submit your move</H1>
<FORM>
  <INPUT TYPE = "button" VALUE = " Rock " +
    onClick = ProcessMove("Rock")
  <BR>
  <INPUT TYPE = "button" VALUE = " Paper " +
    onClick = ProcessMove("Paper")
  <BR>
  <INPUT TYPE = "button" VALUE = "Scissors" +
    onClick = ProcessMove("Scissors")
</FORM>
```

Note that each of the <INPUT> tags makes use of the onClick event handler in order to initiate the execution of a function named ProcessMove(), passing it a text string indicating which of the three buttons were pressed.

Step 3: Creating a Template for Displaying Output

In order to display the results of each round of play, the application needs a way of displaying the player and the computer's moves as well as the results of the game. To accomplish this, add the following statements to the end of the body section.

```
<P><B>Computer Move: <SPAN id="CMove"> </SPAN></B></P>
<P><B>Player Move: <SPAN id="PMove"> </SPAN></B></P>
<P><B>Results: <SPAN id="Msg"> </SPAN></B></P>
```

As you can see, a series of three pairs of <SPAN> </SPAN> tags have been used to help assemble a template through which text can be displayed. Note that each of these statements has been assigned a unique id, allowing the application's JavaScript statements to programmatically update the display of text using these three sets of HTML statements.

Step 4: Developing the Game's Controlling Logic

At this point your work on the applications HTML is complete. Now it is time to breathe life into your new application by adding the JavaScript statements required to control the operation of the game. To begin, add the following statements to the head section of the HTML page:

```
<SCRIPT language = "javascript" type = "text/javascript">
<!-- Start hiding JavaScript statements

// End hiding JavaScript statements -->
</SCRIPT>
```

These statements provide the required HTML and comment tags needed to support the execution to the application's JavaScript. Most of the application's statements reside in a function named ProcessMove(), which, as you have seen, is called upon whenever the player clicks on one of the game's three button controls. To begin work on the development of this function, add the following statements to the head section, inside the opening and closing <SCRIPT> </SCRIPT> tags:

```
function ProcessMove(playerMove) {

}
```

As you can see, the function definition includes a parameter named playerMove, which will be mapped to an argument passed to the function each time it is called, identifying the move selected by the player (e.g., Rock, Paper, or Scissors). When executed, the function compares the player's move against the computer's move, which the function is responsible for generating, in order to determine the results of the game.

Let's begin laying out the statements that make up the function. For starters, add the following statement to the function between the opening and closing curly braces. As you can see these statements generate a random number between 1 and 3, representing the computer's move.

```
randomNo = 1 + Math.random() * 2; //Generate a random number
                                  //from 1 - 10
randomNo = Math.round(randomNo);  //Turn the number into a integer
```

Next, add these statements to the function, immediately following the statement shown above.

```
if (randomNo == 1) computerMove = "Rock"
if (randomNo == 2) computerMove = "Paper"
if (randomNo == 3) computerMove = "Scissors"
```

These three statements are used to assign a text string to a variable named computerMove, based on the value of the randomly generated number. In other words, if the random number is a 1 then the computer is assigned a move of Rock. Likewise, a value of 2 results in a move of Paper and a value of 3 results in the computer being assigned a move of Scissors.

Now that the function knows both the player and the computer's moves, it must compare them in order to determine who won or if a tie occurred. This is accomplished by adding the following statements to the ProcessMove() function, immediately following the statement shown above.

```
switch (computerMove) {
  case "Rock":
    if (playerMove == "Rock") {
      document.getElementById('Msg').innerHTML = "You tie!"
    }
    if (playerMove == "Paper") {
      document.getElementById('Msg').innerHTML = "You win!"
    }
    if (playerMove == "Scissors") {
      document.getElementById('Msg').innerHTML = "You lose!"
    }
    break;
  case "Paper":
    if (playerMove == "Rock") {
      document.getElementById('Msg').innerHTML = "You lose!"
    }
    if (playerMove == "Paper") {
      document.getElementById('Msg').innerHTML = "You tie!"
    }
    if (playerMove == "Scissors") {
      document.getElementById('Msg').innerHTML = "You win!"
    }
    break;
  case "Scissors":
    if (playerMove == "Rock") {
      document.getElementById('Msg').innerHTML = "You win!"
```

```
     }
     if (playerMove == "Paper") {
        document.getElementById('Msg').innerHTML = "You lose!"
     }
     if (playerMove == "Scissors") {
        document.getElementById('Msg').innerHTML = "You tie!"
     }
     break;
}
```

As you can see, these statements set up a `switch` code block made up of three `case` statements, one for each of the computer's possible moves. For example, the first case statement executes when the computer's move is `Rock`. Each `case` statement is followed by three `if` statement code blocks, of which only one will execute, depending on the player's move. Lastly, a `break` statement follows each set of three `if` statements.

The end result of the function's analysis is the display of a text string that announces whether the player has won, lost, or tied. Note that the `document` object's `getElementByID` method is used to retrieve an object reference to the id of the HTML tag (from Step 3) into which the text string is to be displayed. The object's `innerHTML` property is then used to display the game's text message.

The last two statements that make up the `ProcessMove()` function are shown next and should be added to the end of the function. As you can see, these statements also update the display of a text string on the HTML page. The first statement displays a text string representing the computer's move and the second statement displays a string representing the player's move.

```
document.getElementById('CMove').innerHTML = computerMove
document.getElementById('PMove').innerHTML = playerMove
```

Step 5: Executing Your New Game

Okay, you now have everything you need to create the Rock, Paper, Scissors game. As long as you have followed along carefully and did not skip any steps or make any typos, everything should run as explained at the beginning of this chapter. Go ahead and upload the HTML page to your website, load it into your web browser, and take your application for a spin.

 You will find a copy of this application's source code files on the book's companion website, located at http://www.courseptr.com/downloads.

SUMMARY

This chapter wraps up this book's overview of JavaScript programming. An understanding of JavaScript is essential to the development of robust Ajax applications. This chapter showed you how to create and execute functions, identify and react to different browser types, and to manage large collections of data using arrays. You also learned how to use the `<DIV> </DIV>` and `<SPAN> </SPAN>` tags to facilitate the dynamic updating of text on web pages. On top of all this, you learned how to take advantage of browser events to control the execution of functions containing application scripts.

Before you move on to Chapter 4, consider spending a little time improving the Rock, Paper, Scissors game by addressing the following list of challenges.

CHALLENGES

1. As currently written, the Rock, Paper, Scissors game makes the assumption that the player already knows how to play the game. Consider displaying some additional text that outlines the rules of the game.

2. Consider keeping track of the number of games won, lost, and tied and displaying this information at the end of each game so that the player can gauge her overall performance against the computer. (Hint: Create three variables and increment them as appropriate at the end of each round of play.)

UNDERSTANDING THE DOCUMENT OBJECT MODEL

As you have already learned, JavaScript is the programming language used to build Ajax applications. When combined with the `<DIV> </DIV>` and `<SPAN> </SPAN>` tags, you can dynamically insert text at pre-set locations within your applications. However, if you bring the Document Object Model into the equation, you can take complete control over the layout of your application's web pages. Web browsers use the Document Object Model to create a logical representation of your web pages. Using JavaScript to interact with and manipulate the Document Object Model, you can develop Ajax applications that are able to add, delete, and modify web page content instantly without any page refreshes.

Specifically, you will learn how:

- The Document Object Model creates a tree representation of web pages
- To work with different Document Object Model properties and methods
- To walk the Document Object Model tree and retrieve element information
- To use the Document Object Model to modify tree layout and dynamically update the appearance of web pages

Project Preview: The Ajax Story of the Day Application

This chapter's game project is the Ajax Story of the Day application. This application demonstrates how to dynamically utilize the DOM tree in order to tell different parts of a four part story. Figure 4.1 shows how the application appears once it has been initially loaded into the browser.

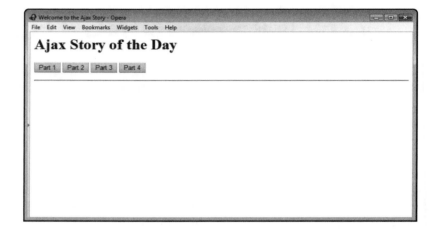

Figure 4.1

The Ajax Story of the Day application as seen running in the Opera browser.

In order to interact with the application and get it to tell its story, the user must click on each of the application's button controls, one at a time, moving from left to right. Each time a button is pressed, a part of the story is displayed. Figure 4.2 shows how the application looks once the user has clicked on the first button.

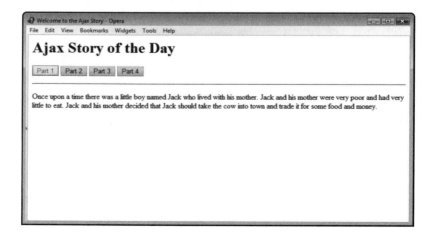

Figure 4.2

To interact with the Ajax Story of the Day application all you have to do is click on the application's buttons.

As Figure 4.2 demonstrates, once a button has been clicked, the application disables it to prevent it from being clicked again. This prevents the user from accidentally redisplaying a portion of the story that has already been displayed. Figure 4.3 shows how the application looks once all of its story has been told.

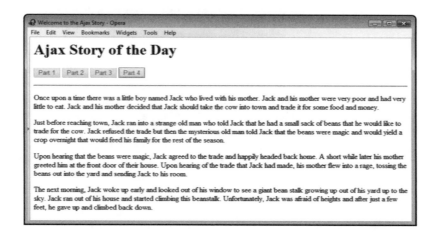

FIGURE 4.3

An example of a complete story presented by the Ajax Story of the Day application.

Each of the four parts of the story told by the application is retrieved from text files stored on the application's web server. As such, the story can easily be changed at any time by simply modifying the text files stored on the web server. For example, you might want to write a number of different four-part stories, replacing the application's text files on the web server every couple of weeks in order to continuously breathe new life into the Ajax application, thus encouraging your website visitors to keep coming back again and again.

AN INTRODUCTION TO THE DOCUMENT OBJECT MODEL

Up to this point in the book, all of the examples that have been presented have relied on the use of the `<DIV>` `</DIV>` and `<SPAN>` `</SPAN>` tags in order to facilitate the display of new text on web pages. However, Ajax developers have another even more powerful tool at their disposal, the HTML *Document Object Model (DOM)*. The DOM generates a logical representation of the items that make up HTML pages. The DOM is not a part of JavaScript. It is provided by the browser. However, your JavaScripts can access DOM objects, including their methods and properties, and programmatically interact with them in order to make dynamic updates to web pages.

Using different DOM methods and properties, you can create and insert new elements into HTML pages, changing the structure of the HTML page, thus altering the page's appearance and content. Every time the browser loads a web page, it renders that HTML page so that it can be viewed. At the same time, the browser also builds a tree-like view in memory of the elements that make up the web page.

Within the DOM, the `document` object provides JavaScript with direct access to the different elements that make up the DOM tree. Your Ajax applications can make changes to a web page's tree, adding, removing, or updating elements, thus dynamically altering page content and appearance.

 Prior to 1998, every browser supported its own unique DOM. In 1998, the first W3C DOM standard was published. In 2004, DOM 3, which is still the current standard, was released. Today all of the major modern web browsers support this version of the DOM. Thanks to the DOM, all modern web browsers will render the same tree for any web page. The DOM represents a huge subject, worthy of its own book. Unfortunately, there is no way that this book can completely cover all the ins and outs of the DOM. If you would like to learn more about the DOM than the essentials covered in this chapter, visit www.w3c.org/DOM.

THE DOM TREE

When an HTML page is loaded, the browser automatically defines a collection of objects based on the content of the HTML page. These objects are organized in a hierarchical top-down order, beginning with the `document` object, tying all of the web pages' elements together in a tree-like structure. The tree is made up of different elements, each of which represents a different web page object.

Using the tree, the browser maintains a map of connections that shows the organization of the web page, which consists of a series of parent, child, and sibling relationships. As you will see a little later in this chapter, you can use these relationships as a means of traversing the DOM tree. Each of the objects in the DOM tree provides access to methods and properties that you can use to programmatically interact with and control the objects. This provides you with the ability to make elements appear and disappear or to modify them in other ways like changing their color, size, etc.

In order to work with DOM trees, you must be familiar with a number of DOM properties and methods. Table 4.1 provides a listing of key DOM properties, which can be used to identify different elements on the DOM tree and to retrieve element (node) names, types, and values.

Using the DOM properties outlined in Table 4.1, you can traverse the DOM tree, moving from parent to child, child to parent, or from sibling to sibling. Table 4.2 provides a listing of key DOM methods that let you make modifications to the DOM tree, creating and appending new elements. As you can see, the DOM also provides access to methods that allow you to retrieve information about tree elements (objects), such as their ID, and to delete them from the DOM tree.

TABLE 4.1   DOM PROPERTIES

Property	Description
childNodes	A collection (e.g., array) of child objects belonging to an object
firstChild	The first child node belonging to an object
lastChild	An object's last child node
NodeName	The name assigned to an object's HTML tag
nodeType	Identifies the type of HTML element (tag, attribute, or text) associated with the object
nodeValue	Retrieves the value assigned to a text node
nextSibling	The child node following the previous child node in the tree
previousSibling	The child node that comes before the current child node
parentNode	An object's parent object

TABLE 4.2   DOM METHODS

Property	Description
appendChild()	Adds a new child node to the specified element
createAttribute()	Creates a new element attribute
createElement()	Creates a new document element
createTextNode()	Creates a new text item
getElementByTagName()	Retrieves an array of item tag names
getElementsById()	Retrieves an element based on its ID
hasChildNotes()	Returns a true or false value depending on whether a node has children
removeChild()	Deletes the specified child node

Using the properties and methods listed in Tables 4.1 and 4.2, you can create new DOM tree elements and add them to specific locations in the DOM tree. Whenever an alteration is programmatically made to the DOM tree, it is immediately reflected in the appearance of the content displayed on the web page—no page refresh required. For example, you might modify the DOM to include new elements like text or images. In doing so, new text and images would automatically appear on the web page. The reverse is also true. If you remove any elements from the DOM tree, the objects that those elements represent disappear from the web page.

Since the DOM tree represents a mapping of every element that makes up a web page, it gives you the ability to alter every part of a web page. There is no need to embed <DIV> </DIV> or <SPAN> </SPAN> tags at strategic locations throughout the web pages just so you have a predefined place to add new content. The DOM tree therefore gives you total control over the look and appearance of any web page. Of course, programming, interacting with, and manipulating the DOM tree does involve added complexity to the design of your Ajax applications. However, in order to develop truly dynamic web pages, a solid understanding of how to work with the DOM is essential for any Ajax developer.

WALKING THE DOM TREE

As previously stated, the document object resides at the top of the DOM tree. You have already worked with the document object extensively in this book. For example, in order to write text to the web page, you have been using the document object's write() method, as demonstrated here:

```
document.write("Easy is as easy does.");
```

As depicted in Figure 4.4, it is through the document object that you are able to access all of the objects that make up an HTML page.

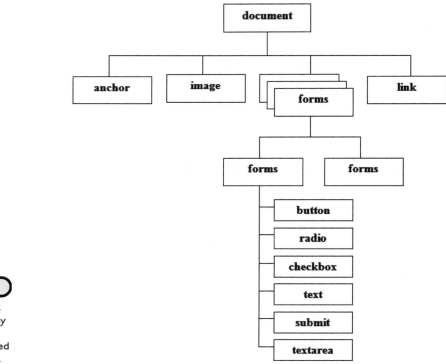

FIGURE 4.4

The document object is the key to accessing elements located on web pages.

As you can see, the document object sits on top of the tree. Beneath it are all of the different objects that make up the web pages. You can access DOM elements in HTML pages in a number of different ways. The most direct way of accessing HTML objects is by referencing tag IDs. Alternatively, you can use various DOM properties. Both of these options are examined in the sections that follow.

Accessing DOM Elements by ID

The advantage of accessing HTML page objects using tag IDs is that it keeps things simple and straightforward. The disadvantage of this approach is that it requires you to supply unique IDs for all HTML tags. The use of this approach is demonstrated here:

```
<HTML>
  <HEAD>
    <TITLE>Demo: Accessing DOM Elements by ID</TITLE>
    <SCRIPT language = "javascript" type = "text/javascript">
    <!-- Start hiding JavaScript statements
      function SetAlarm() {
        document.getElementById('DivTrgt').innerHTML = "Charge!"
      }
    // End hiding JavaScript statements -->
    </SCRIPT>
  </HEAD>
  <BODY onload = " SetAlarm()">
    <H1>Knock Knock!</H1>
    <DIV id="DivTrgt"> </DIV>
  </BODY>
</HTML>
```

As you can see, a function named SetAlarm() has been set up to access an element in the DOM tree named DivTrgt. A reference to this object is retrieved by passing the DOM's getElementById() method the name of the appropriate HTML tag. Once an object reference has been established, you can use the object's innerHTML property to modify its value. In the case of this example, the object being referenced is the <DIV> </DIV> tags located in the page's body section.

Assessing an HTML object using ID references is certainly straightforward, but it takes a little extra time and effort to assign unique IDs to every tag. In addition, this approach is not nearly as flexible as using DOM properties.

Accessing DOM Elements Using DOM Properties

Rather than having to hardcode an ID attribute for every HTML tag you may need to reference in your Ajax applications, you can instead navigate the DOM tree for all its HTML pages. Table 4.1 provides a list of DOM properties that you can use to traverse the elements that make up DOM trees. Using these DOM properties, you can move up, down, and sideways throughout the tree without any need to hard code ID references for specific HTML tags.

To demonstrate how to work with the various DOM properties and methods listed in Tables 4.1 and 4.2, take a look at the following example.

```
<HTML>
  <HEAD>
    <TITLE>Demo: Dissecting the DOM Tree</TITLE>
  </HEAD>
  <BODY>
    <H1>DOM Demo</H1>
    <P>Let's examine this page's DOM tree!</P>
  </BODY>
</HTML>
```

As you can see, this is a small but typical HTML page with a `<TITLE>` tag in the head sections and a level 1 heading and a paragraph in the body section. Figure 4.5 shows how this page looks when loaded by Internet Explorer.

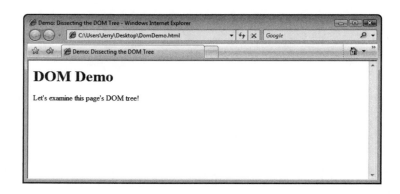

FIGURE 4.5

An example of how the web page looks when loaded by Internet Explorer.

While Figure 4.5 shows how the web page looks when rendered by the browsers, the browser's internal view of the page is maintained in memory using the DOM. Figure 4.6 provides a graphical depiction of the DOM tree that the browser assembles as it loads the web page.

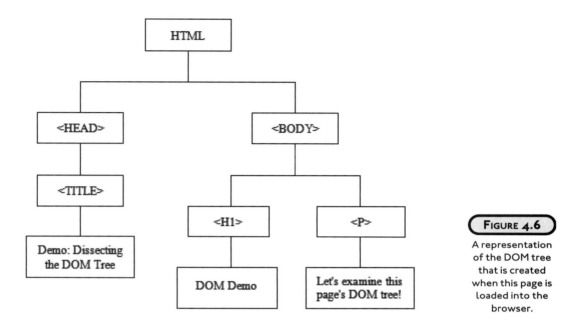

FIGURE 4.6

A representation of the DOM tree that is created when this page is loaded into the browser.

NOTE Although it is not depicted in Figure 4.6, the document object sits at the root of the DOM tree and has just one child object, documentElement. documentElement represents the web page's opening ⟨HTML⟩ tag. You can establish a reference to the opening ⟨HTML⟩ object using the DOM's documentElement property, as demonstrated here:

```
var TreeTop = document.documentElement;
```

As you can see in Figure 4.6, the DOM tree for this HTML page shows the parent/child and sibling relationships for all of the different elements that make up the HTML page. In addition, order is carefully depicted. Using different DOM properties, you can reference any of the elements in the HTML page, as depicted in Figure 4.7.

As you can see in Figure 4.7, to reference an object on the DOM tree you must provide a reference that identifies the location of the element within the tree. In Figure 4.7, a variable named root is defined and assigned a value of document.documentElement. In order to set up the reference, a known reference point had to be used. In the case of the first reference, the point of reference was the documentElement property, which is the root element on the tree. Next, the second reference is established by starting at the location represented by root and then referencing its last child element (e.g., root.lastChild). The first reference is established using the last child of body.

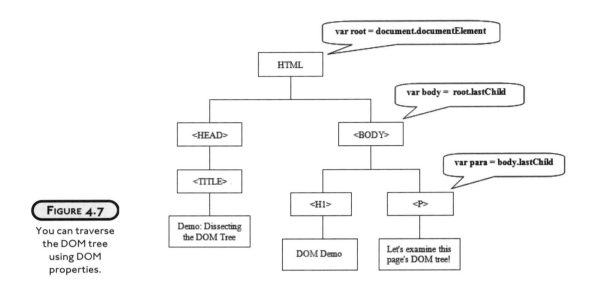

FIGURE 4.7

You can traverse
the DOM tree
using DOM
properties.

A Mixed Navigation Approach

Rather than navigating around a DOM tree and working exclusively with the ID attribute or with DOM properties, a common approach used by Ajax developers is to use a combination of the two approaches. As an example of how to use this approach, let's modify the previous web page, inserting several instances of the ID attribute into a few HTML tags, as shown here:

```
<HTML>
  <HEAD>
    <TITLE>Demo: Dissecting the DOM Tree</TITLE>
  </HEAD>
  <BODY ID = "BodyTag">
    <H1 ID = "HeadTag">DOM Demo</H1>
    <P ID = "ParaTag">Let's examine this page's DOM tree!</P>
  </BODY>
</HTML>
```

Figure 4.8 shows a new depiction of the HTML page's DOM tree view, this time pointing out which tree nodes have been assigned ID attributes.

As an example of how to navigate the DOM tree using a combination of ID attribute references and DOM properties, take a look at Figure 4.9.

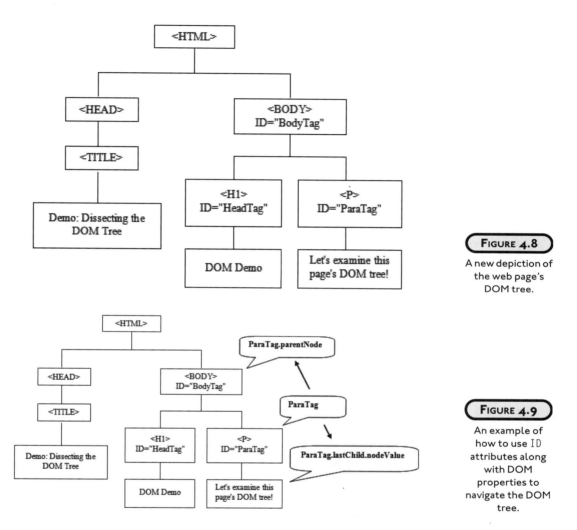

FIGURE 4.8

A new depiction of the web page's DOM tree.

FIGURE 4.9

An example of how to use ID attributes along with DOM properties to navigate the DOM tree.

Now that the HTML page has a number of tags with ID attributes embedded within it, you have greater flexibility when it comes to establishing new element references. Instead of having to start at the root of the DOM tree and work your way down, you can now start at any location within the tree where a tag ID has been set.

DYNAMICALLY UPDATING WEB PAGE CONTENT

Now that you understand how the browser generates a DOM tree for each HTML page, and have seen how to navigate the DOM tree, it's time to learn how to modify the DOM tree in order to facilitate the dynamic update of web page content. To do so, let's create a new web page as shown here:

```
<HTML>
  <HEAD>
    <TITLE>Demo: Working with mouse event handlers</TITLE>
    <SCRIPT LANGUAGE = "JavaScript" TYPE = "Text/JavaScript">
      function ChangePageLayout() {
        var newParagraph = document.createElement("p");
        var newTextNode = document.createTextNode('The DOM Rocks!');
        document.getElementById('trgtDiv').appendChild(newParagraph);
        document.getElementById('trgtDiv').appendChild(newTextNode);
      }
    </SCRIPT>
  </HEAD>
  <BODY>
    <H1>DOM Demonstration</H1>
    <FORM>
      <INPUT type = "button" value = "Click on Me" id = "formButton"
        onclick = "ChangePageLayout()">
    </FORM>
    <DIV id = "trgtDiv"> </DIV>
  </BODY>
</HTML>
```

Figure 4.10 shows how this HTML page looks when initially loaded into the browser.

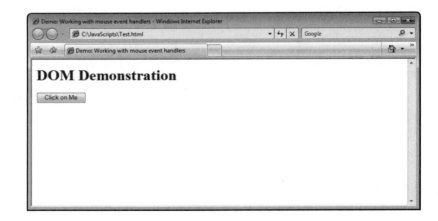

FIGURE 4.10

The web page
currently displays
a level 1 heading
and a button
labeled Click
on Me.

You can create another type of element using the `CreateElement()` method. You can then use the DOM's `AppendChild()` method to attach the new text node to an existing node in the HTML page.

Within the HTML file, a function named `ChangePageLayout()` has been created that when called will create a new HTML paragraph element (e.g., `<P>`) using the DOM's `createElement()` method, assigning it to a variable named `newParagraph`. Next, the DOM's `createTextNode()` method is used to create a text element which is assigned to a variable named `newTextNode`. Using the DOM's `AppendChild()` method, you can attach a new node to any point within the HTML page. The last two statements in the function use the DOM's `appendChild()` method to dynamically modify the DOM tree by adding the two newly created HTML elements to it.

FIGURE 4.11

The HTML appearance of the HTML page has changed to reflect the modifications made to the DOM tree.

NOTE One more thing that you should know when working with the DOM is that you can get the name of any node in the tree using the `nodeName` attribute. An element node represents elements like `<DIV>` and `<P>` tags, which do not have any values. A text node on the other hand, will not have a name but will have a value. You can retrieve a node's value using the `nodeValue` attribute.

BACK TO THE AJAX STORY OF THE DAY APPLICATION

Okay. Let's turn our attention back to the development of the Ajax Story of the Day application. This game will demonstrate how to dynamically modify a web page's DOM tree in order to accommodate the display of text retrieved from a web server, all without any browser refresh, allowing for the seemly display of new content during application execution.

Designing the Application

Like all of the other applications developed in this book, the Ajax Story of the Day application is created using a specific series of steps, as outlined here:

1. Create a new HTML page.
2. Add a form to collect user data.
3. Define a paragraph for displaying story text.
4. Begin the application's JavaScript.
5. Create an XMLHttpRequest object.
6. Retrieve story text from the web server.
7. Modify the DOM tree.
8. Disable game buttons.
9. Create the application's text files.
10. Execute your new Ajax application.

Step 1: Writing the Application's HTML

The first step in the development of the Ajax Story of the Day application is to create the application's HTML page. Start by opening your favorite text or code editor and then adding the following HTML statements to it. Once added, save the HTML page with a name of AjaxStory.html.

```
<HTML>
  <HEAD>
    <TITLE>Welcome to the Ajax Story</TITLE>
  </HEAD>
  <BODY>
    <H1>Ajax Story of the Day</H1>
  </BODY>
</HTML>
```

As you can see this is a fairly vanilla web page, made up of head and body tags along with a title and a level 1 header.

Step 2: Creating the Application's Form

The interface for the Ajax Story of the Day application is made up of four button controls aligned across the top of the web page. To set this up, you need to add a form to the page, which you can do by adding the following HTML statement to the body section of the HTML page.

```
<FORM name = "appForm">
  <INPUT name = "Button1" type = "button" value = "Part 1"
    onclick = "TellStory('Part1.txt')">
  <INPUT name = "Button2" type = "button" value = "Part 2"
    onclick = "TellStory('Part2.txt')">
  <INPUT name = "Button3" type = "button" value = "Part 3"
    onclick = "TellStory('Part3.txt')">
  <INPUT name = "Button4" type = "button" value = "Part 4"
    onclick = "TellStory('Part4.txt')">
</FORM>
```

Each of the four buttons is assigned a unique name and value and is configured to execute the TellStory() function when clicked, passing it the name of a different text file to be downloaded from the application's web server. Just beneath the four button controls, a gray line is displayed. To set this up, add the following HTML tag to the end of the body section, just beneath the form statements that you just added.

```
<HR>
```

Step 3: Adding a Paragraph Element for the Display of Text

To interact with the application, the user must click on the four button controls, in the order that they are presented. Each time a button is clicked, a new portion of the story is displayed on the browser window. Rather than hard coding four sets of <DIV> </DIV> tags at the bottom of the body section to establish a predefined location into which story text can be added, this application instead modifies the DOM tree as necessary each time a new portion of the story needs to be displayed.

When dynamically modifying the DOM tree, the application will use the DOM appendChild() method to repeatedly display new parts of the story. In order to accomplish this, add the following statement to the end of the body section.

```
<P id = "trgtP"> <P>
```

The application will use this paragraph tag to establish the location within the DOM tree where new elements should be appended.

Step 4: Beginning the Development of the Game's Script

The next step in the development of the Ajax Story of the Day application is to begin assembling its JavaScript. Begin by adding the following statement to the head section of the HTML page.

```
<SCRIPT language = "javascript" TYPE = "text/javascript">
<!-- Start hiding JavaScript statements


// End hiding JavaScript statements -->
</SCRIPT>
```

The rest of the steps involved in building this application involve the addition of JavaScript statements and functions belonging to this script.

Step 5: Creating an XMLHttpRequest Object

Since the Ajax Story of the Day application involves the retrieval of data in the form of four text files from its web server, you need to set up an instance of the XMLHttpRequest object. This book has yet to explain how to work with this object, so for now just copy the following statements into the application's JavaScript, exactly as shown.

```
var Request = false;


if (window.XMLHttpRequest) {
  Request = new XMLHttpRequest();
} else if (window.ActiveXObject) {
  Request = new ActiveXObject("Microsoft.XMLHTTP");
}
```

 You will learn all about the XMLHttpRequest object in Chapter 5, "Ajax Basics." For now, all you need to know is that it facilitates the exchange of information with the web server.

Step 6: Retrieving Story Text

The Ajax Story of the Day application is made up of several different functions, each of which performs a unique task. The TellStory() function, shown next, is responsible for telling the application's story. The statements that make up this function should be added to the end of the application's JavaScript.

```
function TellStory(url) {
  if(Request) {
    Request.open("GET", url);
    Request.onreadystatechange = function()
    {
      if (Request.readyState == 4 && Request.status == 200) {
```

```
      ModifyDOM(Request.responseText)
      UpdateInterface(url)
    }
  }
  Request.send(null);
  }
}
```

This function uses the XMLHttpRequest object, established in the previous step, to retrieve a portion of the application's story. The file that is retrieved is passed to the functions as an argument, which is then mapped to the url parameter. Since the inner workings of this function require a good understanding of the use of the XMLHttpRequest object, which is not covered until the next chapter, do not get too hung up on the details of this function. All that you need to know for now is that once the specified text file has been retrieved, it is passed to the ModifyDOM() function, which will then addend the DOM tree and display the text retrieved from the web server. Also, a call is made to the UpdateInterface() function, which is responsible for disabling access to the application's button controls.

Step 7: Updating the DOM Tree

The ModifyDOM() function, shown next, is responsible for modifying the structure of the DOM tree to accommodate the display of each of the four parts of the application's story. Add this function to the application's JavaScript, just below the TellStory() function.

```
function ModifyDOM(storyText) {
  var newText = document.createTextNode(storyText);
  var newLine = document.createElement("p");
  document.getElementById('trgtP').appendChild(newLine);
  document.getElementById('trgtP').appendChild(newText);
}
```

When called, the ModifyDOM() function is passed an argument representing the text of a portion of the application's story (retrieved from the web server). This text is stored in a variable aptly named storyText. The function begins by defining a new text node named newText, made up of the text stored in storyText. Next, a paragraph element node named newLine is then defined. The last two statements in the function append the newLine and newText elements to the end of the trgtP element. If you return to Step 3, you will see that this element was specifically added to the end of the HTML page's body section in order to establish a point of reference and set up a parental element, facilitating the addition of new child elements to the web page.

Step 8: Modifying Button State

The last function to be added to the application's JavaScript is the UpdateInterface() function. Its job is to disable access to each of the application's four button controls. It accomplished its task using plain old JavaScript.

```
function UpdateInterface(selection) {
  if (selection == "Part1.txt") appForm.Button1.disabled = "disabled";
  if (selection == "Part2.txt") appForm.Button2.disabled = "disabled";
  if (selection == "Part3.txt") appForm.Button3.disabled = "disabled";
  if (selection == "Part4.txt") appForm.Button4.disabled = "disabled";
}
```

As you can see, the function passes an argument that indicates which part of the story has just been displayed. Using this information, one of the application's four button controls is then displayed by setting the control's disabled property to a value of disabled. This prevents the player from accidentally clicking on the same button more than once during the telling of the story.

Step 9: Creating the Application's Text Files

In order to finish up work on the Ajax Story of the Day application, you need to create each of the application's four text files. To do so, create four new text files named Part1.txt, Part2.txt, Part3.txt, and Part4.txt and add the text shown below to the appropriate files.

Part1.txt

Once upon a time there was a little boy named Jack, who lived with his mother. Jack and his mother were very poor and had very little to eat. Jack and his mother decided that Jack should take the cow into town and trade it for some food and money.

Part2.txt

Just before reaching town, Jack ran into a strange old man who told Jack that he had a small sack of beans that he would like to trade for the cow. Jack refused the trade but then the mysterious old man told Jack that the beans were magic and would yield a crop overnight that would feed his family for the rest of the season.

Part3.txt

Upon hearing that the beans were magic, Jack agreed to the trade and happily headed back home. A short while later his mother greeted him at the front door of their house. Upon hearing of the trade that Jack had made, his mother flew into a rage, tossing the beans out into the yard and sending Jack to his room.

`Part4.txt`

The next morning, Jack woke up early and looked out of his window to see a giant bean stalk growing up out of his yard up to the sky. Jack ran out of his house and started climbing this beanstalk. Unfortunately, Jack was afraid of heights and after just a few feet, he gave up and climbed back down.

Step 10: Executing Your New Game

All right! At this point, you have all of the information needed to create the Ajax Story of the Day application. Assuming that you have carefully followed along with the instruction that has been provided and did not make any typos along the way, everything should run as described at the beginning of this chapter. To test this application, upload the AjaxStory.html file along with Part1.txt, Part2.txt, Part3.txt, and Part4.txt files to your web servers and then load AjaxStory.html into your web browser and see what happens.

 You will find a copy of this application's source code files on the book's companion website, located at http://www.courseptr.com/downloads.

SUMMARY

This chapter provided you with a detailed overview of the Document Object Model and explained how it can be used to dynamically modify the appearance of web pages without any page refreshes. You learned how the DOM creates a DOM tree representation of all web pages and how to manipulate this tree using the `document` object and various DOM properties and methods. You learned different ways of referencing objects in the DOM tree and to use object relationships as a means of navigating the DOM tree. You also learned how to use the DOM tree to update web page content without using the `<DIV> </DIV>` and `<SPAN> </SPAN>` tags.

Now, before you move on to Chapter 5, "Ajax Basics," I suggest you set aside a few more minutes to work on the Ajax Story of the Day application by implementing the following list of challenges.

CHALLENGES

1. As currently written, there is no programming logic in place that prevents the user from clicking on each of the button controls in the proper order. Consider modifying the application to address this situation, forcing the user to click on the correct button each time the story is told.

2. Rewrite the application's story to tell a story that better suits your own interests. Remember, once you are done writing it, you will need to break it down into four parts, and save those parts in appropriately named text files.

Part

III

Building Ajax Applications

Ajax Basics

To become an effective Ajax programmer you must, at a minimum, understand how to work with HTML, JavaScript, the DOM, and the XMLHttpRequest object. Your knowledge of HTML is assumed. Chapters 1–4 provided you with a working understanding of JavaScript and the DOM. This chapter introduces you to the XMLHttpRequest object and explains how to use it to communicate with web servers and facilitate the exchange of data in your Ajax applications. This chapter will demonstrate how to use the XMLHttpRequest object to retrieve text files and to use the data that is retrieved in different ways. This chapter will also introduce you to Ajax frameworks, which are libraries of JavaScript functions that you can load and integrate into your web applications, allowing you to shorten application time and to create applications capable of performing all sorts of complex operations.

Specifically, you will learn:

- How to instantiate and interact with the XMLHttpRequest object
- How to retrieve data stored in web server text files
- How to create an Ajax application that uses toolbar-driven mouseover effects
- How to integrate Ajax frameworks into your applications

PROJECT PREVIEW: THE AJAX TYPING CHALLENGE

This chapter's game project is the Ajax Typing Challenge. In this application, the user is challenged to type three increasingly lengthy and difficult sentences. Figure 5.1 shows how the application looks when loaded into Internet Explorer.

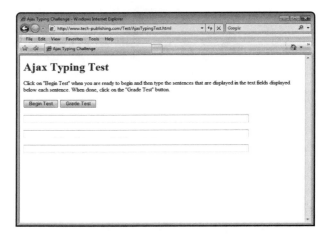

FIGURE 5.1

To begin the Ajax Typing Challenge application, the user must click on the Begin Test button.

As soon as the Begin Test button is clicked, the application connects to the web server and downloads three challenge sentences, which are then displayed on the browser window. As shown in Figure 5.2, the challenge sentences are dispersed between the application's text box fields.

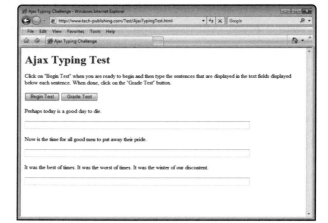

FIGURE 5.2

The user's job is to type each sentence exactly as shown on the screen.

There is no time limit on how long the user can take to complete the typing challenge. Once the user has finished retyping all three sentences, the Grade Test button must be clicked. This instructs the application to grade the test, as demonstrated in Figure 5.3.

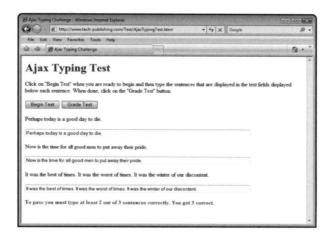

FIGURE 5.3

To pass the Ajax Typing Challenge, the user must correctly type in at least two sentences.

If the user fails the test and wants to retake the test, the player can click on the Begin Test button again. In response, the application clears out any text displayed in the three test fields, allowing the user to try again.

CONNECTING YOUR APPLICATIONS TO WEB SERVERS

Ajax applications take advantage of the browser's ability to execute client-side JavaScript code that can interact with the browser's DOM and make dynamic modifications to a page's DOM tree using data retrieved from a web server. An Ajax application's communication with the web server occurs behind the scenes using methods and properties belonging to the XMLHttpRequest object. Using the XMLHttpRequest object, Ajax applications send and receive HTTP requests and responses.

Microsoft created the XMLHttpRequest object and initially released it in 1999 as an ActiveX object component in Internet Explorer 5. Other web browser developers soon realized the usefulness of this object and added support for it to their own browsers, implementing it as a window object property. Eventually, Microsoft followed suit and re-engineered the XMLHttpRequest object as a window object property starting in Internet Explorer 7.

Ajax applications use the XMLHttpRequest object to initiate and manage the submission of data requests to web servers and to monitor and handle the receipt of server data. A solid understanding of how to work with this object's methods and properties is essential to Ajax application developers. The primary purpose of this chapter is to provide you with detailed instruction on how to instantiate and then use XMLHttpRequest objects in order to manage data retrieval in Ajax applications.

XMLHttpRequest Methods

The XMLHttpRequest object provides access to two methods that facilitate connecting to web servers and submitting requests. A brief explanation of these methods is provided next.

- open(). Establishes a connection to a web server.
- send(). Sends a request to a web server.

The open() method is used to initiate a connection to the web server. Once connected, you will use various XMLHttpRequest properties, discussed in the next section, to send data requests and then to monitor them once they are started (which is done using the send() method).

XMLHttpRequest Properties

In order to specify the type of data that your Ajax applications expect to receive from the web server and to monitor and respond to that data once it has been received from the web server, you need to work with different XMLHttpRequest properties. Table 5.1 lists and describes various XMLHttpRequest properties that you will need to know how to work with in your Ajax applications.

TABLE 5.1	XMLHTTPREQUEST OBJECT ATTRIBUTES
Attribute	**Description**
readyState	A value between 0 and 4 indicating the state of the receipt of data from the web server, where a value of 4 means the data has been received.
status	A status code indicating the overall status of the XMLHttpRequest object's data request, where a value of 200 indicated that everything went well (refer to Table 5.2).
responseText	Stores text data returned by the web server.
responseXML	Stores XML data returned by the web server.
onreadystatechange	Takes a function and calls on it to execute whenever the readystatechange event occurs.

WORKING WITH THE **XMLHTTPREQUEST** OBJECT

Using XMLHttpRequest objects to establish connections to web servers, specifying data requests, and then handling the data that is returned is a multi-step process. An understanding of how these steps work is essential and is covered in great detail in the sections that follow.

Instantiating the XMLHttpRequest Object

The first step in working with the XMLHttpRequest object is to instantiate it. Unfortunately, the XMLHttpRequest object represents another point of divergence between web browsers. The following statement demonstrates how to determine if an Ajax application is running on FireFox, Safari, Opera, or any Internet Explorer browser after version 6.

```
var Request = false;
if (window.XMLHttpRequest) {    //Try FireFox, Safari, Opera, IE 7 or higher
  Request = new XMLHttpRequest();
}
```

Here, the first statement defines a variable named Request that will be used to set up a reference to the XMLHttpRequest object. The second statement executes the window object's XMLHttpRequest property to determine if it is supported. If it is, the second statement creates a new XMLHttpRequest object named Request using the new keyword.

 Once instantiated, you can work with the XMLHttpRequest object using the same sets of properties, methods, and events, regardless of the type of browser in use.

To instantiate the XMLHttpRequest object in a browser running Internet Explorer 5 or 6, you need to use the ActiveXObject() method as demonstrated here:

```
if (window.ActiveXObject) {    //Try ActiveX (Internet Explorer)
  Request = new ActiveXObject("Microsoft.XMLHTTP");
}
```

 Although Internet Explorer 8 was available as a beta release as of the writing of this book, Internet Explorer 7 was the most current official version of that browser, having been that way since October 2006. Still, because large numbers of web surfers are still using Internet Explorer 5 and 6, it is a standard practice to provide support for Internet Explorer 5 and 6 in all Ajax applications, as demonstrated here:

```
var Request = false;
if (window.XMLHttpRequest) {
  Request = new XMLHttpRequest();
```

```
} else if (window.ActiveXObject) {
  Request = new ActiveXObject("Microsoft.XMLHTTP");
}
```

Rather than instantiating the XMLHttpRequest object as just demonstrated, you may sometimes come across examples where other Ajax developers set up instances of the XMLHttpRequest object using an exceptions-based approach, as demonstrated here:

```
var Request = false;
try {
  Request = new XMLHttpRequest();  //Try FireFox, Safari, Opera, etc.
}
Catch(e)
{
  Request = new ActiveXObject("Microsoft.XMLHTTP"); //Try ActiveX (IE)
}
```

Here, a variable named Request is declared, after which a try code block is set up in an attempt to instantiate an instance of the XMLHttpRequest object using the Window object's XMLHttpRequest() method. This will work as long as the browser being used is not Internet Explorer 5 or 6. If this is the case, an error occurs and the Catch() method is executed. This method ignores the error, allowing the application to continue its execution. If this occurs, the XMLHttpRequest object is set up using Internet Explorer's ActiveXObject() method.

Opening a New Connection

The next step after instantiating the XMLHttpRequest object is to establish a connection with the web server using the open() method. This method has the following syntax.

```
open("method", "url" [, asyncFlag [, username [, password]]])
```

Table 5.2 identifies the purpose of each of the open() method's arguments.

The XMLHttpRequest object always creates asynchronous connections with the web server, unless you explicitly tell it not to by assigning a value of false to asyncFlag. Doing so, however, defeats the entire purpose of using Ajax by forcing Ajax applications to halt execution and wait for data to be retrieved.

	TABLE 5.2 XMLHttpRequest Object Open() Method Parameters	

Value	Explanation
method	The HTTP method to be used to establish a connection with the web server (GET, POST)
url	The URL of the file URL to be opened on the web server
asyncFlag	An optional value that when set to true (default) sets up an asynchronous connection (a value of false dictates a synchronous connection)
userName	An optional username if required by the web server
password	An optional password if required by the web server

Executing the open() method

To use the open() method to open a URL on a web server, you must specify either the standard HTML GET or POST option. Of the two, the GET option, as demonstrated below, is all that is usually used to retrieve a moderate amount of data from the web server, and the POST option is usually used when you need to download large amounts of data.

```
if(Request) {
  Request.open("GET", "url");
  .
  .
  .
}
```

Both the GET and POST options configure the XMLHttpRequest object to work with a specified file. However, neither option causes the application to connect to the web server or access the file. You will learn how to make this happen in a couple more steps. Note that before executing the open() method, this example checks to make sure that a valid XMLHttpRequest object has in fact been successfully instantiated (by making sure that the value assigned to the Request object variable is equal to true).

TRICK

Take note of the example shown here. It checks if the value assigned to Request is equal to true.

```
if (Request) {

}
```

This example is functionally identical to the following example. The only difference between these two examples is that the first example takes fewer keystrokes to write and the second example is arguably a little easier to understand. Ajax programmers generally use the former version instead of the latter version, but ultimately it's a matter of personal choice.

```
if (Request = true) {

}
```

Using Absolute and Relative Paths

When specifying the path and filename for an Ajax application, two options are available: absolute paths and relative paths. An absolute path is one that specifies the exact location of the file, as demonstrated here:

```
Request.open("GET", "http://www.tech-publishing.com/Test/Scores.txt");
```

Here, a file named Scores.txt, residing on the web server at http://www.tech-publishing.com/Test/ has been specified. A relative path, on the other hand, specifies the location of a file based on its location on the web server in relation to the application file. For example, the following statement looks for a file named Scores.txt, residing in the same location as the application.

```
Request.open("GET", "Scores.txt");
```

For the sake of simplicity, relative paths are used in all of the examples in this book.

Waiting for the Web Server's Response

Once you have instantiated the XMLHttpRequest object and specified the file that you want to access using its open() method, you need to add the programming logic needed to handle the web server's response. The XMLHttpRequest object cycles through a number of different states as it goes through the process of sending an HTTP request and then waiting for and finally receiving data back from the web server. Specifically, the XMLHttpRequest object exposes two properties that let you know the overall status of an HTTP request. These properties are the readyState and status properties.

By keeping an eye on the value assigned to the readyState property, you can programmatically determine when the application has finished receiving the data. The readyState property can report any of the values shown in Table 5.3.

By keeping an eye on the value assigned to the status attribute, you can determine whether an HTTP request was successful. Specifically, you need to make sure that the value assigned to the status property is 200. Any other value indicates that something has gone awry.

The XMLHttpRequest object also has a property named onreadystatechange that can be used to manage your applications' asynchronous operations. All you have to do to use it is set up a function, as demonstrated here:

TABLE 5.3 XMLHTTPREQUEST OBJECT STATUS ATTRIBUTES VALUES

Value	Explanation
0	Represents an uninitialized state in which the XMLHttpRequest object has been created but not initialized.
1	Represents "sent" state in which the XMLHttpRequest object's open() method has been executed but the sent() method has yet to execute.
2	Represents a "sent" state in which the XMLHttpRequest object is waiting for data to be returned.
3	Represents a state in which the XMLHttpRequest object is in the process of receiving data from the web server.
4	Indicates that the XMLHttpRequest object has finished receiving the data from the web server.

```
Request.onreadystatechange = function() {
  if (Request.readyState == 4 && Request.status == 200) {
    .
    .
    .
  }
}
```

This type of function is referred to as an anonymous function. This function automatically executes whenever there is a change in the state of the request, allowing you to add script statements designed to monitor and keep track of the progress of the application's data request.

Handling the Web Server Response

Now that you have added the programming logic needed to handle the data that will be returned by the web server, you need to specify the type of data that your application expects to receive. This is done by one of the XMLHttpRequest object properties listed here:

- responseText. The data is returned as plain text.
- responseXML. The data is returned as XML.

The following statement demonstrates how to set up your Ajax application to handle text data returned by the web server.

```
RequestObj.innerHTML = Request.responseText;
```

Alternatively, you can set up your application to process XML data, as demonstrated here:

```
RequestObj.innerHTML = Request.responseXML;
```

Wrapping Things Up

Up to this point, you have seen how to instantiate the XMLHttpRequest object, specify a file, set up a server connection, verify the connection, and then prepare the application to retrieve data from the web server. To actually submit the request and retrieve the data, you must execute the send() method, which has the following syntax.

```
send("string")
```

Here, the value that you assign to the string parameter will always be "null" when working with the get mode, as demonstrated here:

```
Request.send(null);
```

Once executed, the send() method initiates the download process, allowing the JavaScript's anonymous function you set up to begin managing the download process.

Putting All the Pieces Together to Create a Working Ajax Application

To help tie together all of the information just presented, let's revisit the Ajax Joke of the Day application that was presented back in Chapter 1. The complete HTML file for this application is shown here:

```
<HTML>
  <HEAD>
    <TITLE>Ajax Joke of the Day Application</TITLE>
    <SCRIPT language = "javascript" type = "text/javascript">
      var Request = false;
      if (window.XMLHttpRequest) {
        Request = new XMLHttpRequest();
      } else if (window.ActiveXObject) {
        Request = new ActiveXObject("Microsoft.XMLHTTP");
      }
      function retrieveJoke(url, elementID) {
        if(Request) {
          var RequestObj = document.getElementById(elementID);
          Request.open("GET", url);
          Request.onreadystatechange = function() {
```

```
            if (Request.readyState == 4 && Request.status == 200) {
                RequestObj.innerHTML = Request.responseText;
            }
        }
        Request.send(null);
      }
    }
  </SCRIPT>
</HEAD>
<BODY>
  <H1>Where do bees go when they get married?</H1>
  <FORM>
    <INPUT type = "button" value = "Fetch Answer"
      onclick = "retrieveJoke('joke.txt', 'DivTarget')">
  </FORM>
  <DIV id="DivTarget"> </DIV>
</BODY>
</HTML>
```

As you can see, this application begins by defining a variable that will be used to represent an instance of the XMLHttpRequest object. Next, an if statement code block is set to determine whether a web browser is running Internet Explorer 7 or above or is a different type of browser altogether. The code statements that set up the variable and instantiate the XMLHttpRequest object have been added to the HTML page, outside of any function, so that they automatically execute when the web page loads.

An initial value of false is assigned to the Request variable so that the application's JavaScript can later check its value in order to verify that the XMLHttpRequest object has been created. A function named retrieveJoke() is then defined. This function executes when the user clicks on a button located on a form defined in the body section of the HTML page. The button's onClick event handler passes the function two arguments. The first argument specifies the name of a text file to be downloaded from the web server, and the second argument specifies the id associated with a pair of <DIV> </DIV> tags located in the body section where the contents of the text files will be displayed once processed by the retrieveJoke() function.

Once executed, the retrieveJoke() function checks to make sure that an instance of the XMLHttpRequest object has been set up and then declares a variable named requestObj and assigns it a value representing the <DIV> </DIV> tags located in the page's body section. Next, the open() method is executed using the GET option, and an anonymous function is set up to handle the text file downloaded by the server, using the RequestObj object's innerHTML property to display the contents of the text file in the HTML page's <DIV> </DIV> tags. Lastly, the send() method is executed, initiating the download process and invoking the execution of the anonymous function. Figure 5.4 shows an example of this application in action.

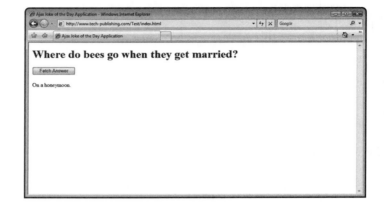

Executing the Ajax Joke of the Day application.

MANAGING CONCURRENT XMLHTTPREQUESTS

Up to this point in the book, the Ajax applications that you have seen have all used a single XMLHttpRequest object. However, as you begin developing more complex Ajax applications, you may eventually need to develop an Ajax application that must respond to different user actions, simultaneously fetching multiple sets of data from the web server. This cannot be done using a single XMLHttpRequest object.

One way to handle this scenario is to define multiple instances of the XMLHttpRequest object. For example, the following statement defines a pair of XMLHttpRequest objects.

```
var Request1 = false;
var Request2 = false;
if (window.XMLHttpRequest) {
  Request1 = new XMLHttpRequest();
  Request2 = new XMLHttpRequest();
} else if (window.ActiveXObject) {
  Request1 = new ActiveXObject("Microsoft.XMLHTTP");
  Request2 = new ActiveXObject("Microsoft.XMLHTTP");
}
```

Using this approach, you will need to create a unique instance of the XMLHttpRequest object for each request that your application may need to initiate. If you create an application that needs to support more than two or three requests at a time, this approach can quickly become troublesome to manage. Instead, a better approach is to use an array to manage your application's `XMLHttpRequest` objects. Remember, JavaScript arrays can be used to store collections of any type of object supported by JavaScript.

The following example demonstrates the logic required to set up an array of `XMLHttpRequest` objects. The array is named `aRequests`. Each `XMLHttpRequest` object in the array can then be referenced as necessary using its index position within the array.

```
var aRequests = new Array();
if (window.XMLHttpRequest) {
  aRequests.push(new XMLHttpRequest());
} else if (window.ActiveXObject) {
  aRequests.push(new ActiveXObject("Microsoft.XMLHttp"));
}
```

 TRICK JavaScript arrays support a function named `push()`, which, when executed, increases the size of the specified array by adding a new element to the end of the array.

USING AJAX TO SET UP MOUSEOVERS

In the previous section, you saw an example of how to create an Ajax application that retrieves a text file from the web server when the user clicks on a button control. Ajax is not limited to retrieving data and modifying web page content only in situations where the user explicitly initiates an action. Ajax applications can just as easily be set up that interact with the web server behind the scenes to provide the user with dynamic content as the mouse pointer is moved around the web page. An example demonstrating how you might set up something like this is provided here:

```
<HTML>
  <HEAD>
    <TITLE>XYZ Website</TITLE>
    <SCRIPT language = "javascript" type = "text/javascript">
    <!-- Start hiding JavaScript statements
      var Request = false;
      if (window.XMLHttpRequest) {
        Request = new XMLHttpRequest();
      } else if (window.ActiveXObject) {
        Request = new ActiveXObject("Microsoft.XMLHTTP");
      }
      function updatePage(fileName, target)
```

```
    {
      if(Request) {
        var targetDiv = document.getElementById(target);
        Request.open("GET", fileName);
        Request.onreadystatechange = function() {
          if (Request.readyState == 4 && Request.status == 200) {
              targetDiv.innerHTML = Request.responseText;
          }
        }
        Request.send(null);
      }
    }
  // End hiding JavaScript statements -->
  </SCRIPT>
</HEAD>
<BODY>
  <IMG src = "home.jpg" onmouseover="updatePage('home.txt', 'TrgtDiv')">
  <IMG src = "products.jpg" onmouseover="updatePage('products.txt',
    'TrgtDiv')">
  <IMG src = "downloads.jpg"
    onmouseover="updatePage('downloads.txt', 'TrgtDiv')">
  <IMG src = "forums.jpg" onmouseover="updatePage('forums.txt',
    'TrgtDiv')">
  <IMG src = "about.jpg" onmouseover="updatePage('about.txt',
    'TrgtDiv')">
  <H1> <DIV id = "TrgtDiv"> </DIV> </H1>
</BODY>
</HTML>
```

Here, a small application made up of five graphic menus located at the top of the browser window has been created. Each of these graphic objects calls upon a JavaScript function named updatePage() whenever the user moves the mouse over one of the images. When this happens, the mouseover event occurs and the onMouseOver() event handler is executed, passing the name of a text file located on the web server where text that provides more information is available and the id of a pair of <DIV> </DIV> tags where data retrieved from the web server should be displayed.

When called, the updatePage() function first checks to make sure that an instance of the XMLHttpRequest object has been instantiated. Next, a variable named trgtDiv is created and used to set up a reference to the <DIV> </DIV> tags. The XMLHttpRequest object's open() method is executed in order to set up a connection to the web server. As soon as the connection is established, an anonymous function is set up to handle the data returned by the web server, dynamically posting it on the web page.

Figure 5.5 shows how this application looks when initially loaded into the browser.

FIGURE 5.5

An example of a series of graphical menus used to control page content.

Each time the user moves the mouse pointer over one of the graphic menus located at the top of the browser window, the application connects to the web server behind the scenes and retrieves data that describes the menu. In total, the application utilizes five different text files. The web server returns a copy of the text stored in one of these files each time it is called. This information is then posted in the browser, instantly with no page refreshes! Figure 5.6 shows how this application looks when the user moves the mouse pointer over the DOWNLOADS menu.

FIGURE 5.6

An example of the content that the application displays when the user moves the mouse pointer over the DOWNLOADS menu.

LEVERAGING AJAX FRAMEWORKS

If you have done any surfing around the Internet to learn about Ajax, chances are that you have come across references to different Ajax frameworks. A *framework* is a collection of program code that is designed to simplify application development. Ajax frameworks consist of collections of JavaScript functions that you can call upon from within your applications. Some

Ajax frameworks also include a server-side component that includes program code that facilitates server-side database searches and data manipulation and processing.

Ajax frameworks range from very small libraries to large, robust code libraries that provide everything needed to build complex applications. The primary advantage of using Ajax frameworks is that they speed up application development by allowing you to incorporate pre-written JavaScript functions into your web pages and JavaScript code. There are literally hundreds of Ajax frameworks to choose from. They range from small general-purpose frameworks that you can download for free on the Internet to large commercial libraries. Some Ajax libraries are highly specialized, designed to support the development of specific types of applications such as online shopping carts.

Popular Ajax Frameworks

Examples of two popular Ajax frameworks include the Yahoo! User Interface Library (YUI) and Dojo. The Yahoo! User Interface Library is written entirely in JavaScript. It is distributed as an open-source library and can be downloaded for free from http://developer.yahoo.com/yui/, as shown in Figure 5.7.

The Yahoo! User Interface Library provides Ajax developers with a wealth of features and capabilities, including support for the development and management of calendars and charts as well as features like text AutoComplete and application menus. The framework provides Ajax developers with the ability to add tree views that can be clicked on and expanded. It also provides a rich text editor that offers advanced text processing features. This framework also supports the creation of tooltips, the generation of animated effects, and support for drag and drop operations. In addition, the Yahoo! User Interface Library also provides a browser history manager that enables Ajax applications to retain backward and forward browser history buttons.

The Dojo Ajax framework is an open-source library written in JavaScript that is designed to support the rapid development of Ajax applications and websites. It is developed by the Dojo Foundation, which is a non-profit institution and can be downloaded for free from http://dojotoolkit.org, as shown in Figure 5.8. Dojo provides Ajax developers with a wealth of features and capabilities, including support for the development of menus, tables, tooltips, charts, and animated effects. Dojo also provides functions specifically designed to support the management of forms and input validation. It also facilitates the development of tree views and calendars and even provides access to a sophisticated rich text editor.

To use most Ajax frameworks, you have to copy the code files that make up the framework to your web server and then add a reference to it in your Ajax application using a statement like the one shown here:

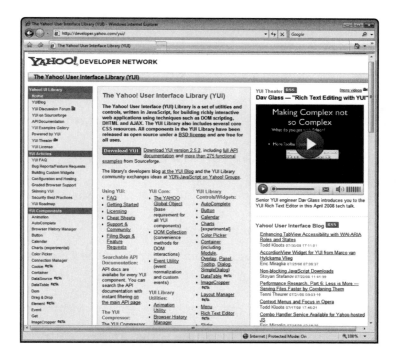

FIGURE 5.7

You can download a free copy of the Yahoo! User Interface Library from http://developer.yahoo.com/yui/.

FIGURE 5.8

You can download a free copy of the Dojo Ajax framework from http://dojotoolkit.org.

```
<SCRIPT language = "javascript" type = "text/javascript" scr = "cba.js">
   .
   .
   .
   .
</SCRIPT>
```

Here, a reference to an Ajax framework named cba.js has been established.

Framework Demo—Using the CBA Framework

As an example of how easy it can be to work with an Ajax framework to simplify application development, let's take a look at a small Ajax framework known as Cross Browser Ajax or CBA. CBA is free to download and use. Compared to the Yahoo! User Interface Library and Dojo, CBA is a small framework, and was only 12.8KB in size at the time this book was published.

To download CBA, visit http://www.crossbrowserajax.com and click on the Download button, as shown in Figure 5.9.

CBA downloads as a JavaScript file named CBA.js, which is stored in a Zip file. To make the framework available to your application, upload CBA.js to the same folder on your web server where your Ajax applications are stored. Once you have performed this task, use the framework in your applications to add the following statement to a JavaScript located in the head section of your Ajax application's HTML files.

```
<SCRIPT language = "javascript" type = "text/javascript" src = "cba.js">
```

Once added, you can then begin calling on any of the JavaScript functions made available through the framework, as demonstrated in the following example.

```
<HTML>
  <HEAD>
    <TITLE>Cross Browser Ajax Demo</TITLE>
    <SCRIPT language = "javascript" type = "text/javascript" src="cba.js">
    </SCRIPT>
  </HEAD>
  <BODY>
    Enter a term: <BR>
    <INPUT type = "textfield" id = "termfield">
    <INPUT type = "button" value = "Get Definition"
      onclick = "cbaUpdateElement('TrgtDiv',
      'http://crossbrowserajax.com/data/examples/quickhelp.php?word=' +
      termfield.value);">
    <P id="TrgtDiv" style = "color:blue"></P>
  </BODY>
</HTML>
```

Here, a web page has been created that consists of a text field and a button. The user is prompted to enter a term in the text field and then to click on the button to look up information about that term. A function named cbaUpdateElement() is called when the button is clicked, and passed two arguments, the id of a pair of <DIV> </DIV> tags where the text returned by the web server will be displayed, and the URL of a PHP program named quickhelp.php, which is passed the search term as an argument.

The cbaUpdateElement() function is one of a number of functions made available to the Ajax application through the CBA framework. When executed, it handles all communication with the web server and makes sure that the text that is returned by the web server is dynamically added to the web page. Thanks to the CBA.js framework, all of this is accomplished without the application developer having to develop any of the JavaScript functions that make the application work. As this application demonstrated, you can use frameworks to significantly reduce the size and complexity of your Ajax applications. Figure 5.10 shows how this application looks when first loaded into the browser.

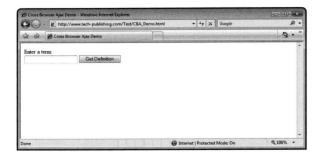

FIGURE 5.10

An example of an Ajax application built by using the Cross Browser Ajax framework.

Figure 5.11 shows how the application looks after the user uses it to look up information on the term xml.

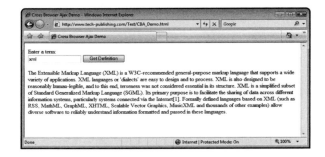

FIGURE 5.11

Using the CBA framework to create an application that retrieves Ajax-related vocabulary terms.

BACK TO THE AJAX TYPING CHALLENGE APPLICATION

Okay! It is time to turn your attention back to the development of this chapter's project, the Ajax Typing Challenge. When loaded, this application challenges the user to type three sentences exactly as shown on the screen. All three of the sentences are retrieved behind the scenes from three text files stored on the application's web server, allowing web server administrators to update challenge sentences at any time.

Designing the Application

To help make things easy to follow along, this application will be developed in a series of steps, as outlined here:

1. Create a new HTML page.
2. Create the application's text files.
3. Create the application's JavaScript and defining global variables.
4. Set up the XMLHttpRequest object.
5. Download and display the game's challenge sentences.
6. Evaluate the player's score.

Step 1: Writing the Application's HTML

The first step in the development of the Ajax Typing Challenge is to create the application's HTML file. Do so by creating a new HTML file named AjaxTypingTest.html and then adding the following HTML statements to it.

```
<HTML>
  <HEAD>
    <TITLE>Ajax Typing Challenge</TITLE>
  </HEAD>
  <BODY>
    <H1 style = "color:blue">Ajax Typing Challenge</H1>
    <FORM>
      <P>Click on "Begin Test" when you are ready to begin and then
      type the sentences that are displayed in the text fields
      displayed below each sentence. When done, click on the "Grade
       Test" button.</P>
      <INPUT type = "button" value = "Begin Test" id = "btnControl1"
        onclick = startQuiz()>
      <INPUT type = "button" value = "Grade Test" id = "btnControl2"
        onclick = gradeQuiz()>
      <P><DIV id = "trgtDiv1"> </DIV></P>
      <INPUT type = "textfield" size = "100" id = "inputField1">
      <P><DIV id = "trgtDiv2"> </DIV></P>
      <INPUT type = "textfield" size = "100" id = "inputField2">
      <P><DIV id = "trgtDiv3"> </DIV></P>
      <INPUT type = "textfield" size = "100" id = "inputField3">
    </FORM>
    <P style = "color:red; font-weight:Bold" id = "trgtP"> </P>
  </BODY>
</HTML>
```

As you can see, this HTML page consists of the required head and body tags. The body section includes a level 1 heading, followed by a form and a pair of <P> </P> tags that have been assigned an id of trgtP, into which the application will display a message informing the user of his grade once the test is complete.

The form consists of two button controls and three textfield controls. The button controls use onClick event handlers to call on JavaScript functions named startQuiz() and gradeQuiz(). Each of the three textfield controls is assigned a unique id, allowing them to later be referenced so that the application's functions can retrieve the user's input from them.

Step 2: Creating the Application's Server-Side Text Files

The Ajax Typing Challenge presents the user with three challenge sentences, which are retrieved from text files stored on the web server. Table 5.4 identifies the names of these three files and shows their contents.

Text File	Contents
TABLE 5.4	**SERVER-SIDE TEXT FILES**
challenge1.txt	Perhaps today is a good day to die.
challenge2.txt	Now is the time for all good men to put away their pride.
challenge3.txt	It was the best of times. It was the worst of times. It was the winter of our discontent.

Before moving on to step 3, take a few moments to create each of these text files and upload them to your web server.

Step 3: Beginning Work on the Application's JavaScript

The next step in the development of the Ajax Typing Challenge application is to begin writing its JavaScript. Begin by adding the following statement to the head section of the HTML page.

```
<SCRIPT language = "javascript" type = "text/javascript">
<!-- Start hiding JavaScript statements
  var Request1 = false;
  var Request2 = false;
  var Request3 = false;
  var sentence1 = "";
  var sentence2 = "";
  var sentence3 = "";
  var numberCorrect;
// End hiding JavaScript statements -->
</SCRIPT>
```

As you can see, in addition to adding the JavaScript's opening and closing tags, these statements also define a number of global variables. The first three variables will be used throughout the application to help manage the application's XMLHttpRequest objects. The next three variables are used to store each of the application's challenge sentences. The numberCorrect variable will be used to keep track of the number of sentences that the user correctly types.

Step 4: Instantiating the XMLHttpRequest Object

The Ajax Typing Challenge application involves the retrieval of three text files from the web server. To facilitate the retrieval of the data stored in these files, you need to set up several instances of the XMLHttpRequest object. This is accomplished by adding the following statements to the end of the application's JavaScript.

```
if (window.XMLHttpRequest) {
  Request1 = new XMLHttpRequest();
  Request2 = new XMLHttpRequest();
  Request3 = new XMLHttpRequest();
} else if (window.ActiveXObject) {
  Request1 = new ActiveXObject("Microsoft.XMLHTTP");
  Request2 = new ActiveXObject("Microsoft.XMLHTTP");
  Request3 = new ActiveXObject("Microsoft.XMLHTTP");
}
```

As you can see, three XMLHttpRequest objects, named Request1, Request2, and Request3 are defined.

Step 5: Retrieving and Displaying Challenge Sentences

The program code that is responsible for administering the testing belongs to a function named startQuiz(). The statements that make up this function are shown below and should be added to the end of the application's JavaScript.

```
function startQuiz() {
  document.getElementById("inputField1").value = "";
  document.getElementById("inputField2").value = "";
  document.getElementById("inputField3").value = "";
  document.getElementById("trgtP").innerHTML = "";

  if (Request1) {
    var RequestObj1 = document.getElementById("trgtDiv1");
    Request1.open("GET", "challenge1.txt");
    Request1.onreadystatechange = function() {
      if (Request1.readyState == 4 && Request1.status == 200) {
        RequestObj1.innerHTML = Request1.responseText;
        sentense1 = Request1.responseText;
      }
    }
    Request1.send(null);
```

```
    }
    if (Request2) {
      var RequestObj2 = document.getElementById("trgtDiv2");
      Request2.open("GET", "challenge2.txt");
      Request2.onreadystatechange = function() {
        if (Request2.readyState == 4 && Request2.status == 200) {
          RequestObj2.innerHTML = Request2.responseText;
          sentense2 = Request2.responseText;
        }
      }
      Request2.send(null);
    }
    if (Request3) {
      var RequestObj3 = document.getElementById("trgtDiv3");
      Request3.open("GET", "challenge3.txt");
      Request3.onreadystatechange = function() {
        if (Request3.readyState == 4 && Request3.status == 200) {
          RequestObj3.innerHTML = Request3.responseText;
          sentense3 = Request3.responseText;
        }
      }
      Request3.send(null);
    }
}
```

The first three statements use the getElementById() method to retrieve an object reference to each of the application's three textfield controls. In addition to the object's value property, empty strings are displayed in these textfield controls. Next, an empty string is written to the <P> </P> tags (id = trgtP) located under the application's form.

Next, three nearly identical sets of code statements are used to retrieve the text stored in each of the application's three text files. These text files are retrieved using the open() method's GET option. An anonymous function is then used to monitor the status of the request. The XMLHttpRequest object's innerHTML property is then used to retrieve the contents of each of the text files. This text data is stored in variables named sentence1, sentence2, and sentence3, respectively.

Step 6: Grading the Results of the Ajax Typing Challenge

Once the user has completed keying in all three of the challenge sentences and clicks on the Grade Quick button, the gradeQuiz() function is executed. The statements that make up this function are shown next and should be added to the end of the application's JavaScript.

```
function gradeQuiz() {
  numberCorrect = 0;
  var result1 = document.getElementById("inputField1").value;
  var result2 = document.getElementById("inputField2").value;
  var result3 = document.getElementById("inputField3").value;
  var score = document.getElementById("trgtP");
  if (sentence1 == result1) {
    numberCorrect++
  }
  if (sentence2 == result2) {
    numberCorrect++
  }
  if (sentence3 == result3) {
    numberCorrect++
  }
  score.innerHTML = "To pass you must type at least 2 " +
    "out of 3 sentences correctly. You got " + numberCorrect +
    " correct.";
}
```

When executed, this function resets the value assigned to numberCorrect to 0, retrieves the value of the text that the user typed into the application's three text fields, and sets up a variable reference named score to the <P> </P> tags that are located under the applications form. Next, three if statement code blocks are set up to analyze each of the sentences typed by the user to see if they match the contents of the text files stored on the web server. If the first sentence typed by the user (sentence1) matches the text retrieved from the web server for the first text file (result1), the value of numberCorrect is incremented by 1. Similarly, the user's second and third sentences are analyzed. Lastly, using the score object's innerHTML, a message is posted in the application's <P> </P> tags that informs the user of the number of sentences that were correctly typed.

The Final Result

All right, at this point you have all of the instructions needed to create your own copy of the Ajax Typing Challenge application. Before testing your new Ajax application, you will need to upload the AjaxTypingTest.html file as well as the application's three text files to your web server. Once uploaded, start your web browser and load the application. Assuming that you have not made any typos and that you carefully followed the instructions provided, everything should work as described at the beginning of this chapter. Once you are confident that the application works like it is supposed to, take a few extra moments to validate its proper execution in other types of browsers.

> You will find a copy of this application's source code files on the book's companion website, located at http://www.courseptr.com/downloads.

Summary

This chapter provided an overview of the XMLHttpRequest object and explained how to use it in your Ajax applications to facilitate the submission of data requests to web servers. This included learning how to instantiate instances of the XMLHttpRequest objects and to use these objects to set up connections, request data, and then download and make the data available to your Ajax application. This chapter demonstrated how to use the XMLHttpRequest objects to facilitate the creation of Ajax applications that use mouse-controlled rollovers. This chapter also introduced you to the use of Ajax frameworks as a means of simplifying and speeding up application development.

Now, before you move on to Chapter 6, "Digging Deeper into Ajax", consider setting aside a little extra time to improve the Ajax Typing Challenge application by addressing the following list of challenges.

Challenges

1. As currently written, the Ajax Typing Challenge only consists of three challenge sentences. Consider beefing things up a bit by adding a number of additional challenge sentences to the application.
2. Make the application easier to use by adding a third button that when clicked displays more robust instructions about how to work with the application.
3. As currently written, the application does not identify mistyped sentences, instead leaving it to the user to figure out which challenge sentences were mistyped. Modify the application to address this issue.

DIGGING DEEPER INTO AJAX

I n the last chapter, you learned how to work with the XMLHttpRequest object to create Ajax applications that were capable of retrieving text files from web servers. In this chapter, you are going to learn how take things a step further by using the XMLHttpRequest object to call upon server-side programs. This will include learning how to pass arguments to server programs and to retrieve data returned by those programs. You will learn how to create Ajax applications that can dynamically manipulate the display of graphics. On top of all this, this chapter will show you how to execute JavaScript returned from the web server and will demonstrate how to develop the chapter's application project, the Ajax Google Suggest application.

Specifically, you will learn how to:

- Incorporate DHTML techniques into your Ajax applications to dynamically modify the display of graphics
- Create an Ajax application that dynamically changes the display of graphics
- Pass arguments to server-side programs
- Incorporate the execution of JavaScripts downloaded from the web server into your applications

PROJECT PREVIEW: THE AJAX GOOGLE SUGGEST APPLICATION

This chapter's application project is the Ajax Google Suggest application. This application, though not a game, is an extremely fun project that demonstrates how to incorporate the execution of JavaScript code passed to an Ajax application from the web server to incorporate Google Suggest terms into an Ajax application. Figure 6.1 shows an example of how the application looks when initially loaded by Internet Explorer.

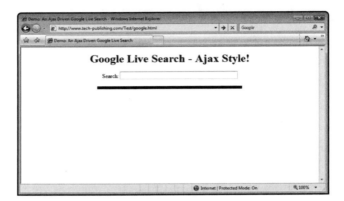

FIGURE 6.1

This application dynamically incorporates the display of data retrieved from Google Suggest.

As soon as the user begins to type in a keyword or phrase, the application captures the user's keystrokes and passes them behind the scenes to the Google Suggest web server, which returns a list of popular matching terms and phrases that the application displays, as demonstrated in Figure 6.2.

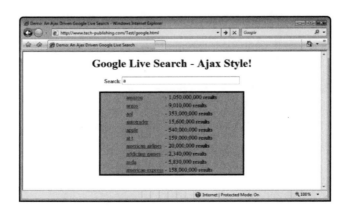

FIGURE 6.2

The Ajax Google Suggest monitors user keystrokes and displays a list of matching keywords and phrases.

As demonstrated in Figure 6.3, the list of terms and phrases that are displayed continually change as the user types in additional characters.

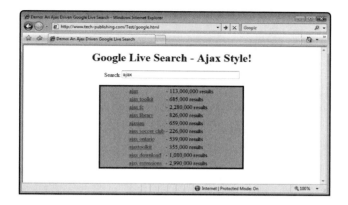

FIGURE 6.3

The terms displayed by Ajax Google Suggest change as the user types in more information.

The user can click on any entry in the list to perform a Google search, as demonstrated in Figure 6.4.

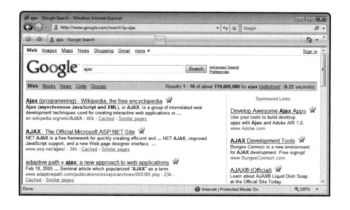

FIGURE 6.4

The application initiates a Google search for the selected keyword or phrase.

USING AJAX TO MANIPULATE GRAPHICS

Although Ajax is limited to working with text and XML, you can use it to develop applications that download graphics from the web server. Even though Ajax cannot directly retrieve graphics, the browser can (thanks to DHTML). With this understanding and a little clever programming, you can create Ajax applications that dynamically download and display graphics. As an example of how Ajax developers often work around Ajax's text-only limitation, consider the following example.

```
<HTML>
  <HEAD>
    <TITLE>Demo: Ajax Graphics Demo</TITLE>
    <SCRIPT language = "javascript" type = "text/javascript">
    <!-- Start hiding JavaScript statements
      function getDataForImage(fileName) {
        var Request = false;
        if (window.XMLHttpRequest) {
          Request = new XMLHttpRequest();
        } else if (window.ActiveXObject) {
          Request = new ActiveXObject("Microsoft.XMLHTTP");
        }
        if(Request) {
          Request.open("GET", fileName);
          Request.onreadystatechange = function() {
            if (Request.readyState == 4 && Request.status == 200) {
              document.getElementById("TrgtDiv").innerHTML = "<IMG src= " +
                Request.responseText + ">";
              delete Request;
              Request = null;
            }
          }
          Request.send(null);
        }
      }
    // End hiding JavaScript statements -->
    </SCRIPT>
  </HEAD>
  <BODY>
    <FORM>
      <INPUT type = "button" value = "Display Shell"
        onclick = "getDataForImage('Shelldown.txt')">
      <INPUT type = "button" value = "Peek Under Shell"
        onclick = "getDataForImage('Shellup.txt')">
    </FORM>
    <DIV id="TrgtDiv"> </DIV>
  </BODY>
</HTML>
```

Here, an Ajax application has been created that consists of two buttons that call on a function named `getDataForImage()`. The first button, labeled `Display Shell`, passes the function the name of a text file named `Shelldown.txt`, which is located on the web server. The second button, labeled `Peek Under Shell`, passes the function the name of a text file named `Shellup.txt`, which is located on the web server.

The `getDataForImage()` function maps the filename argument that is passed to a local variable named `filename` and then instantiates an object named `Request` as an `XMLHttpRequest` object. Next the function uses the `XMLHttpRequest` object's `open()` method to download the text stored in the specified text file. Table 6.1 shows the text that is stored in the application's text files.

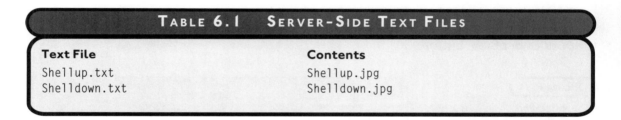

TABLE 6.1	SERVER-SIDE TEXT FILES
Text File	**Contents**
Shellup.txt	Shellup.jpg
Shelldown.txt	Shelldown.jpg

The text that is downloaded is either a string of `"Shelldown.jpg"` or `"Shellup.jpg"`, depending on which button was clicked. Finally, a new `<IMG>` tag is created and the value of the text string downloaded from the server is appended to the tag. The new `<IMG>` tag is placed inside a pair of `<DIV>` `</DIV>` tags (e.g., `TrgtDiv`). The end result of altering the web page DOM tree in this manner is that the browser immediately downloads the graphic files specified in the new `<IMG>` tags and displays them. Of course, this occurs with no screen refresh.

Figure 6.5 shows an example of how the application looks when initially loaded into the browser.

FIGURE 6.5

An example of how the application looks when initially located by Internet Explorer.

Figure 6.6 shows how the application's appearance changes when the user clicks on the Display Shell button.

FIGURE 6.6

The application displays an image of a walnut shell when the user clicks on the Display Shell button.

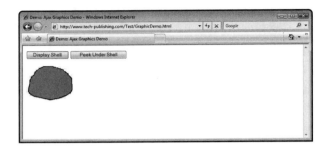

Likewise, Figure 6.7 shows how the application's appearance changes when the user clicks on the Peek Under Shell button.

FIGURE 6.7

The application dynamically displays an image of a walnut with a pea underneath it when the user clicks on the Peek Under Shell button.

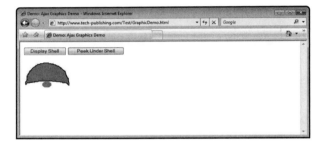

As you can see, even though Ajax does not allow you to work with and directly control graphics, by leveraging its ability to communicate with web servers behind the scenes, along with its ability to modify the DOM tree, you can easily develop Ajax applications that include complicated graphic effects.

SENDING DATA TO WEB SERVERS

Up to this point in the book, all of the Ajax applications that you have seen and worked with have involved the retrieval of text files stored on the web server. However, as previously stated, Ajax can do more than merely download text files from the web server. It can also interact with any web server-based program and upload data as well as download data returned by web server programs.

Strictly speaking, Ajax is a client-side programming tool and you do not need to know how to write web server programs to develop Ajax applications. However, most Ajax applications involve some type of interaction with web server programs that accept and process input provided by Ajax applications and then return data for the Ajax application to process. This means that unless you already have access to prewritten server-based programs that provide the data your Ajax applications need to work with, you are going to need to collaborate with someone that can develop server-side programs for you or you will have to learn how to develop those programs yourself.

Ajax can work with virtually any server-side program, regardless of the programming language used to develop it. One extremely popular server-side programming language is PHP. PHP is a lot like Ajax and is used on thousands of web servers around the world. Chances are extremely good that your local website server provider already has PHP installed and ready to go.

 HINT All of the server-side programming examples demonstrated in this book were created using PHP. You will see a few examples of Ajax applications that interact with PHP scripts as you work your way to the end of this chapter. You do not have to have a working knowledge of PHP in order to follow along and understand the examples. However, Chapter 10 provides a brief PHP primer.

A Quick Example of How to Work with PHP

As has already been stated in this book several times, you do not have to be a PHP programmer to follow along and understand the applications presented in this book. However, a basic understanding is certainly helpful. The following Ajax application consists of two parts, a client-side web page, and a server-side PHP script. It provides an example of a simple application that is designed to call upon a PHP script to pass it some text data (as opposed to retrieving the text data from a file stored on the web server).

 HINT The PHP scripts that you will see in this chapter are very simple. To learn more about PHP and how to use it to develop server-side scripts, read Chapter 9, "Working with Ajax and PHP."

```
<HTML>
  <HEAD>
    <TITLE>Ajax Joke of the Day Application</TITLE>
    <SCRIPT language = "javascript" type = "text/javascript">
      var Request = false;
      if (window.XMLHttpRequest) {
        Request = new XMLHttpRequest();
      } else if (window.ActiveXObject) {
```

```
        Request = new ActiveXObject("Microsoft.XMLHTTP");
      }
      function retrieveJoke(url, elementID) {
        if(Request) {
          var RequestObj = document.getElementById(elementID);
          Request.open("GET", url);
          Request.onreadystatechange = function()
          {
            if (Request.readyState == 4 && Request.status == 200) {
                RequestObj.innerHTML = Request.responseText;
            }
          }
          Request.send(null);
        }
      }
    </SCRIPT>
  </HEAD>
  <BODY>
    <H1>Where do bees go when they get married?</H1>
    <FORM>
      <INPUT type = "button" value = "Fetch Answer"
        onclick = "retrieveJoke('Joke.php', 'DivTarget')">
    </FORM>
    <DIV id="DivTarget"> </DIV>
  </BODY>
</HTML>
```

As you can see, the client-side portion of this application is a modified copy of the Ajax Joke of the Day application, which you learned how to create in Chapter 1. However, instead of retrieving the text for the joke's punch line from a text file stored on the server, the application now calls upon a PHP script named Joke.php, passing the script the id of a pair of <DIV> </DIV> tags into which the text representing the joke's punch line should be written. The only different between this version of the joke.html page and the version that you worked on in Chapter 1 is that in Chapter 1 you specified the text file you wanted to retrieve from the web server, as shown here:

```
<INPUT type = "button" value = "Fetch Answer"
  onclick = "retrieveJoke('Joke.txt', 'DivTarget')">
```

In the new version of the `joke.html` application, you replace the reference to the text file with a reference to a PHP script, as shown here:

```
<INPUT type = "button" value = "Fetch Answer"
  onclick = "retrieveJoke('Joke.php', 'DivTarget')">
```

Of course, in order to work, you have to create a new script named `Joke.php` and upload it to the same folder on your web server where your Ajax application resides. To create the PHP script, all you have to do is create a new file named `Joke.php` and add the following statements to it:

```php
<?php
  echo 'On a honeymoon.';
?>
```

As you can see, the PHP script consists of only three statements. The first and last statements are required opening and closing statements that you will find in all PHP scripts. The second statement consists of an `echo` command and a text string. In PHP, the `echo` command is used to output data provided to it as an argument back to the client-side applications. Note that as is the case with JavaScript, PHP uses the semicolon character to mark the end of the statement. When called to execute, this PHP script returns a text string of `On a honeymoon.` back to your Ajax application.

 While the use of a PHP script in place of text is perhaps a little overkill in this particular example, the primary advantage of calling upon a PHP script instead of simply downloading the contents of a text file is that a PHP script is capable of performing all kinds of complex operations, like reading text files and retrieving data from a server database. Server-side programs can also process application data retrieved from files and databases before returning it back to an Ajax application.

Sending Data to Web Servers for Processing

Okay, now that you have had a sneak peek at how to develop Ajax applications that work with server-side programs, let's take things a step further by learning how to call upon a server-side PHP script and pass it some data for processing.

Two options are available to you. The first option is to use the `open()` method's `GET` option. This will allow you to pass data to the web server using a technique known as URL encoding in which the data being sent is appended to the end of the URL string that is used to connect to the web server. Your second option is to use the `open()` method's `POST` option, which sends encoded data back to the web server.

Using the Get Method to Send Data to a PHP Script

Using the XMLHttpRequest object's open() method's GET option to call on server-side programs and pass them data for processing results in URL-encoded data. URL-encoded data is insecure and easily readable, so it is not a good option for applications that have to deal with highly confidential data.

To use the open() method's GET option, you must append a ? character to the end of the URL string followed by the data that needs to be passed using a *data=value* format. If multiple *data=pair* arguments must be sent, then you must separate them with a & character. If the data being sent contains blank spaces, you must replace those blank spaces with the + character. For example, suppose you wanted to pass two pieces of data representing the number of apples and oranges on hand to a PHP script named test.php located at http://www.someweberserver.com. To accomplish this using the GET option, you would formulate the URL for the request as shown here:

```
http://www.somewebserver.com/test.php?apples=5&oranges=10
```

If you wanted to call on a PHP script named tellstory.php and pass it the contents of a variable named story (whose value is "Once upon a time"), then you would formulate the URL for the request as shown here:

```
http://www.somewebserver.com/tellstory.php?story=Once+upon+a+time
```

 TRICK JavaScript provides a method named escape that you can use to automatically encode data, as demonstrated here:

```
x = escape("Once upon a time")
```

To better understand how to work with the open() method's GET option, let's take a look at an example. In this example, you'll see a graphical menu made up of five menu items, as shown in Figure 6.8.

 FIGURE 6.8

This application consists of five graphic menu options.

HINT If this application looks familiar to you, it should. You worked on a different version of this application in Chapter 5, which retrieved additional information for each menu item from text files stored on the web server. This version of the application replaces the five text files with a small PHP script. In Chapter 7, you will modify the application even further, when you learn how to add dynamic submenu lists to the menus.

The HTML page for this application is shown next. As you can see, five <IMG> tags located in the body section define the application's graphical menus. Whenever the user moves the mouse pointer over one of the menus, the menu's onMouseover() event handler is executed and passed two text strings. The first text string represents the menu item and the second text string identifies a pair of <DIV> </DIV> tags into which text downloaded behind the scenes from the web server is displayed.

```
<HTML>
  <HEAD>
    <TITLE>XYZ Website</TITLE>
    <SCRIPT language = "javascript" type = "text/javascript">
    <!-- Start hiding JavaScript statements
      var Request = false;
      if (window.XMLHttpRequest) {
        Request = new XMLHttpRequest();
      } else if (window.ActiveXObject) {
        Request = new ActiveXObject("Microsoft.XMLHTTP");
      }
      function updatePage(category, target) {
        var url = "options.php?category=" + category;
        if(Request) {
          var targetDiv = document.getElementById(target);
          Request.open("GET", url, true);
          Request.onreadystatechange = function() {
            if (Request.readyState == 4 && Request.status == 200) {
                targetDiv.innerHTML = Request.responseText;
            }
          }
          Request.send(null);
        }
      }
    // End hiding JavaScript statements -->
```

```
    </SCRIPT>
  </HEAD>
  <BODY>
    <IMG src = "home.jpg" onmouseover="updatePage('home', 'TrgtDiv')">
    <IMG src = "products.jpg" onmouseover="updatePage('products',
      'TrgtDiv')">
    <IMG src = "downloads.jpg" onmouseover="updatePage('downloads',
      'TrgtDiv')">
    <IMG src = "forums.jpg" onmouseover="updatePage('forums', 'TrgtDiv')">
    <IMG src = "about.jpg" onmouseover="updatePage('about', 'TrgtDiv')">
    <H1> <DIV id = "TrgtDiv"> </DIV> </H1>
  </BODY>
</HTML>
```

The following example shows an Ajax application that uses the open() method's GET option to call upon a PHP script named options.php, passing it a text string representing the name of a graphical menu whenever the user moves the mouse pointer over the menu.

The graphic image's onMouseover() event handlers call upon a function named updatePage(). This function uses the open() method's GET option to execute options.php, passing it a URL string of option.php?catagory=XXX where XXX represents the name assigned to one of the graphic menu items.

If you want to test the execution of this example, you will also need to upload a copy of the options.php script to your web server. The statements that make up this PHP script are shown here:

```
<?
header("Content-type: text/xml");
if ($_GET["category"] == "home")
  echo 'Welcome to the XYZ website!';
if ($_GET["category"] == "products")
  echo 'Products Page';
if ($_GET["category"] == "downloads")
  echo 'Downloads Page';
if ($_GET["category"] == "forums")
  echo 'Forums Page';
if ($_GET["category"] == "about")
  echo 'About Page';
?>
```

Without getting too involved in the details of how this PHP script works, just note that a series of if statement code blocks, using the $_GET array, are used to analyze the argument passed to the program, and that 1 of 5 echo statements is executed depending on whether the match occurs. The Ajax application captures the outputted text string returned by the PHP script and displays it in the HTML page's <DIV> </DIV> tags, as demonstrated in Figure 6.9.

FIGURE 6.9

This application consists of five menu options.

Using the POST Method to Send Data to a PHP Script

A second way of working with the open() method is to use its POST option. When you work with this option, the data sent by the open() method is internally encoded, making it more secure than the GET option. The following example demonstrates how to rework the previous Ajax application to use the POST method in place of the GET method.

```
<HTML>
  <HEAD>
    <TITLE>XYZ Website</TITLE>
    <SCRIPT language = "javascript" type = "text/javascript">
    <!-- Start hiding JavaScript statements
      var Request = false;
      if (window.XMLHttpRequest) {
        Request = new XMLHttpRequest();
      } else if (window.ActiveXObject) {
        Request = new ActiveXObject("Microsoft.XMLHTTP");
      }
      function updatePage(category, target) {
        if(Request) {
          var targetDiv = document.getElementById(target);
          Request.open("POST", "options.php");
          Request.setRequestHeader('Content-Type',
            'application/x-www-form-urlencoded');
```

```
          Request.onreadystatechange = function() {
            if (Request.readyState == 4 && Request.status == 200) {
              targetDiv.innerHTML = Request.responseText;
            }
          }
          Request.send("category=" + category);
        }
      }
    // End hiding JavaScript statements -->
    </SCRIPT>
  </HEAD>
  <BODY>
    <IMG src = "home.jpg" onmouseover="updatePage('home', 'TrgtDiv')">
    <IMG src = "products.jpg" onmouseover="updatePage('products',
      'TrgtDiv')">
    <IMG src = "downloads.jpg" onmouseover="updatePage('downloads',
      'TrgtDiv')">
    <IMG src = "forums.jpg" onmouseover="updatePage('forums', 'TrgtDiv')">
    <IMG src = "about.jpg" onmouseover="updatePage('about', 'TrgtDiv')">
    <H1> <DIV id = "TrgtDiv"> </DIV> </H1>
  </BODY>
</HTML>
```

As the statements highlighted in bold indicate, the only difference between this and the previous version of the application is that no URL encoding is passed when executing the open() method, and an HTTP header had to specify that a standard HTTP POST request is to be executed. Except for these two changes, everything else remains the same in the Ajax application. However, since the application now passes data to the web server using the POST option in place of the GET option, you must also make a change to the PHP script located on the web server in order for it to be able to properly process the data being passed to it. Specifically, you must replace references to the $_GET array with reference to the $_POST array as shown here.

```
<?
header("Content-type: text/xml");
if ($_POST["category"] == "home")
  echo 'Welcome to the XYZ website!';
if ($_POST["category"] == "products")
  echo 'Products Page';
```

```
if ($_POST["category"] == "downloads")
  echo 'Downloads Page';
if ($_POST["category"] == "forums")
  echo 'Forums Page';
if ($_POST["category"] == "about")
  echo 'About Page';
?>
```

To execute this example, upload the new version of the application along with an updated copy of the PHP file to your web server and then load the HTML page into your web browser. When executed, you should see the same results shown in Figures 6.8 and 6.9.

EXECUTING SERVER-SUPPLIED JAVASCRIPT

In addition to downloading plain text and XML data from web servers, Ajax applications can also download and execute JavaScript statements to accomplish this feat; just download the text representing the JavaScript statements and pass them to a JavaScript function named eval(). This function re-evaluates the text statements passed to it and executes them as JavaScript statements.

Using the eval() functions to execute JavaScript statements downloaded from web servers can be quite convenient. However, it is best, whenever possible, not to rely on this approach when developing your Ajax application. It is a good programming practice to make server-side programs independent of their client-side counterparts.

 There is no reason that server-side programs should have to know the inner workings of your Ajax applications. Still, there are times when you may not have any other choice, like when you want to create an Ajax application that works with any number of third-party web services such as Google Maps or Google Suggest.

Look at the following example to see how JavaScript is downloaded and executed from a web server:

```
<HTML>
  <HEAD>
    <TITLE>DEMO: Executing JavaScript downloaded from the web server</TITLE>
    <SCRIPT language = "javascript" type = "text/javascript">
    <!-- Start hiding JavaScript statements
      var Request = false;
      if (window.XMLHttpRequest) {
```

```
      Request = new XMLHttpRequest();
    } else if (window.ActiveXObject) {
      Request = new ActiveXObject("Microsoft.XMLHTTP");
    }
    function getScript() {
      if(Request) {
        Request.open("GET", "serverjoke.php");
        Request.onreadystatechange = function() {
          if (Request.readyState == 4 && Request.status == 200) {
              eval(Request.responseText);
          }
        }
        Request.send(null);
      }
    }
    function SayJoke(joke, punchLine) {
      window.alert(joke);
      window.alert(punchLine);
    }
  // End hiding JavaScript statements -->
  </SCRIPT>
</HEAD>
<BODY>
  <FORM>
    <INPUT type = "button" value = "Run" onClick = "getScript()">
  </FORM>
</BODY>
</HTML>
```

Here, an Ajax application has been set up to call upon a function named getScript() when its button is clicked. When called, the getScript() function calls upon a PHP script called serverjoke.php, which returns the following JavaScript statements to the Ajax application.

```
SayJoke('What is black, white and red all over?', 'A newspaper!')
```

As you can see, this statement consists of a function call to SayJoke(), passing it two text strings as arguments. Once downloaded, the JavaScript statement is passed to the eval() method, which executes it. The PHP script that this Ajax application calls upon is shown next. As you can see, except for the required opening and closing statements, the PHP script consists of just one statement, which uses the echo command to pass text representing a JavaScript statement to the Ajax application.

```php
<?php
  echo "SayJoke('What is black, white and red all over?', 'A newspaper!')";
?>
```

TRICK In order for this example to work, the programmer that created the PHP script must know that there is a function named SayJoke() in the Ajax application that will call upon it to execute. In addition, the PHP programmer also needs to know the number and type of arguments that the function requires.

Figures 6.10 and 6.11 show the output that is produced when the Ajax application is executed.

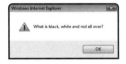

FIGURE 6.10

The application displays its joke in a popup dialog window.

FIGURE 6.11

The application displays the joke's punch line in another popup dialog window.

BACK TO THE AJAX GOOGLE SUGGEST APPLICATION

It is time to return your attention to the development of this chapter's project, the Ajax Google Suggest application. This application takes advantage of Ajax's ability to evaluate and execute JavaScript code downloaded from the web server in order to facilitate the development of a custom implementation of Google's Live Search. Google Suggest is a popular feature of the Google search engine (www.googlesuggest.com) that monitors user keystrokes and displays a list of related keywords and terms, allowing the user to select either a keyword or term or to key in his own search string.

When loaded into the web browser, this application displays a text field into which the user types a search keyword or phrase. The application captures keystrokes as the user types and passes them behind the scenes to Google's web server, where a list of popular matching search terms and phrases is then returned. The application displays the text list that is returned and uses it to display a linked list of terms and phrases that the user can then click on to initiate a Google search. The list of terms and phrases is updated every time the user types or deletes a new character in the application's text field.

The Ajax Google Suggest application will work its magic by capturing and sending user keystrokes to the Google web server using the XMLHttpRequest object. In response, Google's web server returns a JavaScript function similar to this:

```
window.google.ac.Suggest_apply(frameElement, "\x22 ajax", new Array(2,
"ajax", "113,000,000 results", "ajax toolkit", "680,000 results", "ajax
control toolkit", "444,000 results", "ajax fc", "2,270,000 results", "ajax
library", "827,000 results", "ajaxian", "659,000 results", "ajax soccer
club", "225,000 results", "ajax ontario", "540,000 results", "ajax
download", "1,090,000 results", "ajax grips", "649,000 results"), new
Array(""));
```

As you can see, the text string that is returned by the web server consists of a JavaScript function call named window.google.ac.Suggest_apply() along with data for that function to process. The data that is returned is passed as four arguments, using the syntax outlined here:

```
window.google.ac.Suggest_apply(ignoreVar, keyword, aResults, aEmpty)
```

 Unfortunately, the name of the function returned by the web server will not work as a function name in the Ajax application. If you try to add a function named window.google.ac.Suggest_apply() to your Ajax application, the browser will generate an error because based on the name of the function, the browser is instructed to call upon the window object's google property and no such property exists. An easy workaround for this situation is to rename window.google.ac.Suggest_apply() to the name of a function in the Ajax application prior to passing the web server's output string to the JavaScript eval() function (which you will do in step 5).

Designing the Application

The development of the Ajax Google Suggest application will be created in a series of seven steps, as outlined here:

1. Create a new HTML page.
2. Format the display of Google Suggest results using CSS.

3. Begin work on the application's JavaScript and instantiating an XMLHttpRequest object.
4. Create a function to capture user keystrokes and pass them to the application's PHP script.
5. Process the list of terms returned by Google Suggest.
6. Submit the term or phrase selected by the user.
7. Create the application's PHP file.

Step 1: Writing the Application's HTML

The first step in the development of the Ajax Google Suggest application is to create an HTML page for the application named google.html and to add the following statements to it.

```
<HTML>
  <HEAD>
    <TITLE>Demo: An Ajax Driven Google Live Search</TITLE>
  </HEAD>
  <BODY style="text-align:center;">
    <H1>Google Live Search - Ajax Style!</H1>
    Search: <INPUT id = "textField" type = "text" size = 50
      name = "textField" onkeyup = "captureKeystrokes(event)">
      <P><CENTER><DIV id = "trgtDiv"> <div></CENTER></P>
  </BODY>
</HTML>
```

As you can see, the HTML tags that make up the Ajax Google Suggest application are straight-forward. They consist of the required head and body tags. The head section includes a title tag and the body section consists of a level 1 heading and a text field control into which the user will type a search keyword or phrase.

Step 2: Using CSS to Control Search Results

When executed, this application will retrieve a list of popular search keywords or phrases based on the user's input. The output listing returned from Google will be displayed inside a pair of <DIV> </DIV> tags referred to using an id of trgtDiv. To help make the output standout, a pair of embedded CSS style tags will be added to the application that apply a background color, width, and border style to the <DIV> </DIV> tags. These statements that make up the embedded style tags are shown next and should be added to the head section of the HTML page, just under the <TITLE> </TITLE> tags.

```
<STYLE>
  #trgtDiv {
    background-color: #C0C0C0;
```

```
    width: 50%;
    border-style: solid
  }
</STYLE>
```

You will learn more about how to work with CSS in Chapter 8, "Working with Cascading Style Sheets." Figure 6.12 shows the impact that the addition of the CSS embedded style tags have on the appearance of the application.

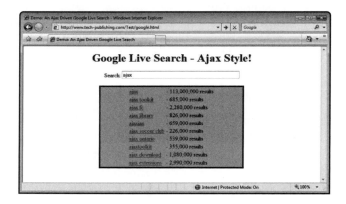

FIGURE 6.12

The Ajax Google Suggest application uses CSS to improve the presentation of its output.

Step 3: Creating the Application's JavaScript and Instantiating the XMLHttpRequest Object

The next step in the development of the Ajax Google Suggest application is to begin assembling its JavaScript. Begin by adding the following statement to the head section of the HTML page, immediately following the CSS style tags that you added in the previous step.

```
<SCRIPT language = "javascript" type = "text/javascript">
<!-- Start hiding JavaScript statements
  var Request = false;
  if (window.XMLHttpRequest) {
    Request = new XMLHttpRequest();
  } else if (window.ActiveXObject) {
    Request = new ActiveXObject("Microsoft.XMLHTTP");
  }
// End hiding JavaScript statements -->
</SCRIPT>
```

As you can see, in addition to adding the JavaScript's opening and closing tags, these statements also define an instance of the XMLHttpRequest object, assigning it an object variable named Request.

Step 4: Capturing and Passing Along User Keystrokes

Each time the user types or deletes a character in the application text field box, the textfield control's onkeyup() event handler executes and calls upon a function named captureKeystrokes(), passing it an argument representing the text that the user has entered. The code statements that make up this function are shown next and should be added to the application's JavaScript.

```
function captureKeystrokes(keyStroke) {
  var keyStroke = (keyStroke) ? keyStroke: window.event;
  var searchString =
    (keyStroke.target) ? keyStroke.target : keyStroke.srcElement;
  if (keyStroke.type == "keyup") {
    if (searchString.value) {
      getGoogleList("google.php?qu=" + searchString.value);
    }
    else {
      document.getElementById("trgtDiv").innerHTML = "<div></div>";
    }
  }
}
```

When called, the function begins by assigning the input to a local variable named keyStroke. Unfortunately, you cannot pass event data this way when working with Internet Explorer. Instead, event data must be retrieved using the window object's event property. To work around this situation, the second statement in the function makes use of the JavaScript ? operator to evaluate and assign a value to keystroke. If keystroke has an assigned value then that value is retained as the variable value. If, on the other hand, keystroke does not have an assigned value, the value of window.event will be assigned.

The ?: operator is one of three logical Boolean operations supported by JavaScript. Its purpose is to assign either of two possible values to a variable based on the result of an evaluated condition, using the following syntax.

```
var result = condition ? value : alternativeValue;
```

The third statement in the function uses the ? operator a second time to establish a reference to the textfield control in which the user has been typing. For a non-Internet Explorer web browser, you can get this value using the event object's target property. However, Internet Explorer does not support this. Instead, you must use the keyEvent object's srcElement property.

Once an object reference of searchString has been established for the textfield control, an if statement code block is used to either retrieve the text string entered by the user and pass them to a function named getGoogleList() or, if the text field is empty (e.g., the user deleted its text), delete any keyword or phrases displayed in the <DIV> </DIV> tags. Note the format of the argument that is passed when the GetGoogleList() function is called. It consists of two strings that are concatenated together ("google.php?qu=" and searchString.value).

Step 5: Processing the List of Terms Provided by Google Suggest

When called, the getGoogleList() function processes the test string passed to it as an argument and sends it to Google's server for processing. The code statements that make up this function are shown next and should be added to the application's JavaScript.

```
function getGoogleList(inputString) {
  if(Request) {
    Request.open("GET", inputString);
    Request.onreadystatechange = function() {
      if (Request.readyState == 4 && Request.status == 200) {
        var responseString =
          Request.responseText.substr(30, Request.responseText.length)
        var functionalCall = "ProcessGoogleResults" + responseString
        eval(functionalCall)
      }
    }
    Request.send(null);
  }
}
```

This function begins by assigning the output that is returned to a variable named responseString. The first 30 characters of the data stored in the response string (e.g., window.google.ac.Suggest_apply) are removed from the string using JavaScript's substr() function. Next, the name of the ProcessGoogleResults() function is appended to the beginning of the string, which is then processed by the eval() function. The end result of this function's work is that the output string returned from Google is modified to point to an internal function named `ProcessGoogleResults()` and then processed like any other JavaScript statement in the application.

Step 6: Submitting the Search Term or Phrase Selected by the User

The last function in the application is the `ProcessGooleResults()` function, which is shown here. This function is executed whenever the output string returned from Google is evaluated and executed (as a JavaScript statement).

```
function ProcessGoogleResults(ignoreVar, keyword, aResults, aEmpty) {
  var googleListing = "<table>";
  if (aResults.length != 0) {
    for (var i = 1; i < aResults.length; i += 2) {
      googleListing += "<tr><td>" +
        "<a href='http://www.google.com/search?q=" +
        aResults[i] + "'>" + aResults[i] +
        '</a></td><td>' + " - " + aResults[i + 1];
    }
  }
  googleListing += "</table>";
  document.getElementById("trgtDiv").innerHTML = googleListing;
}
```

As you can see, this function begins by breaking down its input into four parts, each of which is assigned to a different local variable. Of these four variables, on the string assigned to the first variable, aResult, is used. Actually, aResult is passed through as an array made up of two separate types of information, representing the search terms and their popularity.

 HINT If you go back and look at the sample output that was presented at the beginning of this exercise, you will see that the following statements show an example of what the contents of the array will look like.

```
new Array(2, "ajax", "113,000,000 results", "ajax toolkit",
"680,000 results", "ajax control toolkit", "444,000 results",
"ajax fc", "2,270,000 results", "ajax library", "827,000 results",
"ajaxian", "659,000 results", "ajax soccer club", "225,000 results",
"ajax ontario", "540,000 results", "ajax download", "1,090,000 results",
"ajax grips", "649,000 results")
```

The first item listed in the array is a number that should be disregarded. The rest of the items in the array consist of keywords or phrases followed by an item showing its popularity.

The rest of the statements that make up the ProcessGoogleResults() function are used to define HTML tags required to create a table that displays the contents of the array. The table is made up of two columns, one showing the search keyword or phrase and the other displaying its popularity. Note that each keyword or phrase is turned into a clickable link. This allows the user to perform a Google Search on any of the keywords or phrases that make up the output returned by Google.

Step 7: Creating the Application's PHP Script

The Ajax Google Suggest application also has a server-side component in the form of a PHP script named google.php. The code statements that make up this program are outlined here:

 The Ajax Google Suggest application depends on the google.php script to pass the application's search string to Google Suggest and to collect and return the results of that submission back to the application for processing. The reason that application requires the use of the PHP application instead of trying to directly manage all communications with Google's server is because of security rules that prevent browser applications from directly accessing server programs that run on different Internet domains. To get around this restriction, you must let your web server handle the exchange of information on your behalf, server to server.

```php
<?php
  $objRef = fopen("http://www.google.com/complete/search?hl=en&js=true&qu=" .
    $_GET["qu"], "r");
  while (!feof($objRef)){
    $results = fgets($objRef);
    echo $results;
  }
  fclose($objRef);
?>
```

The first and last statements in the PHP script are the program's required opening and closing tags. The second statement in the PHP script is responsible for submitting your application's search term to Google Suggest using the fopen() function. The output that is returned from Google is stored in the $objRef variable. Next, a loop is set up to process the contents of the data stored in $objRef. Each search term or phrase is retrieved using the PHP fgets() function and then returned as text to the Ajax application, using the echo command. Once all of the output has been received from Google, the connection to Google is closed using the fclose() function and the PHP script halts its execution.

The Final Result

Okay, at this point you have everything you need to create your own copy of the Ajax Google Suggest application. As long as you have followed along carefully and not made any typos, everything should work exactly as was described at the beginning of this chapter. To test the application, upload the `google.html` file along with the `google.php` file to your web server and then load `google.html` into your web browser. Once loaded, type in a few characters and see what happens. Try deleting a character and verify that the application reacts accordingly. Once you have found a keyword or phrase that best matches what you want to search on, click on its entry and make sure that Google performs a search on your behalf.

 You will find a copy of this application's source code files on the book's companion website, located at http://www.courseptr.com/downloads.

SUMMARY

In this chapter, you learned how to use the `XMLHttpRequest` object to interact with programs running on the web server. This included learning how to pass argument data to server-side programs and to retrieve data returned by those programs, using either the `XMLHttpRequest` object's `open()` method's `GET` or the `POST` options. This chapter showed you how to create Ajax applications that can dynamically control the display of graphics. You also learned how to execute JavaScript code returned from the web server and using this programming technique, you created your own Ajax-based implementation of Google Suggest.

Now, before you move on to Chapter 7, "Working with XML," set aside a little extra time to improve the Ajax Google Suggest application by addressing the following list of challenges.

CHALLENGES

1. As currently written, the Ajax Google Suggest application only allows the user to select and submit one of the search terms provided in its output listing. Consider enhancing the application by modifying it to allow the user to submit a search term typed into the Search text field as well.

2. To help make the application easier to work with, display instructions on its usage, perhaps by displaying a Help or Instructions link or graphic and then dynamically display text instructions when the user moves the mouse pointer over it.

Part

IV

WORKING WITH XML

XML is a standard for storing and transporting data in a platform-independent manner. This chapter introduces you to XML and explains how to develop XML applications that can work with data stored in XML files. You will learn how to create XML files and how to access their contents using Ajax. You will learn the basics of XML element syntax and how to formulate XML tags that include text content and optional attribute data. You will also learn how browsers create logical trees for your XML files and how to navigate those trees using JavaScript properties. On top of all this, this chapter will show you how to create the Who Am I? application, which will retrieve data stored in different XML files located on the application's web server.

Specifically, you will learn:

- How to create XML files that are well-formed
- The basic syntax requirements for formulating XML tags
- How to add attributes to XML tags and how to access attribute data from within your Ajax applications
- How white space in XML files can create havoc in Ajax applications and how to work around this problem
- How to use different JavaScript properties to navigate and extract data from XML files

PROJECT PREVIEW: THE WHO AM I? APPLICATION

This chapter's application project is the Who Am I? game. This application challenges players to try to guess the names of different historical figures. The application retrieves data representing questions, answers, and hints from small XML files stored on the application's web server. Each XML file contains information about a different historical figure. The game randomly downloads a different XML file each time the player initiates a new round of play.

Figure 7.1 shows how the game looks when initially loaded into a Firefox web browser.

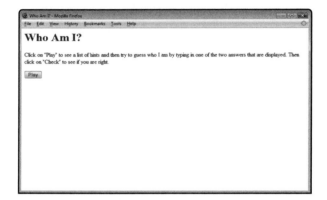

FIGURE 7.1

The player must click on the Play button to start playing the game.

Initially, all the player sees is the name of the game, instructions on how to play, and a Play button. When the user clicks on the Play button, the game generates a random number between 1 and 10, and then based on the value of this number, downloads one of the XML files from the web server. The contents of the downloaded XML file are then processed and used to populate the browser window. As Figure 7.2 shows, the player is presented with three hints, a question, and two different answers from which to choose.

Once the player decides on an answer, it must be typed into the textbox and the Check button must be clicked. The game then compares the player's answer to the answer that was stored in the XML file. Once this analysis is complete, the game notifies the player of the results by displaying a red text message at the bottom of the browser window, as demonstrated in Figure 7.3.

The game allows the player to play as long as she wants, changing the Play button to the Play Again button after the first round of play.

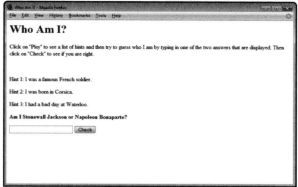

FIGURE 7.2

To submit an answer, the player must type it into the textbox and click on the Check button.

FIGURE 7.3

An example of a question that has been correctly answered.

An Introduction to XML

So far, all of the examples that involve the exchange of data between the web server and Ajax applications have relied on the use of text. However, as its name indicates (the *x* in Ajax stands for XML), Ajax applications are also able to work with XML (*eXtensible Markup Language*) data.

XML is a general-purpose markup language that is similar in many ways to HTML. Both of these markup languages are derived from SGML (Standard Generalized Markup Language), which is used to organize the different types of elements that make up documents. While HTML is used to develop web pages, XML is designed to manage the storage and transfer of data. XML is a widely accepted standard used by Ajax developers for transporting structured data between applications. In terms of Ajax applications, this means passing data from the web server to your Ajax applications where it can be parsed and processed.

Unlike HTML, which consists of a large collection of pre-defined tags (elements), each of which is designed for a specific purpose, XML allows developers to design their own tags to describe any type of data. For example, the following XML file describes instructions to bake a cake.

```
<cake>
  <instructions>oven='microwave'>
    <heat>'300 degrees'</heat>
    <time>'30 minutes'</time>
    <over>conventional</oven>
  </instructions>
  <instructions>oven='conventional'>
    <heat>'300 degrees'</heat>
    <time>'30 minutes'</time>
    <over>conventional</oven>
  </instructions>
</cake>
```

As you can see, two different sets of instructions are provided, one for baking the cake using a microwave and another for baking it in a conventional oven. Take note of the use of attributes to identify each cooking option and how the tags are laid out in a hierarchical structure.

Rules for Formulating XML Tags

To be valid, XML files must be well-formed. A *well formed* XML file is one that conforms to all of XML's syntax rules. These rules include:

- All XML files must have one root element (also referred to as the *document element*), made up of an opening (root) tag and a corresponding closing tag.
- Element attributes must be enclosed within single or double quotation marks.
- An attribute can only appear once in an element tag.
- Tag names cannot begin with a numeric value.
- All elements must be properly nested.
- Tag names cannot include blank spaces or quotation marks.

Examples of illegal XML tags include:

- `<99years>`
- `< "library">`
- `<Good Times>`

XML can be used to transfer any amount of data. Like the HTML DOM, XML organizes data into a logical tree format, the root of which is the document element. The document element is a set of developer-specified tags, within which other XML elements are embedded. For example, the following example shows an XML file that consists only of a document element.

```
<library>Historical Book Collection</library>
```

This document is well-formed. It contains the required document element tags. It has no attributes and since it has no other elements, there are no nesting issues.

 HINT XML is a widely used standard. XML oversight is provided by the World Wide Web Consortium. To review detailed information about the XML standard specification, visit http://www.w3.org/TR/REC-xml.

XML Element Syntax

Most XML elements consist of an opening and a closing tag and may contain zero or more attributes as well as text content. The basic syntax for an XML element is shown here:

```
<openingtag attribute="value">content</closingtag>
```

Here, *openingtag* and *closingtag* mark the beginning and ending of the element, which can contain zero or more attributes using the format shown above. Blanks spaces are used to separate *attributes* when more than one is included. Value assignments must be enclosed within quotation marks. *content* represents optional text contained in the element.

 TRAP While HTML is not case-sensitive, XML tags are. Therefore, in XML, `<Library>` and `<library>` are regarded as two different elements. Because of this, you must take extra care when formulating your XML files to ensure that you do not make mistakes in the capitalization of tag names.

Including the XML Declaration Instruction

If you want, you may include an optional XML declaration instruction in your XML files. The purpose of the XML declaration is to identify the document as an XML file. As a matter of good programming practice, every XML file should include a declaration instruction. The XML declaration statement supports the syntax outlined here:

```
<?xml
version="versionNumber"
encoding="encodingType"
standalone="standaloneValue" ?>
```

The versionNumber attribute specifies the version of XML in use. As of the writing of this book, 1.0 and 1.1 were the only valid versions of XML. Common practice is to specify version 1.0. The optional encodingType attribute is used to specify the character set used by the XML file. Examples of valid options here include UTF-8, UTF-16, and EUC-JP. UTF-8 will suffice for most situations. The standaloneValue attribute, if present, must be set to either yes or no. You should specify a value of no if the XML file has a link to an external DTD or if it has any external entity references and specify a value of yes if the XML file has an internal DTD.

 DTD stands for document type definition. DTDs are used to define rules that govern the creation of XML files. The creation of DTD is outside the scope of this book.

If present, the declaration element must be the first tag in the XML file. In fact, this element must be placed on the first line in the file or an error will occur. If specified, the declaration element must specify a versionNumber attribute. Take note that the XML declaration has no closing tag.

Commenting Your XML Files

Even though XML is considered to be self-describing, you can make your XML files easier to understand and work with by making liberal use of XML comments. XML comments are formatted in the same manner as HTML comments—delimited within <!-- and --> characters. For example, the following statement provides an example of an XML comment:

```
<!--This XML file contains a list of custom information-->
```

You may place XML comments anywhere in an XML file. If you want, you can use XML comments to comment out multiple lines in an XML file, as demonstrated here:

```
<!--
This XML file
contains a list
of custom information
-->
```

 One limitation of XML comments is that you cannot place two consecutive dashes (--) in a row anywhere within a comment; otherwise, and error will occur.

Working with Elements with No Content

XML elements do not necessarily have to contain any content, in which case the element is considered to be an empty element. In XML, an empty element can be represented by an opening tag followed immediately by a matching closing tag, as demonstrated here:

```
<library></library>
```

XML also supports a simplified format for writing an element with empty content, which allows you to omit the closing tag. Following this format, you add the / character to the end of the opening tag. Using this format, the following example is functionally identical to the previous example.

```
<library/>
```

Although empty elements have no content, they can still contain any number of attributes, as demonstrated here:

```
<library location="downtown" phonenumber="765-4321" />
```

As you can see, an attribute consists of a name followed by a value, which is enclosed inside quotation marks. XML tags can have any number of attributes, as long as they are separated from one another by a blank space.

Understanding the Types of Elements in Use

Even in an XML file, a number of different types of nodes can be used. In addition to different types of nodes, XML lets you assign attributes to nodes and supports a number of other elements as outlined in Table 7.1.

	TABLE 7.1	JAVASCRIPT PROPERTIES THAT SUPPORT XML DOM TREE ACCESS	
Value	**Property**		**Description**
1	NODE_ELEMENT		Represents an element
2	NODE_ATTRIBUTE		Represents an attribute belonging to an element
3	NODE_TEXT		Represents a tag's text content
4	NODE_CDATA_SECTION		Represents the XML's CDATA section
5	NODE_ENTITY_REFERENCE		Provides a reference to an entity within an XML document
6	NODE_ENTITY		Represents an expanded entity
7	NODE_PROCESSING_INSTRUCTION		Represents an XML document processing instruction
8	NODE_COMMENT		Represents a comment within an XML document
9	NODE_DOCUMENT		Represents an object within an XML document
10	NODE_DOCUMENT_TYPE		Represents the document type declaration of the <!DOCTYPE> tag
11	NODE_DOCUMENT_FRAGMENT		Represents a document fragment
12	NODE_NOTATION		Represents a notation within the document type declaration

As you will see a little later in this chapter, there will be times when you will need to know information about the type of elements that are specified in XML documents. In these situations, knowing which values represent which properties, as outlined in Table 7.1, is essential.

VERIFYING THAT YOUR XML FILES ARE WELL-FORMED

All XML files must be well-formed. But how can you be sure that your XML files are well-formed and error free? Any software application designed to work with XML can be used to verify whether an XML file is well-formed. Since Internet Explorer and Firefox are both XML-compatible web browsers, you can use either of them to load and verify that your XML files are well-formed. For example, Figure 7.4 shows an example of how a typical well-formed XML file looks when loaded by Firefox.

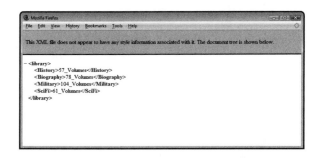

FIGURE 7.4

Using Firefox to verify that an XML file is well-formed.

Figure 7.5 shows an example of an XML file that is not well-formed.

FIGURE 7.5

The document element's closing tag has been mistyped resulting in an XML file that is not well-formed.

Obviously, if your browser flags your XML file as having an error, you must go back and correct it before you can use it in your Ajax application.

UNDERSTANDING XML TREES

When browsers load XML files, they automatically convert them into logical collections of related nodes. These nodes have relationships to one another. For example, consider the following XML file.

```
<?xml version = "1.0" encoding="utf-8"?>
<library>
  <History>57 Volumes</History>
  <Biography>78 Volumes</Biography>
  <Military>104 Volumes</Military>
  <SciFi>61 Volumes</SciFi>
</library>
```

Here, the `<library>` document element node contains four subnodes (`<History>`, `<Biography>`, `<Military>`, and `<SciFi>`). These four nodes are children of the `<library>` names and siblings to one another. Each of the four child nodes also has a child node (text node) of its own that contains text data.

A Depiction of a Small XML File

When processing the XML file that was presented in the previous section, web browsers automatically generate a logical tree representation of the nodes that make up the XML file in memory. Figure 7.6 shows a depiction of the logical tree that is generated when the previous XML file is loaded.

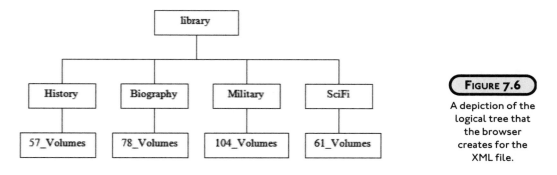

FIGURE 7.6

A depiction of the logical tree that the browser creates for the XML file.

As you can see, the document element `<library>` resides at the root of the tree. It has four child nodes (`<History>`, `<Biography>`, `<Military>`, and `<SciFi>`). Also, each of the child nodes has a text node.

JavaScript Properties That Work with XML Trees

In addition to the XMLHttpRequest object's responseXML property, JavaScript provides access to a large collection of properties that you can use to interact with, navigate, and extract data from XML files. These properties are listed and described in Table 7.2.

TABLE 7.2	JAVASCRIPT PROPERTIES THAT SUPPORT XML DOM TREE ACCESS
Property	**Description**
attributes	Returns a list of attributes belonging to the node
documentElement	Returns a node's document element
parentNode	Rerturns a node's parent node
childNodes	Returns an array listing all of a node's child nodes
firstChild	Returns the first child belonging to a node
lastChild	Returns the last child belonging to a node
name	Returns a node's name
localName	Returns a node's local name
nodeValue	Returns a node's value
nodeType	Returns a node's type
nodeName	Returns a node's name
nextSibling	Returns a node's next sibling (based on its order in the XML DOM tree)
previousSibling	Returns a node's previous sibling (based on its order in the XML DOM tree)

Many of the properties should look familiar to you because they mirror properties of the same name used to navigate DOM trees.

NAVIGATING XML FILES

Using the properties listed in Table 7.2, you can navigate and extract data from XML files. For example, the following series of steps demonstrate how to write a function named getData() that extracts the text that is highlighted in this XML file:

```
<?xml version = "1.0" encoding="utf-8"?>
<library>
  <History>57 Volumes</History>
  <Biography>78 Volumes</Biography>
  <Military>104 Volumes</Military>
  <SciFi>61 Volumes</SciFi>
</library>
```

The first step in creating the getData() function is to lay out the function's opening and closing tags and to define a variable that will be used to download and store an object reference to the XML file.

```
function getData() {
  var Request = false
  var docElement, childOne, childTwo, textNode, targetData;
  if (window.XMLHttpRequest) {
   Request = new XMLHttpRequest();
  } else if (window.ActiveXObject) {
    Request = new ActiveXObject("Microsoft.XMLHTTP");
  }
  if(Request) {
    Request.open("GET", "library.xml");
    Request.onreadystatechange = function() {
      if (Request.readyState == 4 && Request.status == 200) {
        var xmlDoc = Request.responseXML;
        ClearOutWhiteSpace(xmlDoc)
        .
        .
        .
      }
    }
  }
  Request.send(null);
}
```

Here an XML file named library.xml is downloaded and assigned to a variable named xmlDoc. Take note of the highlighted statement shown above. It calls upon a function named ClearOutWhiteSpace(). Some web browsers, including Safari and Firefox, interpret the use of blank spaces in XML files differently from other browsers. To allow the application to process the XML file using the same programming logic, regardless of the browser being used, this method is called to remove white space from the XML file.

The next step in navigating the XML is to set up an object reference to the document element, which you can do using the documentElement property, as shown here:

```
docElement = xmlDoc.documentElement;
```

As an object reference to the root element of the entire XML file, docElement can be used to access all four of the document element's children. The first child of the document element is the `<History>` element, which you can reference using the `firstChild` property, as shown here:

```
docElement = xmlDoc.documentElement;
childOne = docElement.firstChild;
```

The `<Biography>` tag is a sibling of the `<History>` tag. Specifically, it is the first sibling of the `<History>` tag. You can set up an object reference to it using the `nextSibling` property, as shown here:

```
docElement = xmlDoc.documentElement;
childOne = docElement.firstChild;
childTwo = childOne.nextSibling;
```

Now that you have an object reference to the `<Biography>` node, you need to get your hands on its text node object, which you can do using the `firstChild` property, as shown here:

```
docElement = xmlDoc.documentElement;
childOne = docElement.firstChild;
childTwo = childOne.nextSibling;
textNode = childTwo.firstChild;
```

All that is left to do to get your hands on the data belonging to the second node is to retrieve its value, which you can do using the `nodeValue` property, as shown here:

```
docElement = xmlDoc.documentElement;
childOne = docElement.firstChild;
childTwo = childOne.nextSibling;
textNode = childTwo.firstChild;
targetData = textNode.nodeValue;
```

Now that the function has the data it was looking for, let's verify its success by displaying it, as shown here:

```
docElement = xmlDoc.documentElement;
childOne = docElement.firstChild;
childTwo = childOne.nextSibling;
textNode = childTwo.firstChild;
targetData = textNode.nodeValue;
window.alert("There are " + targetData + " in the library.");
```

Figure 7.7 shows the output that is displayed when this Ajax application is executed on an Apple Computer running the Safari web browser.

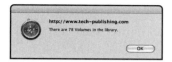

FIGURE 7.7

Using JavaScript
properties, you
can extract data
from any XML file.

Eliminating White Space

Unfortunately, there is a major difference in the way different browsers handle the presence of white space in XML files. While browsers like Internet Explorer work with XML exactly as described in the preceding sections, browsers like Firefox and Safari do not. Specifically, browsers like Safari and Firefox do not ignore the white space that exists between tags in XML files. Instead, these browsers strictly adhere to W3C standards by treating blank space as an empty text node. These browsers also interpret tabs and linefeeds as blank space. As a result of their strict adherence to the standard, navigating the XML tree that these browsers generate for XML pages becomes very challenging.

Rather than creating Ajax applications that process XML trees one way for Internet Explorer and another way for browsers like Safari and Firefox, most Ajax developers simply add an extra function to their applications that strips out the extra spaces from XML tags. An example of such a function is shown here:

```
function ClearOutWhiteSpace(xmlFile) {
  var i = 0;
  for (i = 0; i < xmlFile.childNodes.length; i++) {
    var tag = xmlFile.childNodes[i];
    if (tag.nodeType == 1) {
      ClearOutWhiteSpace(tag);
    }
    if ((tag.nodeType == 3) && (/^\s+$/.test(tag.nodeValue))) {
      xmlFile.removeChild(xmlFile.childNodes[i--]);
    }
  }
}
```

Here, a function named ClearOutWhiteSpace() is passed a variable containing the contents of an XML file. A loop is set up to process every node in the XML file. Note that an array of nodes is generated using the JavaScript childNodes property. An if statement code block is set up to check the node's node type. If it has a value of 1 (refer to Table 7.1), then it may have child elements, so to process the child elements, a recursive call is made to the ClearOutWhiteSpace() function. A second if statement code block is then set up to check the node's node type to see if it is equal to 3 (e.g., it's a text node). This code block also executes a regular expression that looks to see if the node is made up of all white space. If this is the case, then the node is removed by calling on the `removeChild()` method. The end result is an XML file with no extra white space.

Now let's tie together everything that you have learned regarding how to navigate XML files and how to remove extra white space, by creating a small Ajax application that processes the following XML file and extracts and displays the highlighted data.

```xml
<?xml version = "1.0" encoding="utf-8"?>
<library>
  <History>57 Volumes</History>
  <Biography>78 Volumes</Biography>
  <Military>104 Volumes</Military>
  <SciFi>61 Volumes</SciFi>
</library>
```

The statements that make up the Ajax application are shown here:

```html
<HTML>
  <HEAD>
    <TITLE>Demo: Extracting data from an XML file</TITLE>
    <SCRIPT language = "javascript" type = "text/javascript">
    <!-- Start hiding JavaScript statements
      function getData() {
        var Request = false
        var docElement, childOne, childTwo, textNode, targetData;
        if (window.XMLHttpRequest) {
         Request = new XMLHttpRequest();
        } else if (window.ActiveXObject) {
          Request = new ActiveXObject("Microsoft.XMLHTTP");
        }
        if(Request) {
          Request.open("GET", "library.xml");
          Request.onreadystatechange = function() {
            if (Request.readyState == 4 && Request.status == 200) {
              var xmlDoc = Request.responseXML;
              ClearOutWhiteSpace(xmlDoc)
              docElement = xmlDoc.documentElement;
              childOne = docElement.firstChild;
```

```
            childTwo = childOne.nextSibling;
            textNode = childTwo.firstChild;
            targetData = textNode.nodeValue;
            window.alert("There are " + targetData + " in the library.");
          }
        }
      }
      Request.send(null);
    }
    function ClearOutWhiteSpace(xmlFile) {
      var i = 0;
      for (i = 0; i < xmlFile.childNodes.length; i++) {
        var tag = xmlFile.childNodes[i];
        if (tag.nodeType == 1) {
          ClearOutWhiteSpace(tag);
        }
        if ((tag.nodeType == 3) && (/^\s+$/.test(tag.nodeValue))) {
          xmlFile.removeChild(xmlFile.childNodes[i--]);
        }
      }
    }
  // End hiding JavaScript statements -->
  </SCRIPT>
</HEAD>
<BODY onLoad=getData()>
</BODY>
</HTML>
```

When executed, this application downloads the library.xml file, clears out any excess white space, navigates the XML file, and extracts and displays the required data. Check out Figure 7.7 for an example of the output that this application produces.

Processing XML Element Attributes

Some XML element tags also include attribute data. You can programmatically access tag attributes and use them when processing XML files. If an object contains one or more attributes, you can set up an object reference to those attributes using the attributes property. For example, take a look at the following XML file:

```
<?xml version = "1.0" encoding="utf-8"?>
<toys>
  <toy color="red">
    <price>$9.99</price>
    <inventory>in stock</inventory>
  </toy>
  <toy color="blue">
    <price>$9.99</price>
    <inventory>out of stock</inventory>
  </toy>
  <toy color="green">
    <price>$8.99</price>
    <inventory>on backorder</inventory>
  </toy>
</toys>
```

This XML file's <toy> tags include an attribute named color. As the highlighted tag in the XMP file indicates, the third <toy> tag contains information about the color, price, and inventory status of a toy. The following Ajax application downloads the XML file, clears out any extra white space, and then extracts the attribute and content data for the third tag, displaying the results in a popup dialog.

```
<HTML>
  <HEAD>
    <TITLE>Demo: Extracting data from an XML file</TITLE>
    <SCRIPT language = "javascript" type = "text/javascript">
    <!-- Start hiding JavaScript statements
      function getData() {
        var Request = false
        var docElement, childOne, childTwo, textNode, targetData;
        if (window.XMLHttpRequest) {
         Request = new XMLHttpRequest();
        } else if (window.ActiveXObject) {
          Request = new ActiveXObject("Microsoft.XMLHTTP");
        }
        if(Request) {
          Request.open("GET", "toys.xml");
          Request.onreadystatechange = function() {
            if (Request.readyState == 4 && Request.status == 200) {
```

```
           var xmlDoc = Request.responseXML;
           ClearOutWhiteSpace(xmlDoc)
           docElement = xmlDoc.documentElement;
           toyThree = docElement.lastChild;
           toyAttribute = toyThree.attributes;
           colorType = toyAttribute.getNamedItem("color");
           toyColor = colorType.nodeValue;
           toyPrice = toyThree.firstChild.firstChild
           toyStatus = toyThree.lastChild.firstChild
           window.alert("The " + toyColor + " toy is " +
             toyPrice.nodeValue + " and is " +
             toyStatus.nodeValue + ".");
         }
       }
     }
     Request.send(null);
   }
   function ClearOutWhiteSpace(xmlFile) {
     var i = 0;
     for (i = 0; i < xmlFile.childNodes.length; i++) {
       var tag = xmlFile.childNodes[i];
       if (tag.nodeType == 1) {
         ClearOutWhiteSpace(tag);
       }
       if ((tag.nodeType == 3) && (/^\s+$/.test(tag.nodeValue))) {
         xmlFile.removeChild(xmlFile.childNodes[i--]);
       }
     }
   }
 // End hiding JavaScript statements -->
 </SCRIPT>
</HEAD>
<BODY onLoad=getData()>
</BODY>
</HTML>
```

The main statements to focus on are the ones that have been highlighted in bold. The first of these statements uses the JavaScript `attributes` properties to retrieve a list of attributes belonging to a specific node. The resulting object creates a mapping of all the attributes belonging to the specified node. Using this object's getNamedItem() method, you can retrieve a specific attribute by specifying its name (e.g., color). This creates an attribute node for that attribute. Once created, you can use the nodeValue property to reference the attribute node's value.

Now that the application has extracted the attribute data from the third <toy> tag, all that is left to do is retrieve the content of the <price> and <status> tags and then to display the results, as shown in Figure 7.8.

FIGURE 7.8

An example of the output produced by the application when executed using Firefox.

JSON: JavaScript Object Notation—An Alternative to XML

JSON is a lightweight data format that allows you to transfer data using only JavaScript. Unlike XML, you do not have to work with an object model to use JSON. Instead, you are able to access data using lists. Therefore, many Ajax developers find it easy to learn JSON, whereas learning XML takes more time and effort.

A disadvantage of using JSON is that most server-side programming languages, such as PHP, Perl, Ruby, and Java, will not be able to work with it unless you install a JSON library on the web server.

This book uses XML in its examples because XML represents a standards-based method of transporting data that is widely accepted and employed by Ajax developers. Although arguably more difficult to initially learn, XML's mass acceptance makes it an obvious choice. In addition, you do not have to worry about installing any additional libraries on your web server to work with it. XML is used in many different development environments. So learning how to work with XML in your Ajax applications may pay additional dividends later.

 If you are interested in learning more about JSON, visit http://en.wikipedia.org/wiki/JSON.

Back to the Who Am I? Application

It is time to return your attention to the development of this chapter's project, the Ajax Who Am I? application. This application is designed to test the player's knowledge of famous historical figures. Each time the game is played, a set of three hints is displayed to help the user identify the person being described. Two possible answers are then presented and the player is asked to type in the correct answer. The data that is used to generate the hints and answers for each question are stored in small XML files located on the web server. The game randomly downloads 1 of 10 XML files each time the game is played, providing a variety of questions.

Designing the Application

The development of the Ajax Who Am I? application will be created in a series of seven steps, as outlined here:

1. Create the application's XML files.
2. Create a new HTML page.
3. Get started on the application's JavaScript.
4. Set up an instance of an XMLHttpRequest object.
5. Develop the getXML() function.
6. Develop the ClearOutWhiteSpace() function.
7. Develop the checkAnswer() function.

Step 1: Creating the Application's XML Files

The first step in the development of the Who Am I? application is to create each of the 10 XML files that the application will download. These XML files represent a set of 10 individual questions, along with accompanying hints and the answers to the questions. The names of each of these XML files are shown next in bold print, followed by the tags that make up those files.

whoami1.xml

```
<?xml version = "1.0"?>
<question>
  <hint>Hint 1: I was the first president of the United States of
    America.</hint>
  <hint>Hint 2: I am famous for chopping down a cherry tree.</hint>
  <hint>Hint 3: My face is on the one dollar bill.</hint>
  <question>Am I George Washington or Abraham Lincoln?</question>
  <answer>George Washington</answer>
</question>
```

whoami2.xml

```
<?xml version = "1.0"?>
<question>
  <hint>Hint 1: I was an Apollo 14 astronaut.</hint>
```

```
<hint>Hint 2: I was the first man to walk on the moon.</hint>
<hint>Hint 3: I drank a lot of Tang.</hint>
<question>Am I Neil Armstrong or George Bush?</question>
<answer>Neil Armstrong</answer>
</question>
```

whoami3.xml

```
<?xml version = "1.0"?>
<question>
  <hint>Hint 1: I was Prime Minister of Great Britain in WWII.</hint>
  <hint>Hint 2: I was well known for my ability to make extraordinary
    speeches.</hint>
  <hint>Hint 3: I was once the First Lord of the Admiralty.</hint>
  <question>Am I Dwight Eisenhower or Winston Churchill?</question>
  <answer>Winston Churchill</answer>
</question>
```

whoami4.xml

```
<?xml version = "1.0"?>
<question>
  <hint>Hint 1: I was a famous French soldier.</hint>
  <hint>Hint 2: I was born in Corsica.</hint>
  <hint>Hint 3: I had a bad day at Waterloo.</hint>
  <question>Am I Stonewall Jackson or Napoleon Bonaparte?</question>
  <answer>Napoleon Bonaparte</answer>
</question>
```

whoami5.xml

```
<?xml version = "1.0"?>
<question>
  <hint>Hint 1: I was Prime Minister of England from 1979 to 1990.</hint>
  <hint>Hint 2: My nickname was the Iron Lady.</hint>
  <hint>Hint 3: I was the leader of my country's Conservative Party.</hint>
  <question>Am I Tony Blair or Margaret Thatcher?</question>
  <answer>Margaret Thatcher</answer>
</question>
```

whoami6.xml

```
<?xml version = "1.0"?>
<question>
  <hint>Hint 1: I was emperor of the Roman Empire.</hint>
  <hint>Hint 2: I commanded the Roman invasion of Britain in 55 BC.</hint>
  <hint>Hint 3: I conquered Gaul.</hint>
  <question>Am I Marcus Brutus or Julius Caesar?</question>
  <answer>Julius Caesar</answer>
</question>
```

whoami7.xml

```
<?xml version = "1.0"?>
<question>
  <hint>Hint 1: I was a Carthaginian military leader.</hint>
  <hint>Hint 2: I once invaded Italy.</hint>
  <hint>Hint 3: I won battles at Trasimene, Cannae and Trebia.</hint>
  <question>Am I Hannibal or Attila the Hun?</question>
  <answer>Hannibal</answer>
</question>
```

whoami8.xml

```
<?xml version = "1.0"?>
<question>
  <hint>Hint 1: I am a famous biblical character.</hint>
  <hint>Hint 2: I once hiked up Mount Sinai.</hint>
  <hint>Hint 3: I was given the 10 commandments.</hint>
  <question>Am I Moses or Abraham?</question>
  <answer>Moses</answer>
</question>
```

whoami9.xml

```
<?xml version = "1.0"?>
<question>
  <hint>Hint 1: I was the last Pharaoh.</hint>
  <hint>Hint 2: I was the mother of 3 of Mark Antony's children.</hint>
  <hint>Hint 3: I once hid in a carpet so I could meet Julius Caesar.</hint>
```

```
<question>Am I Portia or Cleopatra?</question>
<answer>Cleopatra</answer>
</question>
```

whoami10.xml

```
<?xml version = "1.0"?>
<question>
  <hint>Hint 1: I was the President of the Second Continental Congress.</hint>
  <hint>Hint 2: I was the Governor of Massachusetts.</hint>
  <hint>Hint 3: I am famous for the size of my signature.</hint>
  <question>Am I John Adams or John Hancock?</question>
  <answer>John Hancock</answer>
</question>
```

As you can see, each of these 10 XML files consists of a declaration tag followed by the document element, within which an additional five tags have been placed. The first three of these five tags contain content representing separate text strings containing different hints. The fourth tag contains a text string representing the question to be asked by the application. The last of the five tags contains a text string that specifies the correct answer to the questions.

Step 2: Writing the Application's HTML

The next step is to create the application's HTML. Do so by creating an HTML page named whoami.html and adding the following statements to it.

```
<HTML>
  <HEAD>
    <TITLE>Who Am I?</TITLE>
  </HEAD>
  <BODY>
    <H1 style = "color:blue">Who Am I?</H1>
    <FORM>
      <P>Click on "Play" to see a list of hints and then try to
      guess who I am by typing in one of the two answers that are
      displayed. Then click on "Check" to see if you are right.</P>
      <INPUT type="button" value="Play" id="playBtn" onclick=getXML()>
      <P><DIV id = "hint1Div"> </DIV></P>
      <P><DIV id = "hint2Div"> </DIV></P>
      <P><DIV id = "hint3Div"> </DIV></P>
      <P><DIV id="questionDiv" style="color:blue; font-weight:Bold">
        </DIV></P>
```

```
    <INPUT type="textfield" size="25" style="visibility:hidden"
      id="inputField">
    <INPUT type="button" value="Check" style="visibility:hidden"
      id="checkBtn" onclick=checkAnswer()>
  </FORM>
  <P style = "color:red; font-weight:Bold" id = "resultsP"> </P>
</BODY>
</HTML>
```

As you can see, the HTML tags that make up the Who Am I? application are straightforward. They consist of the required head and body tags. The head section contains a title tag and the body section contains a level 1 header followed by a form. The form tags contain a number of elements that display descriptive text, two button controls, and a text file. Note that the id attribute has been specified for the button and textfield controls, allowing them to be programmatically referenced by the application's JavaScript.

Also note that a number of pairs of <P></P> and <DIV></DIV> tags have been embedded within the form. These pairs of tags will be used to programmatically display questions and their accompanying hints during game play. A final pair of <P></P> tags is included at the end of the body section and will be used to display messages that notify the player as to whether her answers are right or wrong.

 Many of the tags in the HTML file contain additional style attributes that are used to specify the length, color, and visibility of various form controls. You will learn all about the effect that these style attributes have on the appearance and operation of the application in Chapter 9, "Working with Cascading Style Sheets."

Step 3: Getting Started on the Application's JavaScript

The next step in the development of the application is to begin assembling its JavaScript. Start by adding the following statement to the head section of the HTML page:

```
<SCRIPT language = "javascript" type = "text/javascript">
<!-- Start hiding JavaScript statements
  var correctAnswer = "";


// End hiding JavaScript statements -->
</SCRIPT>
```

In addition to specifying the JavaScript's opening and closing tags, one global variable is defined. It will be used to store the answer to questions downloaded and extracted from the application's XML files.

Step 4: Instantiating the XMLHttpRequest Object

Now it is time to add statements to the JavaScript that are responsible for instantiating the XMLHttpRequest object. Do so by adding the following statements to the end of the JavaScript.

```
var Request = false;
if (window.XMLHttpRequest) {
  Request = new XMLHttpRequest();
} else if (window.ActiveXObject) {
  Request = new ActiveXObject("Microsoft.XMLHTTP");
}
```

As you can see, these statements define an instance of the XMLHttpRequest object, assigning it an object variable named Request.

Step 5: Creating the getXML() Function

The getXML () function, shown next, is responsible for downloading a randomly selected XML file from the application's web server and then retrieving and displaying the question and three hints specified as content in the XML file. To create this function, add the following statements to the end of the application's JavaScript.

```
function getXML() {

  if (Request) {
    var RequestObj1 = document.getElementById("hint1Div");
    var RequestObj2 = document.getElementById("hint2Div");
    var RequestObj3 = document.getElementById("hint3Div");
    var RequestObj4 = document.getElementById("questionDiv");

    randomNo = 1 + Math.random() * 9;
    randomNo = Math.round(randomNo);

    Request.open("GET", "whoami" + randomNo + ".xml");
    Request.onreadystatechange = function() {

      if (Request.readyState == 4 && Request.status == 200) {
        var xmlDoc = Request.responseXML;
        ClearOutWhiteSpace(xmlDoc)

        docElement = xmlDoc.documentElement;
        hint1 = docElement.firstChild;
```

```
    hint2 = hint1.nextSibling;
    hint3 = hint2.nextSibling;
    question = hint3.nextSibling;
    answer = question.nextSibling;

    RequestObj1.innerHTML = hint1.firstChild.nodeValue;
    RequestObj2.innerHTML = hint2.firstChild.nodeValue;
    RequestObj3.innerHTML = hint3.firstChild.nodeValue;
    RequestObj4.innerHTML = question.firstChild.nodeValue;
    correctAnswer = answer.firstChild.nodeValue;

    document.getElementById("inputField").value = "";

    var textField = document.getElementById("inputField")
    var checkButton = document.getElementById("checkBtn")
    var playButton = document.getElementById("playBtn")
    var resultsParagraph = document.getElementById("resultsP");
    textField.style.visibility="visible";
    checkButton.style.visibility="visible";
    playButton.style.visibility="hidden";
    resultsParagraph.innerHTML = "";

  }
 }
 Request.send(null);
 }
}
```

The first four statements set up object references to the <DIV></DIV> tags that will be used to display the three hints and the question stored in the XML file. Next, a random number from 1 to 10 is generated and used as input in the formation of a filename representing one of the application's XML files, which is then downloaded and stored in an object variable named xmlDoc. ClearOutWhiteSpace() which is then called to remove blank spaces from the XML file. Object variables are then set up to store references to different XML tags. Next, the text strings stored in those tags are retrieved and displayed. Finally, the last nine statements configure the visibility of the application's button and textfield controls.

Step 6: Creating the ClearOutWhiteSpace() Function

The ClearOutWhiteSpace() function, shown next, takes as an argument an object representing an XML file. It then uses a loop to iterate through each line of the XML file, removing any excess white space. When necessary, the function makes recursive calls to itself to process any white space embedded within child nodes. To create this function, add the following statements to the application's JavaScript, immediately following the getXML() function.

```
function ClearOutWhiteSpace(xmlFile) {
  var i = 0;
  for (i = 0; i < xmlFile.childNodes.length; i++) {
    var tag = xmlFile.childNodes[i];
    if (tag.nodeType == 1) {
      ClearOutWhiteSpace(tag);
    }
    if ((tag.nodeType == 3) && (/^\s+$/.test(tag.nodeValue))) {
      xmlFile.removeChild(xmlFile.childNodes[i--]);
    }
  }
}
```

Detailed instructions on how to build the ClearOutWhiteSpace() function were provided earlier in this chapter.

Step 7: Creating the checkAnswer() Function

The checkAnswer() function is responsible for determining whether the player was able to correctly answer the game's current question. The code statements that make up this function are shown next and should be added to the end of the application's JavaScript.

```
function checkAnswer() {

  var answer = document.getElementById("inputField").value;
  var results = document.getElementById("resultsP");

  if (answer == correctAnswer) {
    results.innerHTML = "That's right!";
  } else {
    results.innerHTML = "Sorry, that's not me.";
  }

  var playButton = document.getElementById("playBtn");
```

```
playButton.style.visibility="visible";
playButton.value="Play Again";

var checkButton = document.getElementById("checkBtn");
checkButton.style.visibility="hidden";
```

```
}
```

The statement retrieves the player's answer from the textfield control. The second statement retrieves a reference to a pair of <P></P> tags located just under the application's form into which the text generated by this function is displayed. Next an if statement code block has been set up to compare the player's answer (stored in answer) to the correct answer for the question (stored in correctAnswer). Based on this analysis either of two messages is displayed (using the innerHTML property belonging to the object reference [results] of the <P></P> tags). Finally, the last five statements change the text displayed on the Play button to Play Again and make it visible while also turning the button labeled Check invisible.

The Final Result

All right, assuming that you followed along with the steps outlined in this chapter and did not make any typos along the way, everything should work as described at the beginning of the chapter. To test the application, upload the whoami.html file along with the 10 accompanying XML files to your web server and then load whoami.html into your web browser. Once loaded click on the Play button and start answering questions. When testing, submit both correct and incorrect answers and make sure the application processes them correctly.

 You will find a copy of this application's source code on the book's companion website, located at http://www.courseptr.com/downloads.

SUMMARY

In this chapter you learned how to develop Ajax applications that work with data made available through XML files. You learned how to create and format XML files. You learned the basics of XML element tag syntax, and to work with element attributes. This chapter explained the problem that some browsers have with white space and provided a solution for removing white space from XML files. On top of all this, you learned how web browsers translate XML files into logical trees and how to navigate and access different parts of XML files using various related JavaScript properties.

Now, before you move on to Chapter 8, "Working with Cascading Style Sheets," set aside a little extra time to improve the Who Am I? application by addressing the following list of challenges.

CHALLENGES

1. This version of the Who Am I? application retrieves questions, answers, and hints from 1 of 10 XML files. It does not take long to exhaust the available supply of files. Make the game more interesting by creating additional XML files and updating the logic that controls the range of files that the game randomly downloads.

2. Rather than make the player type the answers to questions, consider redesigning the XML files to provide answers using two separate tags and then modify the application to separately extract and associate both answers with radio buttons. This will make the game easier to play and will eliminate wrong answers that occur because of typos.

WORKING WITH CASCADING STYLE SHEETS

A lthough CSS is not regarded as a formal Ajax component, Ajax programmers have come to depend upon it for all sorts of things. For example, using
CSS, you can change foreground and background colors, specify font type,
size, and color, turn things visible and invisible, and even move things around the
screen. In short, CSS provides Ajax developers with much needed functionality,
giving them the ability to exercise detailed control over the display of elements
and to programmatically alter all or part of a web page's presentation, instantly,
with no need for page refreshes.

Specifically, you will learn:

- The basics of CSS syntax
- How to use CSS to modify the presentation of text and to modify color and backgrounds
- How to use CSS to control the positioning of elements
- How to work with inline, embedded, and external styles

PROJECT PREVIEW: THE FORTUNE TELLING GAME

This chapter application project is the Fortune Telling game. This Ajax application
uses CSS and JavaScript to create and manage a graphical menu that builds a series

of menu lists based on content downloaded from the application's web server. Figure 8.1 provides a view of the application when initially loaded into the browser.

FIGURE 8.1

The opening view of the Fortune Telling game consists of three menus.

As demonstrated in Figure 8.2, the game's menus provide access to commands that initiate game play, allow the user to modify the game's appearance, and provide information about the game.

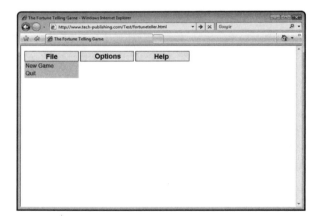

FIGURE 8.2

Menus located across the top of the browser screen control key game functionality.

As shown in Figure 8.3, once game play has been initiated, the player is prompted to ask a question and then click on the Get Answer button.

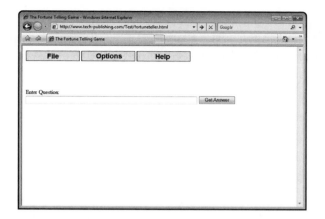

FIGURE 8.3

The player asks questions by typing them and then clicking on the Get Answer button.

In response to the player's question, the game displays a randomly generated answer, as demonstrated in Figure 8.4.

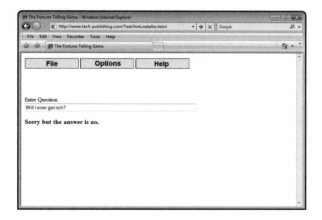

FIGURE 8.4

The game randomly generates answers to player questions.

The Get Answer button is hidden from the screen for three seconds to give the player time to read the game's response, after which the button is redisplayed and the player is permitted to ask another question.

AN INTRODUCTION TO CSS

Cascading Style Sheets or *CSS* is a stylesheet programming language used by web developers to specify the presentation of web page content. Prior to the introduction of CSS, all HTML presentation attributes had to be set using HTML markup. CSS gives web developers the ability to apply a consistent look and feel over web page layout and design. This includes things like font type, size, and color as well as background styles, borders, and the content alignment. Thanks to CSS, web developers no longer have to repeatedly configure the presentation of header elements. With CSS, color, size, and font used to present these tags can be specified just one time and then be consistently applied throughout a web page.

CSS was first introduced back in 1997 and over time slowly worked its way into mainstream web development. Today, CSS represents a widely adopted standard maintained by the World Wide Web Consortium. Today, the W3C regards CSS as the best way to apply presentation markup and has deprecated the use of all HTML presentation markup.

CSS executes locally within the web browser. Its primary purpose is to enable the separation of presentation and content. This separation can help reduce the size of your Ajax applications and simplify overall application design by removing repetition in the specification of layout instructions. It allows you to specify the fonts, colors, and layout of web pages. CSS provides rules that determine how conflicting style rules are applied or *cascaded*.

 Unfortunately, because of differences in support for the CSS specification, different web browsers render different results when processing CSS layouts. The only way to effectively deal with this reality is to extensively test your Ajax applications on different web browsers to ensure that the data in your applications is presented in the way that you want it.

CSS Syntax

CSS adheres to a simple syntax, using English keywords to specify the names of different styles and their values. Style sheets are made up of lists of rules. Each rule is comprised of one or more selectors and a declaration block. A *declaration block* is comprised of a list of declarations. *Declarations* are embedded within braces and consist of a property followed by a colon and then an assigned value. Semicolons are used to separate multi declarations. *Selectors* are used to specify the elements to which styles are applied. Selectors can be set up to apply to specific elements based on matching attributes or to all attributes that match a specific type.

USING CSS TO SPECIFY STYLE, COLOR, AND PRESENTATION

CSS controls the presentation of content on web pages through the specification of rules. These rules are created by assigning values to different CSS style properties. Entire books have been written that discuss the application and use of CSS. This chapter highlights CSS style rules commonly used by Ajax developers and is intended to provide a basic overview of how to put CSS to work in your Ajax applications.

Controlling Font Presentation

CSS gives Ajax developers explicit control of the appearance of fonts, allowing the specification of font type, size, and a number of other attributes. Table 8.1 provides a list of commonly used CSS properties that you can use to work with and control fonts in your Ajax applications.

TABLE 8.1	COMMON CSS FONT PROPERTIES
Property	**Description**
font-family	A prioritized list of font types, such as Arial and Verdana, that specify the font to be used. The list of fonts must be separated by commas. The first available font on the user's computer is automatically used.
font-size	Specifies the size of the font.
font-stretch	Expands or condenses a font's width. Available options include: normal, wider, and narrower.
font-style	Specifies how the font should be displayed. Available options include: normal, italic, and oblique.
font-weight	Specifies font boldness. Available options include: normal, bold, bolder, and lighter.

As an example of how to control the presentation of fonts, look at the following example.

```
<HTML>
  <HEAD>
    <TITLE>Demo: Using CSS to set font attributes</TITLE>
  </HEAD>
  <BODY>
    <H1 style = "font-family:Arial; font-style:italic;">This heading is
      displayed in the Arial font using italics</H1>
    <P style = "font-family:Garamond; font-size:12;">This paragraph is
      displayed in the Garamond font in size 12</P>
  </BODY>
<HTML/>
```

When displayed, this HTML page will look like Figure 8.5.

FIGURE 8.5

You can use CSS to modify different font properties.

Managing the Display of Text

In addition to allowing you to specify different font properties, CSS provides access to a number of additional properties that affect the presentation of text. Table 8.2 is a list of text-related style properties that give you control over things like line height, letter spacing, and indentation.

TABLE 8.2	COMMON CSS TEXT FORMATTING PROPERTIES

Property	Description
color	Specifies the color to be used as the foreground color.
text-align	Sets text alignment. Available options include: left, right, center, and justify.
text-indent	Indents the first line of text.
text-decoration	Applies a decoration to text. Available options include: none, underline, overline, blink, and line-through.
line-height	Specifies the distance between lines.
letter-spacing	Specifies the amount of space between characters.
word-spacing	Specifies the amount of space between words.

As an example of how to use CSS to control the presentation of text, look at the following example.

```
<HTML>
  <HEAD>
    <TITLE>Demo: Using CSS to set text attributes</TITLE>
  </HEAD>
  <BODY>
    <H1 style = "text-align:center;">This heading is centered</H1>
    <P style = "text-decoration:underline; text-align:right;">This
```

```
      paragraph is underlined and right justified</P>
   <P style = "text-align:left;">This paragraph is left aligned</P>
  </BODY>
</HTML>
```

When displayed, this HTML page produces the results shown in Figure 8.6.

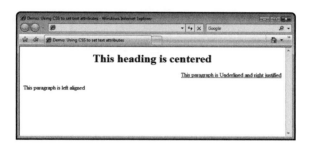

FIGURE 8.6

You can use different CSS style properties to control the presentation of text.

Controlling Color and Background

CSS gives you detailed control over the colors and backgrounds displayed on your web pages. Table 8.3 shows a list of commonly used CSS style properties that you can use to specify things like font and window color and backgrounds.

TABLE 8.3   COMMON CSS COLOR AND BACKGROUND PROPERTIES

Property	Description
background-image	Specifies the URL of an image file to be used as the background.
background-color	Specifies the color to be used as the background color.
background-repeat	Specifies whether the background image should be tiled. Available options include: no-repeat, repeat-x, and repeat-y.
background-position	Specifies the starting position for the background. Available options include: center, top, bottom, right, and left.

HINT A number of different options are available to you for specifying color values. For starters, you may specify colors using hexadecimal color codes (example: #FFFFFF equals white, #000000 equals black, #FF0000 equals red). You may also specify color using the JavaScript rgb() function to which you just pass three numbers in the range of 1 to 255, representing different red, green, and blue values (example: rgb(255, 255, 255) equals white, rgb(0, 0, 0) equals black, and rgb(255, 0, 0) equals red). A third option is to simply type the name of the color you want to use (example: white, black, and red).

As an example of how to work with the properties listed in Table 8.3, look at the following.

```
<HTML>
  <HEAD>
    <TITLE>Demo: Using CSS to set color and background attributes</TITLE>
  </HEAD>
  <BODY style="color:red; background-color:lightgrey;">
    <H1>The text on this page should be red</H1>
    <P>The page's background should be light gray</P>
  </BODY>
</HTML>
```

Figure 8.7 shows how this example appears when loaded into a web browser.

FIGURE 8.7

An example of how to specify foreground and background colors for a web page.

Exercising Control over Content Location

In addition to giving you control over the appearance and presentation of text, CSS lets you take control over the placement of content on the browser window. CSS lets you specify where web page elements are placed using either absolute or relative positioning. Table 8.4 provides a list of CSS properties that affect element positioning.

TABLE 8.4	CSS PROPERTIES THAT AFFECT ELEMENT POSITIONING	
Property	**Property**	**Description**
top	pixel value	Offset from the top of the browser's display area (absolute) or from its default location as determined by the browser.
bottom	pixel value	Offset from the bottom of the browser's display area (absolute) or from its default location as determined by the browser.
left	pixel value	Offset from the top-left side of the browser's display area (absolute) or from its default location as determined by the browser.
right	pixel value	Offset from the top-right side of the browser's display area (absolute) or from its default location as determined by the browser.
position	absolute or relative	Determines whether an element's position is set based on its distance from the upper-left corner to the browser's display area (absolute) or in relation to other elements (relative).
z-index	numeric value	A value that determines the order in which elements appear when they overlap one another.

Using absolute positioning, you specify the location of elements on the browser window using the coordinates systems shown in Figure 8.8.

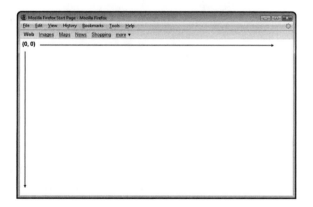

FIGURE 8.8

A depiction of the system of coordinates used when working with absolute positioning.

To get a feel as to how to work with the properties listed in Table 8.4, look at the following example.

```
<HEAD>
  <TITLE>Demo: Using CSS to control element placement</TITLE>
</HEAD>
  <BODY>
    <IMG src="cats.jpg" style="position:absolute; left:100; top:50;
      z-index:20;">
    <IMG src="bird.jpg" style="position:absolute; left:300; top:200;
      z-index:10;">
  </BODY>
</HTML>
```

Here, two images are displayed on the browser window using absolute positioning. Because the coordinates used cause the images to overlap, the image with the highest specified z-index property value is displayed on top. Figure 8.9 shows an example of the effect of absolute position on the display of the two image files.

FIGURE 8.9

Using absolute position to control the display of image files.

Unlike absolute positioning, which specifies a precise location in the browser window, relative positioning sets an element's position relative to other elements on a web page. The problem with absolute positioning is that different users have their computers set up to use different resolutions. As a result, the size of the coordinate system changes from user to user, making it difficult to ensure a consistent look and feel for your web pages. The answer to this challenge is relative positioning. For example, if you create an application that uses relative positioning to control the placement of elements, the browser will automatically reposition the elements based on the resolution being used to display the application. This helps keep elements from overlapping one another or from being pushed out of view off of the edge of the browser window.

As a demonstration of how relative positioning works, take a look at the following example:

```
<HTML>
  <HEAD>
    <TITLE>Demo: Using CSS to control element placement</TITLE>
  </HEAD>
  <BODY>
    <BR><BR><BR>
    The
    <SPAN style="position:relative; top:-5;">little</SPAN>
    <SPAN style="position:relative; top:-10;">boy</SPAN>
    <SPAN style="position:relative; top:-20;">pulled</SPAN>
    <SPAN style="position:relative; top:-30;">his</SPAN>
    <SPAN style="position:relative; top:-40;">little</SPAN>
    <SPAN style="position:relative; top:-50;">red</SPAN>
    <SPAN style="position:relative; top:-60;">wagon</SPAN>
    <SPAN style="position:relative; top:-50;">up</SPAN>
    <SPAN style="position:relative; top:-40;">and</SPAN>
    <SPAN style="position:relative; top:-30;">down</SPAN>
    <SPAN style="position:relative; top:-20;">the</SPAN>
    <SPAN style="position:relative; top:-10;">tall</SPAN>
    <SPAN style="position:relative; top:-5;">hill</SPAN>
    .
  </BODY>
</HTML>
```

Figure 8.10 shows what this page looks like when loaded.

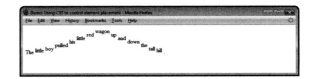

FIGURE 8.10

Using relative positioning to modify the display of text.

ADDING CSS TO YOUR HTML PAGES

So far, all of the examples of CSS that you have seen in this chapter have been applied inline to individual HTML tags. This is a handy option for controlling the presentation of individual elements. However, CSS styling instructions can be applied to HTML pages in other ways, including embedded style elements and external style sheets. Both of these options provide the ability to specify presentation styles globally, throughout an entire web page.

Using Inline Styles

Using inline styles, you embed CSS styles inside HTML tags. For example, the following statements add an inline style to a paragraph tag, instructing the browser to display its text in `blue`.

```
<P style="color:blue";>Once upon a time...<P>
```

If needed, you can include any number of property specifications to an inline style, as long as each one is followed by a semicolon, as demonstrated here:

```
<P style="color:red; font-size:12; text-align:center;">Once upon a time</P>
```

Defining Embedded Style Elements

Working with inline styles is okay for small HTML pages and for pages that require a lot of detailed customization. However, since most HTML pages tend to apply a consistent look and feel to elements of the same type, you will often be better served using embedded style elements.

The format that you must follow when working with embedded style elements is straightforward. You start by adding opening and closing style tags to the head section of your HTML page. Next, you embed style rules inside the `<STYLE>` and `</STYLE>` tags. Related rules are grouped together using declaration blocks, each of which is preceded by a selector that specifies the elements to which the rules will be applied. Selectors can be set up to specify the type of tag to which they apply. Alternatively, you can set them up to work with specific tags by referring to the tag's id. You may add as many rules as you want within each declaration block.

To see how all this works, look at the following example:

```
<HTML>
  <HEAD>
    <TITLE>DEMO: CSS Style Embedded Style Elements</TITLE>
    <STYLE>
    H1 {
      color:blue;
      font-style:italic;
    }
    H2 {
```

```
      color:green;
      background-color:yellow;
    }
    P {
      text-align:center;
      font-weight:bold;
      color:red;
      text-decoration:underline;
    }
    #P1 {
      font-style:italic;
    }
    </STYLE>
  </HEAD>
  <BODY>
    <H1>This text should be blue and italics</H1>
    <P>This text should be centered, bold, red and underlined</P>
    <H2>This text should be green with a yellow background</H2>
    <P id="P1">This text should be centered, bold, red and underlined
      and italic</P>
  </BODY>
</HTML>
```

As you can see, four declaration blocks have been added to the head section of the HTML page. The first block makes changes to the way the pages's level 1 headings are presented. The second block configures the presentation of all level 2 headings, and the third block specifies how all text contained in <P> <P/> tags is to be presented. The fourth block demonstrates CSS's ability to cascade overlapping rules by modifying the presentation of one specific paragraph tag. The fourth block does not prevent the third block from being applied. Instead, it adds to the changes made by the third block. Had the fourth block included any changes that conflicted with the third block, the conflicting property changes in the fourth block (e.g., the more granular block) would override the property specifications outlined in the third block.

Figure 8.11 shows the output that is displayed when this page is loaded.

Working with External Style Sheets

If your Ajax applications make substantive use of CSS, you may find that by moving your styles into external style sheets, you can significantly reduce the overall size and complexity of your application's web pages. Creating an external style sheet is easy. All you have to do is move the declaration blocks from your <STYLE> elements into an external file (less the opening <STYLE> and closing </STYLE> tags).

You can name the external file anything you want, but you must assign a .css file extension to it. For example, the following CSS file, named style.css, is an example of an external style sheet. This external style sheet was created by extracting the embedded style rules from the previous example. As you can see, except for the absence of the <STYLE> and </STYLE> tags, everything else remains unchanged.

```
H1 {
  color:blue;
  font-style:italic;
}
H2 {
  color:green;
  background-color:yellow;
}
P {
  text-align:center;
  font-weight:bold;
  color:red;
  text-decoration:underline;
}
#P1 {
  font-style:italic;
}
```

With the CSS style sheet removed, the HTML file is now significantly smaller, as shown here:

```
<HTML>
  <HEAD>
    <TITLE>DEMO: CSS Style Embedded Style Elements</TITLE>
    <LINK rel="stylesheet" href="style.css">
  </HEAD>
  <BODY>
    <H1>This text should be blue and italics</H1>
    <P>This text should be centered, bold, red and underlined</P>
    <H2>This text should be green with a yellow background</H2>
    <P id="P1">This text should be centered, bold, red and underlined
      and italic</P>
  </BODY>
</HTML>
```

Take note of the new <LINK> tag that has been added to the head section of the HTML page. This new tag is what instructs the web browser to load and apply the external style sheet to the HTML page. The <LINK> tag has two attributes. The rel attribute is required and is set to stylesheet, and the href attribute is used to tell the browser the stylesheet's URL.

The use of embedded versus external style sheets is strictly a matter of personal preference. If your Ajax applications make limited use of CSS, embedded style sheets may be all you need. However, large and complex Ajax applications, with significant numbers of CSS rules, may benefit from external style sheets.

BACK TO THE FORTUNE TELLING GAME

Okay, now it's time to return your attention back to the development of this chapter's project, the Fortune Telling game. Through the development of this application, you will learn how to create and manage application menus using a combination of JavaScript and CSS. You will gain further experience working with both inline and external styles. In addition, you will be introduced to a number of new JavaScript methods.

Designing the Application

The development of the Ajax Fortune Telling game will be created in a series of 13 steps, as outlined here:

1. Assemble the application's external style sheet.
2. Put together the application's external text files.
3. Create a new HTML page.

4. Start the application's JavaScript.
5. Develop the ProcessEvent() function.
6. Develop the getMouseData() function.
7. Develop the populateMenus() function.
8. Develop the RemoveMenus() function.
9. Develop the DisplayMenu() function.
10. Develop the ExecuteCommand() function.
11. Develop the StartPlay() function.
12. Develop the AnswerQuestion() function.
13. Develop the ResetScreen() function.

Step 1: Creating the Application's External Style Sheet

The Fortune Telling game makes liberal use of CSS to control the presentation of data. Specifically, it uses an external style sheet to apply CSS rules that affect the display of items displayed in each of the application's menus. To create the external style sheet for this application, create and save a file named style.css and add the following statements to it.

```css
#fileMenu {
  position: absolute;
  font-family: arial;
  background-color:lightgrey;
  visibility: hidden;
}
#optionsMenu {
  position: absolute;
  font-family: arial;
  background-color:lightgrey;
  visibility: hidden;
}
#helpMenu {
  visibility: hidden;
  font-family: arial;
  background-color:lightgrey;
  position: absolute;
}
```

As you can see, the external style sheet is organized into three parts, one per menu, specifying that the menus are initially hidden. Font type, background color, and absolute positioning are also specified.

Step 2: Creating the Application's Server Files

In addition to its external style sheet, this application also uses three text files stored on the web server, which you will need to create. Each text file contains a comma-separated list of items belonging to an application menu (each menu's name is the same as the name of the text file). The names of these three text files are shown next in bold, followed by a text string that shows each file's contents.

file.txt

```
New Game, Quit
```

options.txt

```
White Background, Grey Background
```

help.txt

```
Instructions, About
```

Step 3: Writing the Application's HTML

The next step in the development of the Fortune Teller game is to create an HTML page for the application named `fortuneteller.html` and add the following statements to it.

```
<HTML>
  <HEAD>
    <TITLE>The Fortune Telling Game</TITLE>
    <LINK rel="stylesheet" href="style.css">
  </HEAD>
  <BODY onmousemove = "ProcessEvent(event)" onclick = "RemoveMenus()">
    <IMG id="fileIMG" src="file.jpg" style="left:0; top:0; width:150;
      height:29;">
    <DIV id="fileMenu" style="left:10; top:44; width:150; height: 48;
      visibility:hidden;"></DIV>
    <IMG id="optionsIMG" src="options.jpg" style="left:150; top:0;
      width:150; height:29;" >
    <DIV id="optionsMenu" style="left:165; top:44; width:150; height: 48;
      visibility:hidden;"></DIV>
    <IMG id="helpIMG" src="help.jpg" style="left:300; top:0; width:150;
      height:29;" >
    <DIV id="helpMenu" style="left:319; top:44; width:150; height: 48;
      visibility:hidden;"></DIV>
    <FORM>
```

```
       <BR> <BR> <BR>
       <DIV id = "Label"> </DIV>
       <INPUT type="textfield" size="75" style="visibility:hidden"
         id="inputField">
       <INPUT type="button" value="Get Answer" style="visibility:hidden"
         id="checkBtn" onclick=AnswerQuestion()>
       <H3><DIV id = "answer"> </H3>
     </FORM>
   </BODY>
</HTML>
```

As you can see, these HTML tags include a `<LINK>` tag that points the application to its external style sheet. In addition, three `<IMG>` tags are included that display the application's graphical menus. Each graphic is 150 x 29 pixels in size. The three graphics are displayed side by side at the top of the browser display area. In addition, three sets of `<DIV>` `</DIV>` tags are included, each of which lines up with one of the graphics menus. The application will use the `<DIV>` `</DIV>` tags to display each menu's list of menu items, whenever the user moves the mouse pointer over them.

 HINT You will find copies of the three graphic images needed to build this application's menus on the book's companion website, located at http://www.courseptr.com/downloads/.

Step 4: Starting the Application's JavaScript

The next step in the development of the application is to begin assembling its JavaScript. Start by adding the following statement to the head section of the HTML page.

```
<SCRIPT language = "javascript" type = "text/javascript">
<!-- Start hiding JavaScript statements
  var aMenuList;
  var Request = false;
  if (window.XMLHttpRequest) {
    Request = new XMLHttpRequest();
  } else if (window.ActiveXObject) {
    Request = new ActiveXObject("Microsoft.XMLHTTP");
  }
// End hiding JavaScript statements -->
</SCRIPT>
```

In addition to specifying the JavaScript's opening and closing tags, one global variable is defined. It will be used to create a global array that contains the list of menu items retrieved from the application's three text files. Also defined here is an instance of the XMLHttpRequest object, which is assigned a name of Request.

Step 5: Creating the ProcessEvent() Function

The ProcessEvent() function is responsible for processing mouse data, passed to it as an argument, in order to determine when to show and when to hide each menu's item listing. Create this function by adding the following statements to the application's JavaScript.

```
function ProcessEvent(event) {
  var e = new getMouseData(event);
  var appMenu;
  if ((e.x > 10) && (e.x < 470) && (e.y > 20) && (e.y < 50)) {
    if (e.x < 160) {populateMenus(1);}
    if ((e.x > 160) && (e.x < 310)) {populateMenus(2);}
    if (e.x > 310) {populateMenus(3);}
  }
  appMenu = document.getElementById("fileMenu");
  if (appMenu.style.visibility == "visible"){
    if (((e.x < 10) || (e.x > 150)) || ((e.y < 20) || (e.y > 100))) {
      RemoveMenus();
    }
  }


  appMenu = document.getElementById("optionsMenu");
  if (appMenu.style.visibility == "visible"){
    if (((e.x < 150) || (e.x > 300)) || ((e.y < 20) || (e.y > 100))) {
      RemoveMenus();
    }
  }
  appMenu  = document.getElementById("helpMenu");
  if (appMenu.style.visibility == "visible"){
    if (((e.x < 300) || (e.x > 450)) || ((e.y < 20) || (e.y > 100))) {
      RemoveMenus();
    }
  }
}
```

Every time the user moves the mouse, the onmousemove() event handler embedded in the <BODY> tag is executed, calling this function and passing it a mousemove event. The function begins by calling on another function named getMouseData(). It then creates a new event object named e based on the data returned by the getMouseData() function. Next, a series of if statements execute, calling on a function named populateMenus() when the user moves the mouse pointer over one of the application's menus. The rest of the function is organized into three nearly identical sets of statements that call on the RemoveMenus() function whenever the user moves the mouse pointer away from the graphic menus and their resulting menu items.

The getMouseData() function works by comparing the X,Y location of the mouse pointer to known coordinate locations representing the location of the three menus and their menu lists (when visible). A more elegant but more involved solution for determining when to display menu lists and when to hide them would be to retrieve references to all three <IMG> tags and all three <DIV> </DIV> tags and then to programmatically determine the coordinate information for these elements. This approach would facilitate the display of menu lists that vary in regards to the number of elements that are displayed. However, to keep things as simple as possible, this function relies on using known coordinates.

Step 6: Creating the getMouseData() Function

The getMouseData() function, shown next, is responsible for creating a browser-independent event object that retrieves and assigns the mouse pointer's X and Y coordinates. Like all of the functions in this application, you must place this function's statements inside the application's JavaScript.

```
function getMouseData(event) {
  if(event) {
    this.x = event.clientX;
    this.y = event.clientY;
  } else {
    this.x = event.pageX;
    this.y = event.pageY;
  }
}
```

The getMouseData() function is an example of a *JavaScript Constructor* function, which is a type of function used to construct a new class. A *class* is an object-oriented term that basically refers to a template that can be used as the basis for instantiating new objects. JavaScript Constructor functions create a new class based on the name of the argument that they are passed, and then, using the this keyword, allow you to define properties for the class. Objects can then be created using the new keyword. Objects automatically inherit all of the features of the classes upon which they are based, including their properties.

Step 7: Creating the populateMenus() Function

The populateMenus() function, shown next, is responsible for retrieving the contents of one of the application's text files stored on the web server and passing that data to a function named DisplayMenu().

```
function populateMenus(menu) {
  var menuList;
  if (menu == 1) {menuList = "file.txt"}
  if (menu == 2) {menuList = "options.txt"}
  if (menu == 3) {menuList = "help.txt"}
  if(Request) {
    Request.open("GET", menuList);
    Request.onreadystatechange = function() {
      if (Request.readyState == 4 && Request.status == 200) {
        DisplayMenu(menu, Request.responseText);
      }
    }
    Request.send(null);
  }
}
```

Step 8: Creating the RemoveMenus() Function

The RemoveMenus() function, shown next, is responsible for making the currently visible menu items invisible (whenever the user moves the mouse pointer away from it and its associated graphic menu).

```
function RemoveMenus() {
  var fileMenu = document.getElementById("fileMenu");
  if (fileMenu.style.visibility == "visible"){
    fileMenu.style.visibility = "hidden";
  }
  var optionsMenu = document.getElementById("optionsMenu");
  if (optionsMenu.style.visibility == "visible"){
    optionsMenu.style.visibility = "hidden";
  }
```

```
var helpMenu = document.getElementById("helpMenu");
if (helpMenu.style.visibility == "visible"){
  helpMenu.style.visibility = "hidden";
  }
}
```

Step 9: Creating the DisplayMenu() Function

The job of the DisplayMenu() function, shown next, is to display a menu items list for the specified menu (passed to it as an argument).

```
function DisplayMenu(choice, menuList) {
  var menu;
  aMenuList = menuList.split(", ");
  var menuTable = "<table width = '99%'>";

  for (var i = 0; i < aMenuList.length; i++) {
    menuTable += "<tr><td " + "onclick='" + "ExecuteCommand(" + i
    + ")" + "'>" + aMenuList[i] + "</td></tr>";
  }

  menuTable += "</table>";

  if (choice == "1"){menu = document.getElementById("fileMenu");}
  if (choice == "2"){menu = document.getElementById("optionsMenu");}
  if (choice == "3"){menu = document.getElementById("helpMenu");}

  menu.innerHTML = menuTable;
  menu.style.visibility = "visible";
}
```

The first thing this function does is use a built-in JavaScript function called split() to populate the global aMenuList array with the list of menu items downloaded from the menu's associated text file. An HTML table is then created that contains one row for each menu item. Note the embedded onclick() event handler, which is used to execute a function named ExecuteCommand() whenever the user clicks on a menu item. The function ends by identifying the menu that has been selected and making that menu's list of menu items visible (inside the <DIV> </DIV> tags that were placed immediately after each of the application's <IMG> tags).

Step 10: Creating the ExecuteCommand() Function

Whenever the user clicks on a menu item, the ExecuteCommand() function is called. Its job is to execute whatever command the user has clicked on. The program statements that make up this function are shown next and should be added to the end of the application's JavaScript.

```javascript
function ExecuteCommand(command) {
  if (aMenuList[command] == "New Game") {
    StartPlay()
  }
  if (aMenuList[command] == "Quit") {
    window.close();
  }
  if (aMenuList[command] == "White Background") {
    document.bgColor="#FFFFFF";
  }
  if (aMenuList[command] == "Grey Background") {
    document.bgColor="#CCCCCC";
  }
  if (aMenuList[command] == "Instructions") {
    window.alert("Click on the New Game command located on the " +
    "File menu to begin game play. Next, type your question and " +
    "click on the Get Answer button to see your fortune.");
  }
  if (aMenuList[command] == "About") {
    window.alert("The Fortune Telling Game - Copyright 2008");
  }
}
```

As you can see, this function is passed an argument that tells it which menu item the user clicked on. This argument is a numeric value representing the index position of the menu item in the global aMenuList array. A total of six if statement code blocks are then used to analyze and process the selected menu item. When the user clicks on the File menu's New Game command, a function named StartPlay() is executed. When the File menu's Quit command is clicked, the window object's close() method is executed. The close() method only works on Internet Explorer and when executed it initiates the closing of the browser window.

The next two code blocks execute when the user clicks on one of the menu commands located on the Options menu. When executed, they assign a color of white or gray to the document object's bgcolor property (demonstrating that there are other ways to manipulate background colors than just using CSS properties). The last two if statement code blocks execute when the user clicks on one of the Help menu's commands, executing the window object's alert() methods in order to display instructions for playing the game or additional information about the game.

Step 11: Creating the StartPlay() Function

The StartPlay() function is called whenever the user clicks on the File menu's New Game menu item (command). Its job is to manipulate the DOM by displaying a little text and making the game's text field and button control visible.

```
function StartPlay() {
  document.getElementById('Label').innerHTML = "Enter Question:"
  document.getElementById("inputField").style.visibility="visible";
  document.getElementById("checkBtn").style.visibility="visible";
}
```

Step 12: Creating the AnswerQuestion() Function

After entering a question and clicking on the game's Get Answer button, the AnswerQuestion() function is called. This function begins by hiding the Get Answer button and then generates a random number from 1 to 10. A switch code block then determines which answer should be displayed.

```
function AnswerQuestion() {
  var checkButton = document.getElementById("checkBtn");
  checkButton.style.visibility="hidden";
  randomNo = 1 + Math.random() * 9;
  randomNo = Math.round(randomNo);
  switch (randomNo) {
  case 1:
    document.getElementById('answer').innerHTML = "Yes!";
    break;
  case 2:
    document.getElementById('answer').innerHTML = "No.";
    break;
  case 3:
    document.getElementById('answer').innerHTML = "Maybe.";
    break;
  case 4:
    document.getElementById('answer').innerHTML = "Doubtful.";
```

```
      break;
  case 5:
    document.getElementById('answer').innerHTML =
      "Not in this lifetime.";
    break;
  case 6:
    document.getElementById('answer').innerHTML =
      "The answer is unclear.";
    break;
  case 7:
    document.getElementById('answer').innerHTML =
      "Ask this question again later.";
    break;
  case 8:
    document.getElementById('answer').innerHTML =
      "Today is your lucky day... Yes!";
    break;
  case 9:
    document.getElementById('answer').innerHTML =
      "Sorry but the answer is no.";
    break;
  case 10:
    document.getElementById('answer').innerHTML = "No way!";
    break;
  }
  setTimeout("ResetScreen()", 3000)
}
```

The last thing the AnswerQuestion() function does is call upon a built-in JavaScript function called setTimeout(), passing it the name of a function to be executed and a numeric value representing the number of milliseconds to wait before executing the specified function. So, in the case of this application, a value of 3000 is passed to setTimeout(), instructing it to wait for three seconds before calling on the ResetScreen() function.

Step 13: Creating the ResetScreen() Function

The last of the application's functions is the ResetScreen() function. It is called after a three-second pause in order to give the player sufficient time to read the game's answer. Once executed, it makes the Get Answer button visible and clears out both the player's question and the game's answer, making the game ready for another question.

```
function ResetScreen() {
  document.getElementById("checkBtn").style.visibility="visible";
  document.getElementById("inputField").value="";
  document.getElementById('answer').innerHTML = "";
}
```

The Final Result

Assuming that you have followed along carefully with the instructions that have been provided, your copy of the Fortune Telling game should be ready for execution. To test the application when you are done, upload the `fortuneteller.html` file along with the `style.css` file and the game's three text files (`file.txt`, `options.txt`, and `help.txt`) to your web server. When you are ready, load `fortuneteller.html` into your web browser and put it through its paces.

 You will find a copy of this application's source code, along with the graphic files needed to build it on the book's companion website, located at http://www.courseptr.com/downloads.

SUMMARY

This chapter provided an overview of CSS and demonstrated its use in Ajax applications. You learned the basics of CSS syntax and how to use CSS to modify the presentation of text and to modify colors and backgrounds. You also learned how to use CSS to control the positioning of elements on the browser window. Using this information, you learned how to develop custom menus for your applications. This chapter also demonstrated how to work with both inline and embedded styles and explained the benefits and use of external style sheets.

Now, before you move on to Chapter 9, "Working with Ajax and PHP," set aside a little extra time to improve the Fortune Telling game by addressing the following list of challenges.

CHALLENGES

1. Using your new knowledge and understanding of CSS, spend a few minutes sprucing up the appearance of the Fortune Telling game.

2. As currently written, the Fortune Telling game does not force the player to enter any text before generating an answer. Modify the game to prevent the player from submitting blank questions.

3. Modify the game to give it a broader range of answers from which to draw on when answering player questions.

WORKING WITH
AJAX AND PHP

I n this chapter, you will learn the basics of PHP programming. PHP is a server-based scripting language designed to support the development of server-based programs. PHP scripts are capable of reading and writing files stored on web servers and working with database management systems. Learning how to create PHP scripts will provide the ability to develop server-based programs designed to support the needs and requirements of your Ajax applications.

Specifically, you will learn how to:

- Develop PHP scripts and integrate PHP with HTML
- Store and retrieve data using variables and arrays
- Perform conditional and iterative programming logic
- Develop and work with functions
- Use PHP to read and write files stored on your web server

PROJECT PREVIEW: SCRAMBLE—THE WORD GUESSING GAME

This chapter's application project is Scramble—The Word Guessing Game. This game involves the development of both client- and server-side components. On the client side, your Ajax application will provide the player with a graphical user interface and will manage the overall execution of the game, using data downloaded from a PHP script executed on the application's web server. Figure 9.1 shows how the application looks when initially loaded using a Firefox web browser.

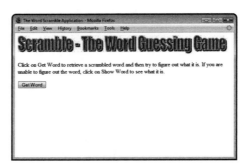

FIGURE 9.1

The game initially displays its name, instructions for playing, and a button.

To begin game play, the player must click on the Get Word button. This prompts the Ajax application to connect to the web server and execute a PHP script named scramble.php, which returns a randomly selected word for the player to try to unscramble. As Figure 9.2 shows, the PHP script automatically scrambles the word before being downloaded and displayed.

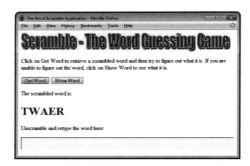

FIGURE 9.2

A scrambled word, downloaded from the web server, is displayed.

The player's job is to try to unscramble the word, using the text field located at the bottom of the screen to retype it, as demonstrated in Figure 9.3.

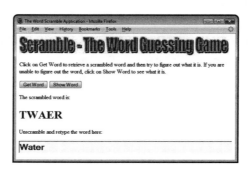

FIGURE 9.3

The player can take as long as necessary to unscramble the word.

If the player is unable to unscramble the word, the player can click on the Show Word button to instruct the game to display the word, as demonstrated in Figure 9.4.

The player can click on the Show Word button to find out what the scrambled word is.

After either unscrambling the word or giving up, the player can initiate a new round of play by once again clicking on the Get Word button, in which case the Ajax application reconnects to its PHP script on the web server and downloads a new word.

INTRODUCTION TO PHP

PHP is an extremely popular server scripting language that is commonly used to support web page development. *PHP*, which standards for *PHP: Hypertext Preprocessor*, runs on most web servers. PHP was first released in 1995. It is developed by the PHP Group and made available for free use.

To execute your PHP scripts, your web server must have PHP installed. Because it is simple and free for commercial use, PHP has been widely deployed on web servers around the world. Chances are very good that your web service provider already has it installed and ready for use. PHP runs on all major web servers and most operating systems. PHP includes a library of built-in functions that allow it to work with most major database management systems.

Although Ajax applications can work with any server-based programming language (Ruby, Perl/CGI, ASP, Python, etc.), PHP is a very popular option. Thanks to its many similarities to JavaScript, it is relatively easy to learn, yet powerful enough to build any type of server-based web application.

You do not have to know how to write web server-based programs to be an Ajax programmer. However, a basic understanding of how web server programs are created and executed is certainly helpful. As such, PHP was selected as the programming language used to develop the server-side programs presented in this book. The purpose of this chapter is to provide a basic PHP primer so that you will be able to better understand how the PHP scripts presented in this book work. This will provide a good appreciation of the work involved in the development of server-based portions of many web applications.

THE BASICS OF WORKING WITH PHP

In order to execute, PHP code must be embedded inside a pair of opening and closing delimiter tags. Typically, most PHP programmers use either <?php and ?> as delimiter tags or <? and ?>. All PHP statements must be embedded within delimiter tags. When used with HTML, PHP's delimiter tags identify PHP statements so that the PHP parser can recognize and process them.

Embedding PHP into Your HTML Pages

One of the neat things about PHP is that you can mix it together with HTML. This is helpful when you only need to add a limited amount of PHP program code to get the job done. To intermix PHP and HTML all you have to do is create a PHP file (a text file with a .php file extension) and add the standard HTML tags to it. Once this has been done, you can add whatever amount of PHP code is required as demonstrated here:

```
<HTML>
  <HEAD>
    <TITLE>Demo: Embedding PHP into an HTML page</TITLE>
  </HEAD>
  <BODY>
    <H1>The following line was generated using PHP</H1>
    <?php
      echo "Using PHP to support Ajax applications is easy.";
    ?>
  </BODY>
<HTML/>
```

As you can see, this PHP file contains all of the HTML elements required for a typical HTML page as well as a small PHP script that uses the echo function (explained in a couple pages) to display a text string (as part of the HTML page). To test the execution of this example, you will need to upload it to your web server and then load the PHP script into your web browser, as demonstrated in Figure 9.5.

Note, that like JavaScript, it is considered to be good form to end all PHP statements with a semicolon.

FIGURE 9.5

An example of a PHP script containing HTML that when loaded displays both HTML and PHP content.

Writing Standalone PHP Scripts

In addition to embedding PHP scripts into your HTML pages, you can create PHP script files and upload them to your web server for execution. PHP files have a .php file extension and can be of any size. You can set them up to generate and return HTML or you can use them to return data when requested, directly to your Ajax applications. For example, the following PHP script, named GetText.php has been set up to return a text string when called by an Ajax application.

```php
<?php
  echo 'Here I am!';
?>
```

As you can see, this PHP script is pretty basic, using the echo function to return a text string. The following Ajax application provides an example of how to call upon and process the text string returned by the GetText.php script.

```html
<HTML>
  <HEAD>
    <TITLE>Demo: Retrieving text from a PHP script</TITLE>
    <SCRIPT language = "javascript" type = "text/javascript">
      var Request = false;
      if (window.XMLHttpRequest) {
        Request = new XMLHttpRequest();
      } else if (window.ActiveXObject) {
        Request = new ActiveXObject("Microsoft.XMLHTTP");
      }
      function getText(url, elementID) {
        if(Request) {
          var RequestObj = document.getElementById(elementID);
          Request.open("GET", url);
          Request.onreadystatechange = function()
```

```
      {
        if (Request.readyState == 4 && Request.status == 200) {
            RequestObj.innerHTML = Request.responseText;
        }
      }
      Request.send(null);
    }
  }
  </SCRIPT>
</HEAD>
<BODY>
  <H1>Demo: Retrieving text from a PHP script</H1>
  <FORM>
    <INPUT type = "button" value = "Get Text"
      onclick = "getText('GetText.php', 'DivTarget')">
  </FORM>
  <DIV id="DivTarget"> </DIV>
</BODY>
</HTML>
```

Figure 9.6 shows the output that is generated when the Ajax application is executed.

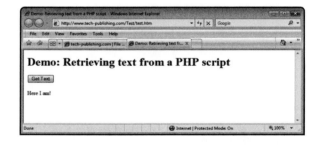

FIGURE 9.6

An example of web page content retrieved from a PHP script.

Note that all of the Ajax and PHP examples that you will see in this chapter assume that the Ajax applications and PHP scripts reside in the same location on the web server.

PHP CODING

One of the things that make PHP easy for Ajax developers to learn is its many similarities to JavaScript. As you will learn in the sections that follow, PHP's support for variables, arrays, conditional logic, and loops is very similar to its JavaScript counterparts. Support for functions, both built-in and functions that you create yourself, also work very similarly.

Returning Data Back to Your Ajax Application

As you have already seen, you can return data back to your Ajax applications from your PHP scripts using the echo function, as demonstrated here:

```
<HTML>
  <HEAD>
    <TITLE>Demo: Embedding PHP into an HTML page</TITLE>
  </HEAD>
  <BODY>
    <H1>The following line was generated using PHP</H1>
    <?php
      echo "Using the echo function to display data.";
    ?>
  </BODY>
<HTML/>
```

Alternatively, PHP also lets you return data using its print function, as shown here:

```
<HTML>
  <HEAD>
    <TITLE>Demo: Embedding PHP into an HTML page</TITLE>
  </HEAD>
  <BODY>
    <H1>The following line was generated using PHP</H1>
    <?php
      print "Using the print function to display data.";
    ?>
  </BODY>
<HTML/>
```

Use of either of these two functions is up to you. Using the print function may make things seem more intuitive, but the echo function runs a little faster and is used more often.

In addition to text, PHP also lets you return XML. To do so, you need to include a header statement at the beginning of your PHP script, after which you can begin returning your XML content, as demonstrated here:

```php
<?php
  header ('Content-Type: text/xml');
  echo '<?xml version = "1.0" encoding="utf-8"?>';
  echo '<cats>';
  echo '<name>Garfield</name>';
  echo '<name>Bill</name>';
  echo '</cats>';
?>
```

When called, this PHP script returns the XML data shown in Figure 9.7.

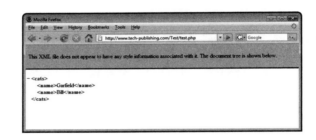

FIGURE 9.7

An example of XML data created and returned by a PHP script.

Commenting Your PHP Code

As with Ajax applications or any other programming applications, it is important to comment your code in order to leave behind an explanation of how things work. PHP gives you three different ways of adding comments to your PHP scripts. As with JavaScript, you can use the // characters to add a comment, as demonstrated here:

```php
//The following statement returns a text string
echo "Hello World!";
```

If you prefer, you may replace the // characters with the # character, as demonstrated here:

```php
#The following statement returns a text string
echo "Hello World!";
```

If you want to create multi-line comments, you can use the /* and */ characters, as demonstrated here:

```php
/* Everything that you see here is
just a part of a multi-line
comment. */
```

Storing Data in Variables

Like JavaScript, PHP lets you store individual pieces of data in variables. PHP variables must begin with the $ character. Like JavaScript, PHP variables are weakly typed, meaning that you do not specify their data type. Instead, PHP automatically determines a variable's type based on the data assigned to it and the context in which it is used. The following example demonstrates how to assign a value of 100 to a variable named $total.

```
$total = 100;
```

PHP variable names can only consist of letters, numbers, and the underscore (_) character.

Managing Collections of Data Using Arrays

Using arrays, you can store collections of data when your PHP scripts execute. PHP arrays do not have to be pre-defined. Instead, all you have to do is start adding data to an array and PHP will recognize what you are doing and create the array for you. For example, the following statement creates an array named $aNames and adds an initial element to it.

```
$aNames[0] = "Washington";
```

Once created, you can continue to populate the array with additional data, as demonstrated here:

```
$aNames[0] = "Washington";
$aNames[1] = "Lincoln";
$aNames[2] = "Adams";
```

Alternatively, you can create and populate new arrays using the array() function, as demonstrated here:

```
$aNames = array("0" =>"Washington", "1" => "Lincoln", "2" => "Adams");
```

As you can see, the array function works by passing it pairs of data in the form of "index" => "value", with each item entry separated by commas. Once populated, you can access array contents by specifying the name of the array and the index value of the data to be retrieved, as demonstrated here:

```
echo "The second item stored in the array is: " . $aNames[1];
```

 In PHP, the . character serves as the concatenation operator.

Data Assignments

PHP provides a number of different operators that you can use when assigning data. These operators include:

- =
- =+
- -+
- *=
- /=

The following statements demonstrate how each of these operators works.

```
$x = 5;            //x equals 5
$x = $x += 1;      //x equals 6
$x = $x -= 1;      //x equals 5
$x = $x *= 2;      //x equals 10
$x = $x /= 2;      //x equals 5
```

Performing Mathematic Calculations

PHP supports many of the same arithmetic operators provided by Javascript. These operators include:

- +
- -
- *
- /
- ++
- −

The following statements demonstrate how each of these operators works.

```
$x = 5 + 1;        //x equals 6
$x = $x - 1;       //x equals 5
$x = $x * 5;       //x equals 25
$x = $x / 5;       //x equals 5
$x++;              //x equals 6
$x--;              //x equals 5
```

One difference between JavaScript and PHP occurs with the application of the concatenator operator. JavaScript uses the + operator to add numeric values and to concatenate strings. PHP also uses the + operators to add numeric values but uses the . operator to concatenate strings. The following PHP statement demonstrates how to concatenate three strings together to create a larger one.

```php
$firstName = "Jerry";
$lastName = "Ford";
$name = $firstName . " " . $lastName;
```

Comparing Values

PHP provides a number of operators that allow you to compare different values. These operators include:

- ==. Equal to
- !=. Not equal to
- <. Less than
- >. Greater than
- <=. Less than or equal to
- >=. Greater than or equal to

Performing Conditional Logic

Like JavaScript, PHP supports the development of conditional logic using variations of the if statement and the switch statement. As the next several sections will demonstrate, there is not a lot of difference between PHP and JavaScript when it comes to these statements.

The if Statement

The if statement is used to determine whether a specified condition is true or false. The following statements demonstrate how to use the if statement to set up a conditional code block in a PHP script.

```php
<?php
$x = 10;
if ($x == 10) {
  echo "We have a match!";
}
?>
```

Since $x is equal to 10, an echo statement is executed, returning a text string to the calling application.

The else Statement

Using the else statement, you can modify a conditional code block to perform an alternate set of statements in the event its tested condition evaluates as false. The following example demonstrates how this works in PHP.

```php
<?php
$x = 5;
if ($x == 10) {
  echo "We have a match!";
} else {
  Echo "Houston, we have a problem.";
}
?>
```

The else-if Statement

There may be a time in which you want to test for more than one possible outcome to a conditional test. One way of accomplishing this is with the else if statement, as demonstrated here:

```php
<?php
$x = 5;
if ($x == 10) {
  echo "We have a match!";
} else if ($x == 5){
  echo "We have a match!";
}
?>
```

In this example, a test has been set up to look for either of two possible values and a text string is displayed if a match occurs.

The switch Statement

As is the case with JavaScript, PHP lets you compare one value against a number of values using the switch statement. The following example demonstrates how to use this statement in PHP.

```php
<?php
$x = 5;
```

```
switch($x) {
  case 1:
    echo "The variable equal to 1";
    break;
  case 2:
    echo "The variable equal to 2";
    break;
  case 3:
    echo "The variable equal to 3";
    break;
  case 4:
    echo "The variable equal to 4";
    break;
  case 5:
    echo "The variable equal to 5";
    break;
  default:
    echo "The variable equal to 1, 2, 3, 4. or 5";
  }
?>
```

The Ternary Operator

Like JavaScript, PHP also supports the use of a ternary operator as an alternative means of performing conditional logic. The following example demonstrates the use of this operator.

```
<?php
$x;
$y = 100;
$x = ($y == 50) ? 50: 100;
  echo $x;
?>
```

Working with Loops

PHP supports a number of different types of loops, providing you with plenty of processing power for performing repetitive logic and managing collections of data like arrays. PHP also provides statements that let you break out of loops early or skip loop iterations.

The for Loop

PHP's for loop allows you to repeat the execution of one or more statements a specified number of times. As is the case in JavaScript, PHP's for loop has three parts: a variable declaration, a tested condition, and an increment/decrement statement. The following PHP script demonstrates how to use the for loop to return a string of characters back to a calling application.

```php
<?php
for ($i = 1; $i <= 5; $i++) {
  echo $i . "<BR>";
}
?>
```

When executed, this example returns the following output.

```
1
2
3
4
5
```

The foreach Loop

You can use PHP's foreach loop to automatically process the contents of arrays and other collections of data. The great thing about using this type of loop is that it does not require you to know in advance how many elements will need to be processed. Instead, the loop automatically ensures that all items are processed, as demonstrated here:

```php
<?php
$aPets = array("cat", "dog", "fish");
foreach ($aPets as $i) {
  echo $i . "<BR>";
}
?>
```

This PHP script generates an array named $aPets and populates it with three entries. A foreach loop is then executed, which iterates through each item in the array and returns it to the application that called upon the PHP script. When executed, this example returns the following output.

```
cat
dog
fish
```

The while Loop

As is the case with JavaScript, PHP's while loops repeat a collection of statements as long as a tested condition remains true. The following example shows a PHP script that uses a while loop to output five numbers.

```php
<?php
$i = 0;
while ($i < 5) {
  $i++;
  echo $i . "<BR>";
}
?>
```

When executed, this example returns the following output.

```
1
2
3
4
5
```

The do...while Loop

If you want to set up a loop that will always run at least one time, regardless of the value of its tested condition, you can use the do...while loop. Unlike the while loop, which tests its condition prior to executing, the do...while loop does not test its condition until the end of the loop. The following example demonstrates how this loop works.

```php
<?php
$i = 5;
do {
  echo $i . "<BR>";
  $i--;
} while ($i < 3);
?>
```

Here, the loop executes one time, returning a value of 5 and then decrementing the value assigned to $i by 1. The loop then checks to see if the value of $i is less than 3. Since it is not, the loop stops executing.

Breaking Out of Loops

PHP lets you prematurely terminate the execution of loops using the break keyword. Once the loop is halted, script execution resumes with the next statement that follows the loop. A demonstration of how to use the break keyword is provided here:

```php
<?php
for ($i = 1; $i < 5; $i++) {
  if ($i == 3) {
    break;
  }
  echo $i . "<BR>";
}
?>
```

When executed, this example returns the following output.

```
1
2
```

Continuing Loop Execution

Depending on what your PHP script may be doing, it may be useful to skip an iteration of a loop when certain situations occur. You can do this using the continue keyword, as demonstrated here:

```php
<?php
for ($i = 1; $i < 6; $i++) {
  if ($i == 3) {
    continue;
  }
  echo $i . "<BR>";
}
?>
```

When executed, this script returns the following output.

```
1
2
4
5
```

WORKING WITH FUNCTIONS

PHP provides strong support for working with functions. This includes allowing you to create and execute your own custom functions, receiving arguments and returning data when necessary. In addition, PHP also provides programmers with access to a large collection of built-in functions, which can be used to speed up development by providing access to pre-written code.

Creating and Executing Custom Functions

PHP functions are laid out using the same format as JavaScript functions. For example, the following PHP script includes a function named `DisplayString()` that when called displays a text string.

```
<HTML>
  <HEAD>
    <TITLE>Demo: Using an embedded PHP script to display text</TITLE>
  </HEAD>
  <?php
  function DisplayString() {
    echo "What's up doc?";
  }

  displayString();
  ?>
  <BODY>
  </BODY>
</HTML>
```

As the following example demonstrates, PHP functions can also be set up to process any number of arguments and to return data.

```
<HTML>
  <HEAD>
    <TITLE>Demo: Processing PHP arguments and returning data</TITLE>
  </HEAD>
  <?php
  function AddNumbers($a, $b) {
    $c = $a + $b;
    return $c;
  }
```

```
echo "Player Score = " . AddNumbers(500, 100);
?>
<BODY>
</BODY>
</HTML>
```

When executed, this example returns the following output.

```
Player Score = 600
```

Taking Advantage of Built-in PHP Functions

PHP really helps make the web programmer's job a lot easier by providing easy access to tons of pre-defined functions. This not only lets you work faster by saving you from having to re-invent a solution to perform an already solved task but also gives you access to program code that has been extensively tested and proven reliable. PHP provides functions that work with arrays, date and time, XML, strings, math, databases, the file system, etc. You have already learned how to work with two PHP string functions, echo and print. Examples of other functions that you will learn to work with in this chapter include:

- `str_shuffle`. Randomly shuffles the contents of a string.
- `rand`. Generates a random number within a specified range.

PROCESSING APPLICATION INPUT

As you learned in Chapter 6, "Digging Deeper into Ajax," Ajax can pass data to PHP scripts using either of the standard HTTP GET and POST requests. Your PHP scripts can then access this data using a pair of built-in global variables. These variables are automatically populated when PHP scripts are called with an external argument. These variables are used to store arrays named $_GET or $_POST. As you would expect, the type of array that a PHP must use to access incoming arguments depends on how its script is called (e.g., either with the HTTP GET or POST request).

Retrieving Arguments Passed Using the GET Option

When the open() method's GET option is used to pass data to a PHP script, the script can gain access to those arguments via the $_GET global array. The following example shows a PHP script that is designed to access and process an argument passed to it from a client-side application that uses the open() method's GET option.

```php
<?php
if ($_GET["color"] == "red")
```

```
  echo 'This color goes well in well-lit rooms.';
if ($_GET["color"] == "blue")
  echo 'This is a great color for boys.';
if ($_GET["color"] == "green")
  echo 'Perfect for small rooms in need of some cheer.';
?>
```

In addition to creating an Ajax application that calls upon this PHP script, you can also call it directly from a web browser by entering its URL, as demonstrated here:

```
http://www.yourserver.com/color.php?color=blue
```

As you can see, this URL string calls upon the PHP script and passes it an argument of blue, as demonstrated in Figure 9.8.

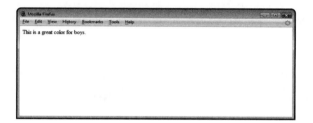

FIGURE 9.8

An example of the output generated when the PHP script is passed a value of blue as an argument.

Retrieving Arguments Passed Using the Post Option

If the Ajax application calls upon the PHP script using the open() method's POST option instead of its GET option, then the script would need to be modified as shown here to retrieve the data using the $_POST array.

```
<?php
if ($_POST["color"] == "red")
  echo 'This color goes well in well-lit rooms.';
if ($_POST["color"] == "blue")
  echo 'This is a great color for boys.';
if ($_POST["color"] == "green")
  echo 'Perfect for small rooms in need of some cheer.';
?>
```

STORING AND ACCESSING DATA

In addition to returning data embedded within PHP scripts to Ajax applications, PHP scripts can also access data stored in files and databases and make that data available. This enables you to create more complex applications that are capable of retaining data across different executions of the application. For example, you might create an Ajax game that allows players to track their success via a score. At the end of each game you could have your Ajax application communicate behind the scenes to its web server to see if the player's score is one of the 10 all time highest scores, and if it is, you could then have the Ajax application capture the player's name and save it in either a file or database on the server where such information would be maintained.

Creating and Accessing Files

In order to read from or to write to a file using PHP, you must first open the file. To do so, you need to use the `fopen` function, which has the following syntax.

```
fopen(filename, mode)
```

filename specifies the URL of the file on the web server and *mode* specifies the manner in which the file should be opened. Table 9.1 lists all of the different types of modes that PHP's `fopen` method supports.

TABLE 9.1	MODES SUPPORTED BY THE FOPEN FUNCTION
Mode	**Description**
r	Opens a file for read only.
r+	Opens a file for read and write.
w	Opens a file for write only. If the file already exists it is truncated. If it does not exist, it gets created.
w+	Opens a file for read and write. If the file already exists it is truncated. If it does not exist, it gets created.
a	Opens a file in append mode for writing. If it does not exist, it gets created.
a+	Opens a file in append mode for reading and writing. If it does not exist, it gets created.
x	Creates and opens a file for writing. If the specified file exists, a value of `false` is returned.
x+	Creates and opens a file for reading and writing. If the specified file exists, a value of `false` is returned.

The `fopen` function retrieves a file handle, which you can then use to programmatically refer to and interact with the file in your PHP script.

Writing to Files

After you have used the fopen function to establish access to a file on your web server, you can write to it using the PHP fwrite function, passing the function a file handle and the data to be written. The following PHP script demonstrates how this works.

```
<HTML>
  <HEAD>
    <TITLE>DEMO: Writing data to a text file</TITLE>
  </HEAD>
  <BODY>
    <?php
      $file = fopen("story.txt", "w");
      $data = "Once upon a time a little girl went to visit her friend. ";
      $data = $data . "Along the way \she met a wolf dressed in ";
      $data = $data . "sheep's clothing.";
      if (fwrite($file, $data) != true) {
         echo "Error occurred writing to file.";
      }
      fclose($file);
    ?>
  </BODY>
</HTML>
```

Here, a file named story.txt, located in the same location as the PHP script, is referenced. Next, a variable named $data is used to build a text string that is to be written to the file. Once the string has been assembled, it is written by calling on the fwrite method, which it wrapped up inside a conditional code block that monitors the success of the write operation, returning an error message if anything goes wrong. Note that in this example, the file is opened using write (w) mode.

 TRICK Take note of the placement of the \n characters in the text string that the script writes to the text file. This pair of characters is used to instruct PHP to begin writing to a new line and is an essential string manipulation tool.

Once all writing has been complete, the access to the file must be terminated (closed) in order to ensure that the file is properly saved. This is accomplished by executing the fclose function, passing it the file handle for the file.

Reading from Files

Now that you have learned how to write a file to the web server, let's take a look at the steps involved in reading data from that file. To do this, you need to use PHP's fopen function, passing it the URL of the file to open and specifying the mode to use as demonstrated here:

```
<HTML>
  <HEAD>
    <TITLE>DEMO: Reading data to a text file</TITLE>
  </HEAD>
  <BODY>
    <?php
      $file = fopen("story.txt", "r");
      while (!feof($file)){
        $data = fgets($file);
        echo $data . "<BR>";
      }
      fclose($file);
    ?>
  </BODY>
</HTML>
```

Once the script has opened a file for reading ("r" mode), it uses a while loop to iterate through the contents of the file, line by line, executing as long as the end of the file has not been reached (!feof($file)). Each time the loop runs, it uses the fgets method to retrieve a line from the file, which is stored in a variable named $data. The echo function is then used to display the contents of $data. Figure 9.9 shows the output that is generated when this example is executed.

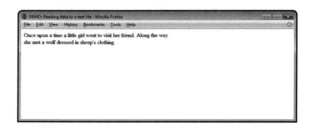

FIGURE 9.9

This example retrieves and displays the data previously written to story.txt.

A Few Words About Working with Databases

As previously mentioned, in addition to working with files, PHP can also interact with database management systems. PHP provides support for most major databases, including Oracle, MySQL, MS SQL, and so on. PHP provides programmers with access to an extensive set of functions that supports database access. However, database programming is an extensive topic all by itself and it is outside the scope of this book to address it.

BACK TO SCRAMBLE—THE WORD GUESSING GAME

Now it is time to turn your attention back to the development of this chapter's project, Scramble—The Word Guessing Game. This application challenges the player to unscramble words which contents have been scrambled. The selection of the word to be used and the scrambling of that word are performed behind the screens on the application's web server. Once downloaded and displayed, the Ajax application provides the game's user interface and manages all interaction with the player.

Designing the Application

The development of Scramble—The Word Guessing Game will be created in a series of five steps, as outlined here:

1. Create a new HTML page.
2. Begin to develop the application's JavaScript file.
3. Develop the GetWord() function.
4. Create the StartGame() function.
5. Create the scramble.php script.

Step 1: Writing the Application's HTML

The first step in the development of Scramble—The Word Guessing Game is to create an HTML page for the application named scramble.html and add the following statements to it.

```
<HTML>
  <HEAD>
    <TITLE>The Word Scramble Application</TITLE>
  </HEAD>
  <BODY>
    <IMG src="scramble.jpg">
    <BR>
    <P>
      Click on Get Word to retrieve a scrambled word and then try to
      figure out what it is. If you are unable to figure out the word,
```

```
          click on Show Word to see what it is.
        </p>
        <FORM>
          <INPUT type = "button" value = "Get Word"
            onclick = "StartGame()">
          <INPUT type = "button" value = "Show Word" style="visibility:hidden"
            id="showBtn" onclick="window.alert('The word is ' + aWordArray[0])">
        </FORM>
        <DIV id="ScrambledHeading" style="visibility:hidden">The scrambled
          word is:</DIV>
        <H1><DIV id="ScrambledDiv" style="color:midnightblue"></DIV></H1>
        <DIV id="UnscrambledHeading" style="visibility:hidden"><P>Unscramble
          and retype the word here:</P></DIV>
        <FORM>
          <INPUT type="textfield" size="45" style="color:midnightblue;
            background-color:honeydew; font-size:24; font-weight:bold;
            visibility:hidden" id="inputField">
        </FORM>
      </BODY>
</HTML>
```

As you can see, the HTML tags that make up Scramble are straightforward. They consist of the required head and body tags, some text, and a pair of forms containing the application's textfield and button controls.

Step 2: Beginning the Application's JavaScript

The second step in the creation of the application is to begin the development of its JavaScript, which is located in the head section. Begin the development of the script by adding the following statements to your HTML file's head section.

```
<SCRIPT language = "javascript" type = "text/javascript">
<!-- Start hiding JavaScript statements

  var Request = false;
  var aWordArray = new Array(2);



// End hiding JavaScript statements -->
</SCRIPT>
```

In addition to laying out the script's opening and closing tags, these statements also define two variables. The first variable will be used in setting up an instance of the XMLHttpRequest object and the second variable sets up an array that will be used to store data downloaded from the scramble.php script.

Step 3: Creating the GetWord() Function

The rest of the application is organized into two functions. The first of these functions is the GetWord() function, which is shown here. Like all of the functions in this application, you must place this function's statements inside the application's JavaScript.

```
function GetWord(url, elementID) {

  if (window.XMLHttpRequest) {
    Request = new XMLHttpRequest();
  } else if (window.ActiveXObject) {
    Request = new ActiveXObject("Microsoft.XMLHTTP");
  }

  if(Request) {
    var RequestObj = document.getElementById(elementID);
    Request.open("GET", url, true);
    Request.onreadystatechange = function() {
      if (Request.readyState == 4 && Request.status == 200) {
        aWordArray = Request.responseText.split(" ");
        RequestObj.innerHTML = aWordArray[1];
      }
    }
    Request.send(null);
  }
}
```

This function is passed two arguments, specifying the URL of the scramble.php script and the id of a pair of <DIV> </DIV> tags in which data returned by the script will be displayed. Next, an instance of the XMLHttpRequest object is established and then a connection is made to the application's web server and the PHP script is opened. When called, the PHP script will return one of ten randomly selected text strings.

Each text string is composed of a word followed by a blank space and then a scrambled copy of that same word. Upon successfully downloading the text string, the function uses the JavaScript split() function, breaking up the string into a two- item array. The first item in the array contains the unscrambled copy of the word and the second item contains the scrambled version of the word. The scrambled version of the word is then displayed so that the player can see it.

Step 4: Creating the StartGame() Function

The `StartGame()` function, shown here, is called whenever the player clicks on the game's `Get Word` button. When called, this function enables the display of all of the HTML elements that were defined but hidden in the HTML tags defined in the web page's body section. This allows the player to see and begin interacting with the application's interface.

```
function StartGame() {

  document.getElementById("showBtn").style.visibility="visible";
  document.getElementById("inputField").style.visibility="visible";
  document.getElementById("inputField").value="";
  document.getElementById('ScrambledDiv').innerHTML = "";
  document.getElementById("ScrambledHeading").style.visibility="visible";
  document.getElementById("UnscrambledHeading").style.visibility="visible";

  GetWord("scramble.php?x=" + Math.round(1 + Math.random() * 9),
    "ScrambledDiv");
  //GetWord("scramble.php", "ScrambledDiv");

}
```

In addition to setting up the game's interface, the function also executes the `GetWord()` function, which connects to the `scramble.php` script behind the scenes in order to download a word for the player to guess.

 Note that the `GetWord()` function is called and passed a randomly generated number between 1 and 10, corresponding to the 10 possible sets of words generated by the `scramble.php` script. If omitted and replaced with the statement that has been commented out, then the application will not work correctly on Internet Explorer but will work just fine on Firefox. Specifically, Internet Explorer will not be able to retrieve and display successive sets of words after downloading an initial word. Firefox, on the other hand, works just fine. To get around this problem, the call made to the `scramble.php` script has been changed to include the passing of an argument corresponding to the range of values that the PHP script may return, after which Internet Explorer is able to download successive sets of words. This unusual quirk is yet another example of the many challenges that Ajax developers face in trying to create cross-browser applications.

Step 5: Creating the scramble.php Script

The scramble.php script is responsible for returning one of ten randomly selected sets of words to the Ajax application. The statements that make up this script are shown here:

```php
<?php
  $randomNo = rand(1, 10);
  switch($randomNo) {
    Case 1:
      $word = "BUILDING";
      break;
    Case 2:
      $word = "GLOBE";
      break;
    Case 3:
      $word = "COUCH";
      break;
    Case 4:
      $word = "WATER";
      break;
    Case 5:
      $word = "WATCH";
      break;
    Case 6:
      $word = "STAPLER";
      break;
    Case 7:
      $word = "HOUSE";
      break;
    Case 8:
      $word = "TELEVISION";
      break;
    Case 9:
      $word = "APPLE";
      break;
    Case 10:
      $word = "TOAST";
      break;
  }
```

```
  echo $word . " " . str_shuffle($word);
?>
```

This script begins by generating a random number from 1 to 10 using the rand function. A switch code block is then set up in order to analyze the value that was assigned to $randomNo. A total of ten case statements have been added to the switch code block, each of which assigns a different word to a variable named $word. Once the value of $word has been set, a string is built that consists of three parts: the value of $word, a blank space, and a scrambled copy of the word generated using the str_shuffle function. This string is then returned to the Ajax application, where it is split into an array and then presented to the player.

The Final Result

Alright, you should have all the instruction you need to complete the development of Scramble—The Word Guessing Game. Assuming that you follow each of the four previously outlined steps without making any typos, you should find that your new Ajax application operates precisely as was outlined at the beginning of this chapter. To test the application when you are done, upload the scramble.html file along with the scramble.php and the scramble.jpg files to your web servers and then load scramble.html into your web browser.

 You will find a copy of this application's source code files on the book's companion website, located at http://www.courseptr.com/downloads.

SUMMARY

This chapter taught you how to develop server programs using PHP. You learned how to integrate PHP and HTML. You learned how to add comments to PHP files, store and access data using both variables and arrays, perform conditional and repetitive logic and to work with built-in and custom functions. In addition to learning the basic of PHP programming, this chapter explained how to read from and write to files stored on the web server, giving your PHP scripts the ability to permanently store and access data that can then be shared with your Ajax applications.

Before you move on to Chapter 10, why don't you set aside a little more time to improve Scramble—The Word Guessing Game by addressing the following list of challenges.

CHALLENGES

1. Currently, the `scramble.php` script only has ten words from which to choose. To make the game more interesting and less redundant, expand this collection by adding new words and modify the application accordingly.

2. As currently written, the game requires the player to make a determination as to whether or not the current word has been correctly unscrambled. Consider modifying the game to automatically monitor the player's keystrokes and respond once the word has been correctly retyped.

3. To make things more exciting, consider modifying the game to limit the amount of time the player has to unscramble the current word to 30 or 60 seconds and then declare the game lost if the player is unable to beat the clock.

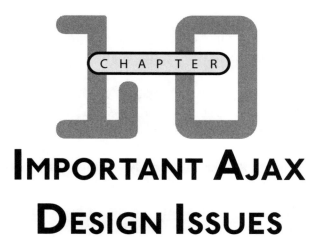

IMPORTANT AJAX
DESIGN ISSUES

As with any application development framework, Ajax applications are subject to a number of issues that Ajax developers must be aware of. In some cases, solutions already exist for dealing with these problems. In other cases, the jury is still out on the best way of handling things. This chapter provides a non-exhaustive list of Ajax development issues and, where possible, will suggest solutions or alternative ways of getting things done.

Specifically, this chapter will discuss:

- Issues and programming challenges specific to Ajax application development
- The importance of not overusing Ajax
- The importance of following good development practices

PROGRAMMING HURDLES THAT ALL AJAX DEVELOPERS FACE

Ajax is a proven technology, but in many ways it has yet to fully mature. It breaks some rules and raises a number of challenges, some of which have yet to be fully overcome. Many of the technologies that it relies on, including the DOM, CSS, and JavaScript all suffer from some form of inherent problems. In addition, there are plenty of users surfing the Internet with web browsers that are not able to support the execution of Ajax applications.

It is important that you are aware of these concerns and that you keep them in mind as you develop your own Ajax applications. That's what this chapter is all about.

Recognize That Not All Browsers Support JavaScript

While close to 90 percent of all browsers currently in use support the execution of JavaScript, there are still a great many users surfing the Internet whose browsers do not support it. In addition, there are countless numbers of users who, for one reason or another, have disabled their browser's JavaScript support. Rather than simply writing off all of these users, you may want to provide them with an alternative source of content.

You should strongly consider taking steps to ensure that users with browsers that do not support JavaScript are not forgotten. Consider adding the display of some static content, such as a logo and contact information on your web pages at all times. To take things a step further, consider developing a non-Ajax version of your application. If this is not feasible, then perhaps you should display a message apologizing for any inconvenience and explaining to your users the browser requirements of the application.

Another alternative is to use the <NOSCRIPT> and </NOSCRIPT> tags. Every web browser recognizes these HTML tags. They allow you to specify a message that will automatically be displayed by browsers that do not support JavaScript. JavaScript-enabled browsers, on the other hand, know to ignore any text embedded within <NOSCRIPT> and </NOSCRIPT> tags.

 The text displaying inside the <NOSCRIPT> and </NOSCRIPT> tags will only be displayed in the event the user's browser is unable to execute your application's JavaScript(s).

The following HTML page shows how you might use the <NOSCRIPT> and </NOSCRIPT> tags to provide information to any browser, regardless of whether it supports JavaScript.

```
<HTML>
  <HEAD>
    <TITLE>Demo: Working with the NOSCRIPT tag</TITLE>
  </HEAD>
  <BODY>
    <SCRIPT language = "javascript" type = "text/javascript">
    <!--Start hiding JavaScript statements
      document.write("Welcome to the XYX website!");
    // End hiding JavaScript statements -->
    </SCRIPT>
    <NOSCRIPT>
```

```
      The XYX website uses Ajax to provide an enriched end user experience.
      Your browser is not equipped to execute Ajax. You can view this site
      using the latest release of all the major web browsers, including
      Internet Explorer, FireFox, and Opera.
    </NOSCRIPT>
  </BODY>
</HTML>
```

Here, a welcome message will be displayed in any JavaScript-enabled web browser that loads the web page. If the web page is loaded by a browser that does not support JavaScript, an alternative message is displayed, informing the user of the application's browser requirements.

Do Not Let Ajax Alienate Your Users

Thanks to new technologies like Ajax, the distinction between desktop and web page applications is rapidly disappearing. As a result, it is very tempting to create web-based versions of desktop applications. Photo management applications like Flickr and online office suites like Google Docs are great examples of these types of applications. Web-enabled applications eliminate distribution issues and greatly simplify maintenance and upgrades. However, there are many people who are either unable or unwilling to give up their desktop applications.

Even in today's era of ultra-high-speed internet connections, there are still millions of people using slower dial-up connections. For these people, the luster and allure of Ajax applications often gives way to disillusion and disappointment when they find that the Ajax application with which they want to work is too large and complex to run efficiently over their slow internet connections. For these individuals, the traditional desktop application model still works best. For example, users with slow internet connections often prefer to use desktop email clients like Microsoft Outlook instead of Ajax-driven online email services like Gmail. Google accommodates these users by allowing them to remotely connect to its web servers using POP.

Online gaming is another area that concerns a lot of people, especially if the game permits participants to communicate directly with one another through texting. Given that the threat of online predators is very real, many parents are wary of permitting their children to play games online, preferring standalone desktop versions of computer games. So, as you begin to consider Ajax as a viable alternative to desktop development, remember that a large segment of internet users will not be able to run your applications. If you do not find a way of accommodating their needs, your competition will.

Ajax Applications Disable the Browser's Back and Forward Buttons

Web browsers are designed to monitor user actions and keep a record of all the web pages that the user loads in a browser history object. This works perfectly for websites and applications that are based on the traditional web model of using linked pages to provide successive levels of content. Internet users have come to anticipate and expect the consistent application of this behavior as they move from website to website across the internet.

However, Ajax applications do not comply with this approach. Ajax applications allow content to be dynamically updated without requiring page refreshes. As a result, Ajax breaks the browser's Back and Forward buttons.

Consider a situation in which a user loads a web page that uses Ajax and interacts with it for several minutes during which time a number of updates are made to the page's content. If the user then clicks the browser's Back button, expecting to see the application's previous state, disappointment occurs when the browser instead loads the web page visited just prior to the loading of the Ajax-powered page. Seeing that things did not occur as expected, the user might then click on the browser's Forward button, expecting to see the application restored to its last state only to find that the web page is loaded in its initial state and data regarding previous states has been lost. The end result is often a confused and frustrated user.

Currently, no one has come up with a perfect solution for overcoming this issue. One way of dealing with it is to create applications that provide their own version of the Back button. This would require that the application capture and store information about current and previous states, so that the application's state can be modified by reloading a previous state. This approach, however, requires significant effort on the part of the Ajax developer. Another possible solution would be to provide the application with a small number of permanent links to specific states of the application.

The impact of this limitation on your Ajax application will vary based on the type of applications you develop. If you make your Ajax applications resemble desktop applications, then your users won't intuitively expect back and forward functionality. On the other hand, if your web application needs to retain a traditional web application look and feel, then perhaps you should consider implementing linked, multi-page applications and limiting the use of Ajax to specific page-by-page tasks.

 Currently, a number of possible solutions to this issued have been created, but all involve a non-trivial level of effort to employ. Presentation of these solutions is outside the scope of this book. To learn more about them, open your browser and perform a search on "Fixing Ajax's Back Button."

Don't Make Unexpected Changes

The ability to interact with the DOM and dynamically modify the format and content of web pages gives Ajax developers the ability to manipulate web pages in any number of different ways. However, it is important that you use this ability with discretion and that you take great care not to make drastically unexpected changes when making updates.

As a simple example, consider an Ajax application that is designed to display news articles. If during the operation of the application, new information is made available on the web server, the application can download and display it. However, if the new text is just suddenly inserted into the middle of the page, all kinds of problems can occur. For starters, the user may be reading the article and may lose her place if everything suddenly shifts position to make room for the new information. If the information is displayed at the beginning or in the middle of the article, the user may not notice it if that portion of the article has already been read. In this scenario, it would be better to either post the new information at the end of the article or to notify the user that new information is available and display a prompt requesting permission to display it. To help make the newly inserted text easy to identify, it might also be a good idea to modify its background or foreground colors.

Ajax Applications Are Not Easily Bookmarked

Because Ajax application development allows the content on a single web page to be refreshed whenever necessary and does not provide a built-in mechanism for keeping track of the different states of an application as updates occur, users are not able to bookmark different states of the application. As a result, a user may interact with an application for several minutes before finally seeing the information that she was looking for displayed. If the user then creates a browser bookmark for the web page, expecting the current state of the page to be saved, she will be disappointed upon later returning to find that the application has returned back to its initial state. As with the problems surrounding the browser's Back and Forward buttons, various solutions exist for dealing with this issue. Coverage of these proposed solutions, easily attained through a quick browser search, is outside the scope of this book.

Ajax Applications Pose Problems for Search Engines

Search engines collect information about websites using a mechanism referred to as a *spider* and store the information that is collected in a database sometimes referred to as an *index*. When web surfers use search engines, they type in keywords or phrases that the search engine then uses to search its index for possible matches. A search engine's spider cannot tell the difference between content and navigational text. As a result, spiders must index everything they find. Ajax applications that retain large amounts of content on web servers, dynamically downloading it when needed, lower the search engine relevancy ranking (for your website's popularity ranking for the keyword or phrase).

If you register your main web page with a search engine, its spider will look for that page when visiting your website. You may want to ensure that you retain a certain amount of relevant text, representing keywords and phrases that you want the spider to index. In addition, if you dynamically download content that includes links to other pages that make up your Ajax applications, the spider will not be able to find them.

To mitigate these concerns, you should consider leaving some links in place on the original HTML page. Alternatively, consider including a link to a hypertext link sitemap. You might also want to provide a static version of your most relevant content somewhere on your website so that the spider can find and index it.

Dynamic Updates Are Not Always Easily Noticed

The dynamic nature of Ajax applications means that new data can be retrieved from web servers behind the scenes at any time. All of this dynamic update may be disconcerting to some users, especially if the users are not able to determine when it is occurring. To overcome this type of issue, you may want to consider providing some type of visual indicator that notifies users when data is being retrieved or the web page has just been updated.

One effective way to let the user know that something has changed in the current state of an application is to take advantage of the ability to control text and background color. For example, if new text is posted onto a page, you might make it stand out by altering its color. You can accomplish this using CSS as demonstrated by the following statement:

```
document.getElementById("DivTrgt").style.color = "blue";
```

Here, the text posted inside a pair of <DIV> </DIV> tags is displayed in blue. This identifies the text as something new and helps ensure that the user does not miss it. If an update includes a sizable amount of text, a better way of drawing attention to it may be to alter its background color, as demonstrated here:

```
document.getElementById("DivTrgt").style.background-color = "yellow";
```

Data Exchange Behind the Scenes May Make Users Uncomfortable

If your Ajax applications involve the collection of information from the user and you have set things up so that every time the user provides you with a piece of information that information is immediately uploaded to a web server for processing, some users will begin to get uncomfortable, preferring instead to exercise a measure of control over their experience with the application. You should keep this in mind as you develop your applications.

If your web page includes a lengthy form, consider waiting until the user has completely filled it out and is satisfied with all of the information that has been entered before submitting it for processing to your web server. You can easily set this up by requiring that the user click on a button to initiate the processing of the form. Many users find this approach much more preferable than having the application try to process every item on the form as soon as the user fills it in. This approach denies users the chance to double-check their work and change their minds about what they entered before allowing it to be submitted. Most users want to feel at least partially in charge of any interaction they become involved with on the internet.

Ajax Applications Do Not Run on a Single Platform

As you work on the development of your Ajax applications, it is important that you always keep in mind that Ajax applications do not run on a single platform. Instead, they may run on different web browsers like Internet Explorer, Safari, FireFox, Opera, plus a host of lesser-known browsers. In order to ensure that your applications operate like you expect them to, you need to test them using as many different web browsers as possible. Otherwise, you run the risk that your application won't work like you expect for a given browser and you will end up alienating an entire group of users.

Not everybody keeps up with the latest technologies. There are millions of people on the internet working with browsers that are 1 or 2 versions old. As such, they may not fully support all of the different technologies that make up Ajax. Therefore, you should also consider testing your applications with previous versions of all the browsers that you want to support. If they do not work correctly, you may want to modify your application. Alternatively, you may instead consider displaying a message that politely informs the user what browser and browser version is needed to access and operate the application.

Don't Build Slow Ajax Applications

Ajax is capable of developing some really cool and powerful applications. Ajax applications tend to be larger and much more complex than their non-Ajax counterparts. As you develop your own Ajax applications, keep the overall user experience in mind and don't get carried away with trying to do all of the things that Ajax is capable of doing. Just because you can build something does not mean that you should. Instead, keep your focus on what your application actually needs to do to be useful and effective and avoid weighing your applications down with fancy but non-useful special effects and gimmicks.

You also need to resist the temptation of abusing Ajax's ability to retrieve data. Just because you can retrieve data behind the scenes does not mean that your Ajax applications should download every possible piece of data available to them. A well-designed application only requests the data that it needs to run. Perhaps you can leverage web server scripting to filter out and prevent the download of unnecessary data. Applications that download too much data can impact other network users by needlessly consuming network bandwidth. If you try to make your Ajax applications process more data than can be reasonably processed, your applications will get bogged down and your user's experience will suffer. As a result, your users may develop the impression that Ajax applications are not so cool after all.

If there is no way around imposing some delays in your Ajax applications as data is downloaded from the web browsers, you should consider providing users with a visual indicator that lets them know that data is being retrieved. Otherwise, the behind the scenes nature of Ajax applications can lead to significant frustration when applications seemingly slow down for no reason.

An easy way to provide a visual indicator is to use an animated GIF file, like an hourglass file, to indicate that a download is in progress. Users are much more likely to be patient as long as they know that the application is still working. Using the statement shown below, you could display the animated GIF at the beginning of the download process.

```
document.getElementById("ImgTrgt").style.visibility = "visible";
```

Once the download is complete, you could suppress the display of the GIF using a statement like the one shown here:

```
if (Request.readyState == 4 && Request.status == 200) {
  document.getElementById("ImgTrgt").style.visibility = "hidden";
}
```

Other ways of letting users know that an application is currently busy include temporarily changing the appearance of the mouse pointer or displaying an information message in a popup dialog window or on the browser's status bar.

Ajax Applications May Create New Security Concerns

Ajax-enabled applications are typically larger and more complex than their non-Ajax counterparts. This is partially the result of the addition of new client-side JavaScript code. Client-side Javascript is easily viewable and therefore inherently insecure. It is therefore important that extra care be taken when developing client-side scripts to ensure that sensitive information like user IDs and passwords are not accidentally disclosed.

Instead, the overall design of the application should move the processing of sensitive information to the web server, where it can be kept safe from public view. In addition, a careful code review should be performed to ensure that no sensitive data accidentally makes it way into the application's JavaScript code.

Don't Overuse Ajax

It is easy to get caught up in the latest tools and technologies. However, it is important that you do not get caught in the habit of using Ajax simply for the sake of using Ajax. Some applications, especially those that still use a page-based presentation, may not benefit from the use of Ajax. Instead, these types of sites typically perform better using the traditional web development model of web pages connected through static links. If you are working on a new application that requires the browser's Back button, then Ajax may not be the right tool for this application, since Ajax breaks the Back button.

Small web applications may not derive sufficient benefit from Ajax to justify the time, additional effort, and complexity required to develop Ajax versions of the application.

Follow Good Development Practices

Regardless of all of Ajax's capabilities, there is no substitute for following good programming practices when developing your web applications. A poorly designed Ajax application is bound to disappoint your users. Characteristics of poorly designed applications include:

- A non-intuitive user interface
- Poor application design leading to slow or inconsistent performance
- The inclusion of unnecessary or overly complex features
- Poor document and user help

One of the easiest traps that Ajax developers can fall into is creating application interfaces that do not follow any type of standard conventions. Because of its flexibility, it is easy to create Ajax applications that are non-intuitive, requiring that users click on interface elements that are not easily identified in order to initiate certain tasks or to interact with the application. Doing so makes applications more difficult to learn and leads to user frustration and can result in user rejection of perfectly good applications.

Poor application design includes things like the movement of excessive amounts of processing load on either the server of the client or the user or excessive or overly large graphics and other multimedia files. Loading down your applications with non-essential features can also degrade an application's performance.

At a minimum, you should provide adequate documentation and help for all your Ajax applications. In addition, you should make liberal use of comments when writing your application's HTML, CSS, XML, and JavaScript statements to make sure that you leave behind an adequate explanation of why you developed the application the way you did.

HINT If your application is designed to loop and behave like a traditional desktop application, then that is exactly how you should make it operate. There is no place for links in these types of applications. Users will not expect to see them so avoid using them to navigate around desktop-like applications. On the other hand, if your application has a traditional web application look and feel, your users will expect to see and click on links. Do not disappoint them.

You can learn more about best practices for Ajax applications by visiting AjaxPatterns website located at http://www.ajaxpatterns.org, as shown in Figure 10.1.

FIGURE 10.1

The AjaxPatterns website provides comprehensive information regarding Ajax application development practices.

SUMMARY

In this final chapter, you learned about a number of environment issues and programming challenges faced by all Ajax application developers. Where possible, solutions and suggestions that help address these issues were suggested. Despite the inherent challenges facing Ajax development, Ajax has proven itself to be a significant and powerful tool that—when used correctly—is helping to transform the face of the Internet.

WHAT'S ON THE COMPANION WEBSITE?

Having completed all ten of this book's chapters, you now have a solid foundation upon which you can continue to build and learn. Rather than looking at this book as the end of your Ajax education, you should view it as the beginning. There is much more left to learn and experience than could ever be covered in any one book.

As you continue to advance your Ajax education and begin tackling larger and more complex projects, you will find that it really helps if you amass a collection of reliable source code that you can continue to reference and use as examples of how specific types of tasks are performed. If you have been recreating the computer games presented in this book, then you already have access to such a collection, to which you should continue to add as you learn more about Ajax programming.

By referring to and studying this book's examples you will not only continue to learn more about how to program, you will be better positioned to leverage the work you have already done. By copying, pasting, and modifying portions of the code statements that make up these examples into new applications, you can adapt them to perform different tasks. Not only will this speed your development time but it will also save you the trouble of having to reinvent the wheel, freeing you up to focus on new challenges.

DOWNLOADING THE BOOK'S SOURCE CODE

The best way to use this book to learn Ajax is to set aside the time required to re-create each sample application using the instructions provided in each chapter. In the event that you have had to skip the development of one or more of these applications, you can download and test the execution of each chapter's sample applications by visiting this book's companion website, located at http://www.courseptr.com/downloads.

Table A.1 provides an overview of all the application projects that you will find on the companion website.

TABLE A.1 SOURCE CODE AVAILABLE ON THE COMPANION WEBSITE	
Chapter	**Application Name**
Chapter 1	Joke of the Day
Chapter 2	Number Guessing game
Chapter 3	Rock, Paper, Scissors
Chapter 4	Ajax Story of the Day
Chapter 5	Ajax Typing Challenge
Chapter 6	Ajax Google Suggest
Chapter 7	Who Am I?
Chapter 8	The Fortune Telling Game
Chapter 9	Scramble – The Word Guess Game

WHAT NEXT?

To become an effective Ajax developer you need to dedicate time and effort to your craft. This means sitting down and creating all sorts of new Ajax projects, experimenting and learning how and why things work. By reading this book and following along with all of the Ajax examples that have been demonstrated, you have made an excellent start at learning how to integrate the use of Ajax in website development. Now that you have completed this book, don't think of it as the end of your Ajax education but rather as the beginning of it.

To continue improving your programming skills and to further your Ajax education, you need to continue to learn more about all of the technologies covered in this book, including:

- HTML
- DOM
- XMLHttpRequest
- CSS
- XML
- JavaScript
- Ajax

To help you to keep your momentum going, this appendix provides a starter list of online resources that you can explore to learn more about all of the technologies listed above.

HTML RESOURCES

If you feel that your knowledge of HTML is lacking or is a little rusty, then the following set of websites should help you get up to speed. These websites provide an overview of HTML and its history, give you access to details about the HTML specification for HTML 4.01, and provide a link to a tutorial you can complete to get a quick HTML refresher.

Wikipedia's HTML Page

If you want a quick high-level overview of HTML, then one of the best places to visit is http://en.wikipedia.org/wiki/HTML, as shown in Figure B.1. Here you will find information about the history of HTML, learn about its major elements, and get access to a wide range of links, including links to a number of excellent online tutorials.

FIGURE B.1

Wikipedia's HTML page provides a comprehensive overview of HTML.

W3C's HTML 4.01 Specification Page

Another important resource that every serious web page developer should be aware of is the HTML 4.01 Specification page provided at http://www.w3.org/TR/html401, as shown in Figure B.2. Here you will learn about the specification for HTML 4.01. Among the information provided at this site is an excellent overview of forms, scripts, and style sheets.

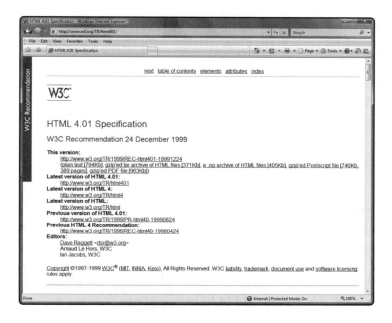

FIGURE B.2

W3C's HTML 4.01
Specification Page
provides access to
detailed HTML
information.

HTML.net's Free HTML Tutorial

If you feel you just need a quick HTML refresher, then spend a little time taking the tutorial provided at http://www.html.net/tutorials/html/introduction.asp, as shown in Figure B.3.

FIGURE B.3

HTML.net's Free
HTML tutorial
provides a quick
and easy HTML
refresher course.

Here you will receive basic HTML instruction as well as a quick overview of cascading style sheets. This should be all the information that you need to follow along and understand the HTML examples presented in this book.

THE HTML DOCUMENT OBJECT MODEL

The Document Object Model (DOM) is a platform-independent object model used to represent different elements in an HTML page as a logical tree structure. Using the DOM, web developers can access and manipulate different items that make up web pages. A solid understanding of the DOM is therefore essential to any Ajax web developer.

Wikipedia's Document Object Model Page

One of the best places on the web to get a quick overview of the Document Object Model is at http://en.wikipedia.org/wiki/Document_Object_Model, as shown in Figure B.4.

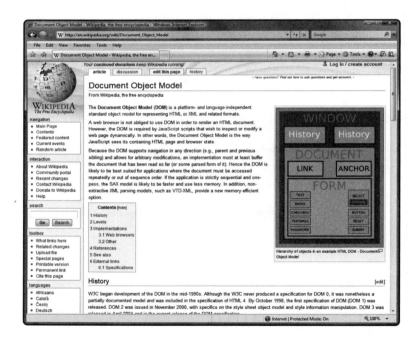

FIGURE B.4

Wikipedia's Document Object Model Page provides a well-rounded overview of the DOM.

This website provides DOM background information and discusses the different browsers that support it. This site also offers access to links of dozens of other websites where you can find additional DOM information.

W3C's Document Object Model (DOM) Page

To dig really deep into the Document Object Model, you need to visit the W3C Document Object Model web page located at http://www.w3.org/DOM/, as shown in Figure B.5.

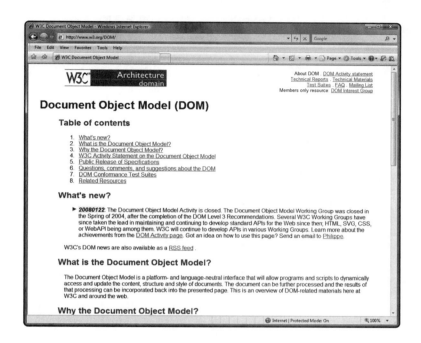

FIGURE B.5

W3C's Document Object Model (DOM) Page provides access to detailed DOM specifications.

Here you can view DOM technical reports and keep your eye on Document Object Model mail lists.

HTML DOM Tutorial

If all you feel you need is a quick tutorial review of the Document Object Model, then consider visiting http://www.w3schools.com/HTMLDOM/default.asp, as shown in Figure B.6.

This site also provides access to dozens of Document Object Model examples and a Document Object Model reference that provides detailed descriptions of every DOM object.

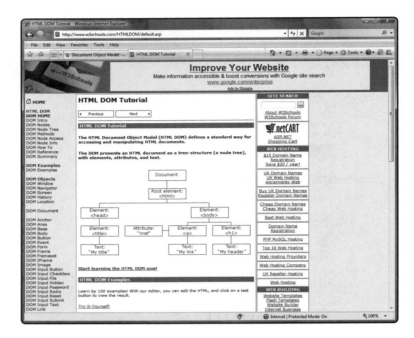

FIGURE B.6

This HTML DOM Tutorial can be used to quickly brush up on the Document Object Model.

XMLHTTPREQUEST RESOURCES

XMLHttpRequest is an object that provides Ajax developers with the ability to send and receive data to and from a web server using HTTP without requiring the submission of a form. This object facilitates asynchronous communication with web servers, allowing for web page updates without requiring web page refreshes.

Wikipedia's XMLHttpRequest Page

One of the best online resources for learning more about the XMLHttpRequest object is Wikipedia's XMLHttpRequest page located at http://en.wikipedia.org/wiki/Xmlhttprequest, as shown in Figure B.7.

Here you will find more information about the XMLHttpRequest object and its history, along with detailed explanation of its property and method syntax as well as code examples and links to numerous other related websites.

FIGURE B.7

Wikipedia's XMLHttpRequest Page provides a comprehensive overview of the XMLHttpRequest object.

W3C's XMLHttpRequest Object Page

You can also find a lot of information on the XMLHttpRequest object by visiting http://www.w3.org/TR/XMLHttpRequest/, as shown in Figure B.8.

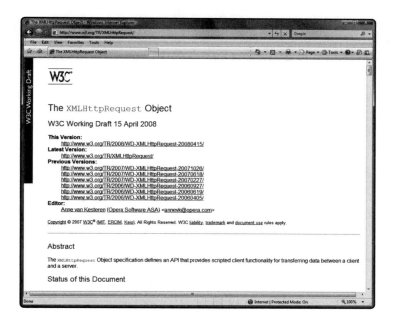

FIGURE B.8

W3C's XMLHttpRequest Object Page provides access to detailed XMLHttpRequest specifications.

Here you will find detailed specifications covering every aspect of the XMLHttpRequest object. You will also find an abundance of code examples and plenty of links to other related websites.

XMLHttpRequest Tutorial

If all you need is a quick tutorial, then visit http://jibbering.com/2002/4/httprequest.html, as shown in Figure B.9.

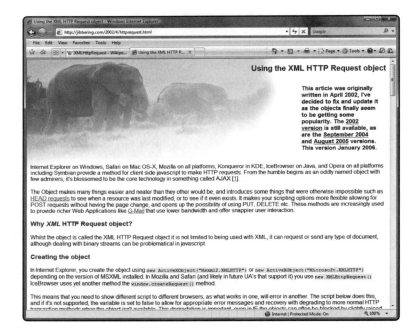

FIGURE B.9

XMLHttpRequest Tutorial provides a good overview of how to work with the XMLHttpRequest object.

Here you will find a good explanation of how to use the XMLHttpRequest object and will see tons of code examples that demonstrate its use. You will also find an example of how to use the XMLHttpRequest object in conjunction with JSON to transfer data.

RESOURCES FOR CASCADING STYLE SHEETS

Cascading Style Sheets or CSS is a standard used to define the layout of an HTML page, specifying how and where page elements should be laid out. Using CSS you can create style templates that specify the layout of different web page items. Using CSS, you can specify the font, spacing, border and other visual and organizational characteristics of text displayed on web pages.

Wikipedia's Cascading Style Sheets Page

An understanding of the use of cascading style sheets to control the presentation of data in Ajax applications is important to any web programmer, especially Ajax developers. One of the best sites to visit to get an overall understanding of cascading style sheets is the cascading style sheets page at Wikipedia, located at http://en.wikipedia.org/wiki/Cascading_style_sheets, as shown in Figure B.10.

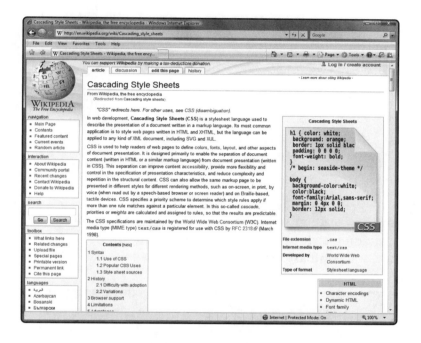

FIGURE B.10

Wikipedia's Cascading Style Sheets page provides an excellent overview of CSS.

Wikipedia Cascading Style Sheets page provides historical information about CSS and discusses its uses and limitations. You will also find dozens of links to other websites dedicated to discussing CSS.

W3C's Cascading Style Sheets Page

If you want to dig further into the technical specifications behind cascading style sheets, you can visit the W3C Cascading Style Sheet page located at http://www.w3.org/Style/CSS/, as shown in Figure B.11.

In addition to detailed information about CSS specifications, this website also provides information about different browsers that support cascading style sheets as well as links to various CSS authoring tools.

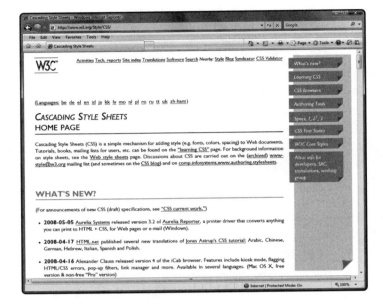

FIGURE B.11

W3C's Cascading
Style Sheets page
provides access to
detailed CSS
specifications.

CSS Tutorial Page

If you have not worked with cascading style sheets in the past, then you may find that
you will benefit from a cascading style sheets tutorial. One such tutorial can be found at
http://www.w3schools.com/Css/default.asp, as shown in Figure B.12.

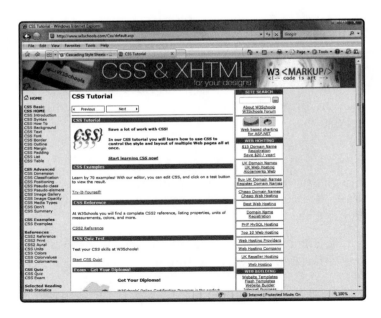

FIGURE B.12

You can use the
Cascading Style
Sheets Online
Tutorial to quickly
ramp up on your
understanding
of CSS.

You will learn how to use CSS to specify font, border, margin, and padding to the display of text. You will also learn how to format lists and tables. In addition to the tutorial, you will find over 70 examples of how to work with CSS and can test your comprehension of what you have learned through a free quiz.

JavaScript Resources

JavaScript is broadly supported scripting language used in the development of web pages to add features that make web pages more dynamic and interactive. Originally developed by Netscape, JavaScript has since been embraced by the international community and standardized by the European Computer Manufacturers Association (ECMA) as ECMAScript.

Wikipedia's JavaScript Page

JavaScript was originally developed by Netscape and first appeared in 1995. It provides the programming language used to create Ajax applications. As such, a solid understanding of JavaScript is fundamental to your success as an Ajax developer. If you feel that your understanding of JavaScript needs a little enhancement, begin by visiting http://en.wikipedia.org/wiki/Javascript, as shown in Figure B.13.

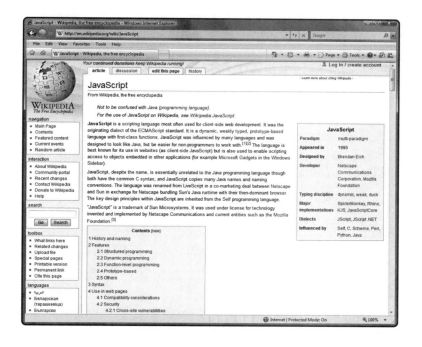

Figure B.13

Wikipedia's JavaScript Page provides an excellent overview of JavaScript programming.

In addition to providing a little background information and a high-level overview of the language, you will find links to dozens of different websites that you can visit to learn even more.

JavaScript.com

Another excellent source of JavaScript information is JavaScript.com located at http://www.javascript.com/, as shown in Figure B.14. This site gives you access to all kinds of sample scripts from which you can learn. In addition, this site offers reference articles that provide in-depth discussions and instructions on how to perform specific tasks.

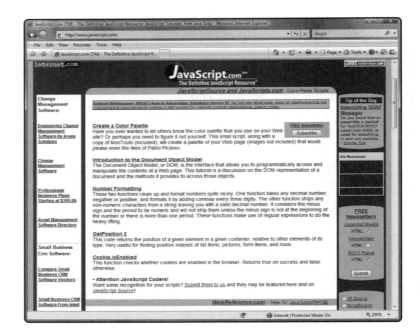

FIGURE B.14

JavaScript.com provides access to tons of sample scripts and articles.

JavaScript Tutorial

If your knowledge and understanding of JavaScript is not quite as strong as you'd like it to be, you may find the tutorial located at http://www.w3schools.com/JS/default.asp, as shown in Figure B.15, to be helpful.

This website provides a top-to-bottom overview of JavaScript programming syntax and will present you with all kinds of examples from which you can learn. You will also find a free quiz that you can take to measure your understanding of what you will learn.

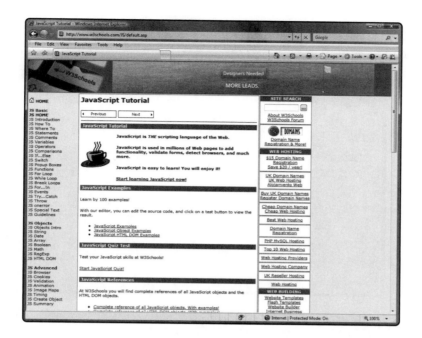

FIGURE B.15

This JavaScript tutorial walks you step by step through the basics of JavaScript programming.

XML RESOURCES

The eXtensible Markup Language or XML is a document processing standard used to describe the structure of data. XML provides web developers with the ability to define custom tags and define a structure for describing data that is passed between applications in a platform-independent manner.

Wikipedia's XML Page

Although this book has provided an overview of XML, there is still much left to learn about this complex and powerful technology. To learn more, visit http://en.wikipedia.org/wiki/Xml, as shown in Figure B.16.

Wikipedia's XML page provides a well laid out explanation of XML, not limited to its use in Ajax web development. You will learn more about the history behind XML and about its many advantages and disadvantages. In addition to the abundance of links to other XML related websites, you will also find a link to a free online XML Wikibook (http://en.wikibooks.org/wiki/XML), where you can learn everything you ever wanted to know about XML.

Wikipedia's XML page provides a comprehensive overview of XML.

W3C's Extensible Markup Language (XML) Page

Another website you can visit to learn more about XML is http://www.w3.org/XML/, as shown in Figure B.17. This website provides a good overview of XML and information and links for different groups currently working on the development and standardization of XML.

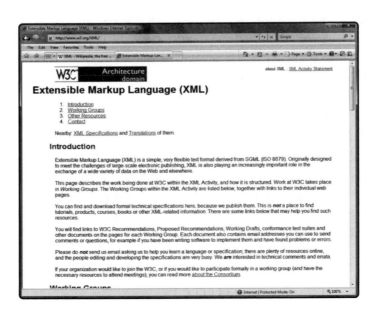

FIGURE B.17

Visit the W3C's Extensible Markup Language (XML) page to keep abreast of the ongoing development of XML.

This site also posts information on different XML events and provides links that you can visit to learn more about XML books, training classes, tutorials, and many other types of resources.

XML Tutorial

If you feel you need additional instruction on the use of XML, then consider visiting the XML tutorial provided at http://www.w3schools.com/xml/default.asp, as shown in Figure B.18. Here you will find a complete review of XML syntax and all of its major elements.

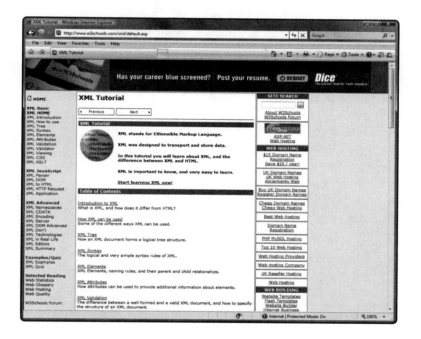

FIGURE B.18

This XML tutorial provides another opportunity to review the fundamentals of XML development.

In addition to basic XML instruction, this site also provides specific instruction on how to use XML with JavaScript, including how to use it to work with the DOM.

LOCATING AJAX RESOURCES ONLINE

Asynchronous JavaScript and XML or Ajax is a collection of technologies that together can be used to build interactive web applications that look and perform very similarly to desktop applications. Using Ajax, web developers are able to update the content of web pages without requiring page reloads, resulting in a faster and most satisfying user experience.

Wikipedia's Ajax Page

All of the websites previously listed in this appendix dealt with specific technologies that you will need to understand as an Ajax developer. In addition to keeping up to date on all of these individual technologies, you will want to also keep your focus on Ajax-specific topics and developments. One particularly good website to keep your eyes on is http://en.wikipedia.org/wiki/Ajax, as shown in Figure B.19.

FIGURE B.19

Wikipedia's Ajax page provides access to community-driven content covering all aspects of Ajax development.

Wikipedia's Ajax page is maintained by a global community of contributors for the purpose of defining and explaining the application of Ajax. This site provides a comprehensive explanation of Ajax's advantages, disadvantages, and uses and provides access to all kinds of helpful links.

Jesse James Garrett's Ground-Breaking Article

Another Ajax web page that every Ajax developer should visit is http://www.adaptivepath.com/ideas/essays/archives/000385.php, as shown in Figure B.20. Here you will find a copy of the article written by Jesse James Garrett where he originally coined the term Ajax and helped introduce it to the world.

FIGURE B.20

This is the article
that helped jump
start Ajax.

In this article Jesse not only articulates the first comprehensive definition of Ajax, he also explains the fundamental shift that it introduced to web page development. Also included at the end of the article is a question and answer section where Jessie addresses a number of commonly asked Ajax questions.

Keeping an Eye on Ajax Blogs

In addition to all of the online resources previously discussed in this appendix, there are a couple of good blogs, listed below, that you might want to consider visiting on a regular basis to keep abreast of what other Ajax web developers are talking about.

- http://ajaxblog.com/
- http://ajaxian.com/
- http://www.ajax-blog.com

When you visit these blogs you will find information on Ajax, Ajax frameworks, tutorials, resources, JavaScript, PHP and much more.

INDEX